Film Actors
Organize

ALSO BY KERRY SEGRAVE AND FROM MCFARLAND

Actors Organize: A History of Union Formation Efforts in America, 1880–1919 (2008)

Obesity in America, 1850–1939: A History of Social Attitudes and Treatment (2008)

Women and Capital Punishment in America, 1840–1899: Death Sentences and Executions in the United States and Canada (2008)

Women Swindlers in America, 1860–1920 (2007)

Ticket Scalping: An American History, 1850–2005 (2007)

America on Foot: Walking and Pedestrianism in the 20th Century (2006)

Suntanning in 20th Century America (2005)

Endorsements in Advertising: A Social History (2005)

Women and Smoking in America, 1880 to 1950 (2005)

Foreign Films in America: A History (2004)

Lie Detectors: A Social History (2004)

Product Placement in Hollywood Films: A History (2004)

Piracy in the Motion Picture Industry (2003)

Jukeboxes: An American Social History (2002)

Vending Machines: An American Social History (2002)

Age Discrimination by Employers (2001)

Shoplifting: A Social History (2001)

Movies at Home: How Hollywood Came to Television (1999)

American Television Abroad: Hollywood's Attempt to Dominate World Television (1998)

Tipping: An American Social History of Gratuities (1998)

American Films Abroad: Hollywood's Domination of the World's Movie Screens from the 1890s to the Present (1997)

Baldness: A Social History (1996; paperback 2009)

Policewomen: A History (1995)

Payola in the Music Industry: A History, 1880–1991 (1994)

The Sexual Harassment of Women in the Workplace, 1600 to 1993 (1994)

Women Serial and Mass Murderers: A Worldwide Reference, 1580 through 1990 (1992)

Drive-in Theaters: A History from Their Inception in 1933 (1992; paperback 2006)

BY KERRY SEGRAVE AND LINDA MARTIN AND FROM MCFARLAND

The Continental Actress: European Film Stars of the Postwar Era; Biographies, Criticism, Filmographies, Bibliographies (1990)

The Post-Feminist Hollywood Actress: Biographies and Filmographies of Stars Born After 1939 (1990)

Film Actors Organize
Union Formation Efforts in America, 1912–1937

KERRY SEGRAVE

McFarland & Company, Inc., Publishers
Jefferson, North Carolina, and London

LIBRARY OF CONGRESS CATALOGUING-IN-PUBLICATION DATA

Segrave, Kerry, 1944–
 Film actors organize : union formation efforts in America, 1912–1937 / Kerry Segrave.
   p.   cm.
 Includes bibliographical references and index.

 ISBN 978-0-7864-4276-8
 softcover : 50# alkaline paper

 1. Actors — Labor unions — United States — History — 20th century.   2. Actors' Equity Association — History.   3. Screen Actors Guild — History.   I. Title.
 PN2016.S46   2009
 331.88'11791430280973 — dc22   2008050692

British Library cataloguing data are available

©2009 Kerry Segrave. All rights reserved

No part of this book may be reproduced or transmitted in any form or by any means, electronic or mechanical, including photocopying or recording, or by any information storage and retrieval system, without permission in writing from the publisher.

Cover photograph: Actors strike, 1919 (Billy Rose Theatre Division, New York Public Library for the Performing Arts, Astor, Lenox and Tilden Foundations)

Manufactured in the United States of America

McFarland & Company, Inc., Publishers
 Box 611, Jefferson, North Carolina 28640
  www.mcfarlandpub.com

Contents

Preface	1
1. Early Efforts and Equity's First Attempt, to 1923	3
2. A Brief Lull, 1924–1927	18
3. AMPAS and Salary Cuts; Equity's Second Attempt, 1927	33
4. A Second Brief Lull, 1928–1929	58
5. Equity's Third Attempt, 1929	68
6. Organizing Founders; Salary Cuts, Again, 1930–1933	111
7. The Coming of SAG, 1933–1936	126
8. SAG Negotiations and First Contract, 1936–1937	149
9. Conclusion	167
Notes	183
Bibliography	195
Index	205

Preface

This book looks at the efforts made by actors in the motion picture industry to organize themselves into a trade union, from the earliest attempt, which took place around 1912, through the formation of the Screen Actors' Guild (SAG) in 1933. The book's coverage ends in 1937, the year that SAG received formal recognition from the film studios as the bargaining agent for the film players and the year in which SAG signed its first contract with the motion picture industry cartel.

Over that period of time many groups surfaced briefly to try and organize the players but all disappeared quickly. Earliest attempts were centered on the New York City area but the focus quickly switched to California as the film industry had mostly relocated to Hollywood by around the middle 1910s. During the years before 1920 there were only two actors' unions of note in America, the White Rats, representing mostly vaudeville performers, and Actors' Equity Association, representing mostly stage players. Both made half-hearted attempts to organize film players before 1920 but each was busy enough in its own sphere trying to survive. The White Rats failed to survive but after Equity successfully fought a stage strike in 1919 its future seemed assured. Thus, Equity seemed the logical candidate to organize the film players.

And over the course of the 1920s Equity launched three major, concentrated efforts to do just that. However, it failed each time, for reasons both internal and external. During the lulls between those efforts the film producers attempted to take advantage of the situation and impose salary cuts on the players. The producers failed in those efforts, for reasons both internal and external, but such behavior tended to draw Equity back into

Preface

action to launch another organizing drive. This book looks at all those efforts, at the working conditions of actors during the period, and at the strategies employed by the producers to keep out the unions. Everything was used by the producers, from the formation of a company union to a media blackout imposed on the unionists by an anti-union press that was only too happy to side with the film cartel.

By the time the 1930s arrived the situation was bad enough for the film players that a union was seen more and more as a necessity. Disenchantment with the company union had reinforced that idea but Equity, having made many mistakes in its earlier organizing efforts, was no longer acceptable to the players as the organization to turn to. Thus SAG was formed and within a few years it had achieved recognition and a first contract. Since the film screenwriters and directors formed unions of their own at roughly the same time as SAG it meant that Hollywood and the film industry had become fully unionized.

1
Early Efforts and Equity's First Attempt, to 1923

The organization of film actors into a trade union was slow in coming, relative to most professions and trades. Writers and directors were equally slow to organize in Hollywood while motion picture craftspeople and technicians organized themselves earlier. Part of the slow start had to do with the nature of the film business; a wider variation in salaries and conditions than were found in most industries. As well, there was a perceived independent nature found in actors, making them less amenable to team work, and so on, compared to most occupations. Additionally, there was a certain amount of snobbery involved; actors were artistes, not stage hands or carpenters, laborers who had earlier unionized and allied themselves with the American Federation of Labor. Then, of course, there was the notorious and egregious anti-union atmosphere found in Los Angeles. Because of that bias the unionization of any part of the Hollywood film industry was delayed, compared to unionization in other parts of America. The earliest effort to organize a union among the film actors seems to have been in 1912, although no details apparently were ever reported, except as a brief line a year later in an account of attempt number two. Motion picture studios had not fully transferred production to California in the first few years of the 1910s, although they soon would, and those first few efforts to organize took place in New York and vicinity.

After working undercover for months a band of progressive, reformist actors gave up in despair in their attempt to organize an actors' union

Film Actors Organize

among the rank and file of movie players in the New York area and, in July 1913, it was reported that everyone involved in that attempt remembered a similar try at forming movie actors into a union, begun more than a year earlier, also suddenly came to naught. The plan abandoned in July 1913 was similar in scope to the earlier effort. However, the leaders of the 1913 movement believed they had the fight won, up to the last moment. Those would-be reformers had hoped to be able to come out in the open soon and deliver a strike threat to the movie producers unless certain changes were made in the method of hiring, working and feeding film players. Each of the reformers leading the movement, believing that to be discovered agitating meant a sweeping application of the blacklist by the producers, had been working undercover. At a meeting of actors held on the evening of July 24 at the Hotel Astor in New York word came from one of the actors that the film producers were on to the plot. According to a reporter, "Practically every move made by the organizers had been reported to headquarters by a stool pigeon. The first overt move that sounded like organized war from any group of picture actors meant the gate." As a result of that warning, the whole organizing effort was called off.[1]

One abuse objected to by those 1913 would-be reformers was the practice of studios calling actors to be on the set at 9:00 A.M. six days a week and keeping them there through until 5:00 P.M., but not using them. That, of course, meant no pay. The salaried and jobbing movie actors also wanted a more "humane" commissary department. A banana, a cheese sandwich, and a bottle of ginger ale were declared to not be a substantial lunch. The actors were willing to buy their own meals, if the movie men would establish satisfactory eating arrangements. Another thing the jobbing malcontents among the actors wanted was consideration of their qualities. "They don't want the actor, for instance, who is recognized as a Shakespearean authority to be paid the same pittance for a classic impersonation that a movie actor shanghaied from a laundry receives, a condition now prevailing in all studios," noted a journalist. Jobbing film players also wanted directors to more efficiently systematize their work so film extras would not needlessly spend their small capital on car fare in order to get to movie studios in the outlying regions, without fair assurance of a day's employment. The small pay for extras meant a lot of them had to walk to and from the studio and that often meant an early morning start

1. Early Efforts and Equity's First Attempt, to 1923

to a long walk. "A movement for the modification and elimination of these evils was originally behind the organization of the Screen Club," it was said. "But time reduced the club to a purely social body, where favors might be courted and exchanged between the directors who joined and the actors who belonged." Those 1913 reformers had hoped to organize a body as effective as the stage hands' union, and later to seek affiliation with the International Alliance of Stage Employees. But on that July evening in 1913 the dream was pronounced dead.[2]

As a result of abuses of film extras by agents and middlemen a mass meeting was held in New York in August 1916 at which plans were formulated for the formation of an organization for mutual protection, and for affiliation of that union with the American Federation of Labor. Catalyst for the move was the activity of several agents who had been getting orders from the studios for film extras but instead of taking a nominal fee for their services, had been paying the extras only about 40 percent of the money received from the studios. Also, the agencies would advertise in the daily papers for extras and, after tentatively engaging them, would keep them calling at their offices for three to four days prior to telling them of the film location, or that the order had been cancelled by the producers. An example was an advertisement inserted by William A. Sheer, an extras' agent, in one of the New York morning papers about five weeks earlier. That ad solicited experienced horsemen to be used in motion picture productions. More than 500 men called at the Sheer office and left their names and were tentatively engaged at a salary of $1.75 a day to begin work on a movie at Whitestone, Long Island. They were told to call at the office a few days later and at that time were told to call again the next day. On that second occasion more excuses were given and they were told to call again in a few days. Stalling such as that continued for some 10 days until Sheer's brother George told them they would receive a post card in the mail when they were needed. By that time many of the men were angry and complained those stalling tactics kept them from looking for other work, as well as subjecting them to the expense of car fare to get repeatedly to the Sheer office.[3]

Another example from the Sheer office involved the agent sending one of his employees to Tenth Avenue in Manhattan to get a number of men of the tough-guy type for a movie, in response to a producer's order. Those recruited men, numbering about 20, were taken to Sheer's office and then

Film Actors Organize

sent to the studio. There, only six were accepted; the remainder insisted Sheer either put them to work or pay them for their time. He refused to do either and the men uttered threats. Police were summoned and the men charged with disorderly conduct. On the following day all were found guilty and fined in the Magistrate's Court. When a reporter spoke to Sheer about the horsemen incident, the agent said he had been asked by the director of the picture to get 500 men and hold them in readiness for a movie that would start production any day. Sheer said he only took the names and addresses of the horsemen and did not ask them to call at his office until they were notified of the location. But he had admitted that many of those recruited horsemen had shown up at his office every day. Meanwhile, delays in staring the movie continued. It was cases such as these that caused the extras to get together for the purpose of unionizing. They planned to have a membership fee of $5 a year and to maintain their own employment office from which extras would be hired and dispensed, thus avoiding the abuses so often received at the hands of agents and middlemen. Scale of wages the new group planned to press for was as follows: in films using 100 extras or less, $3 per person per day; films using over 100 extras, $2 a person; full dress and fancy dress extras, $5 a day; for hazardous work, $7.50 a day; and for night work, after 6:00 P.M., time and a half. Also, no commission was to be deducted from the extras' pay by this fledgling union's employment office. Several of the film producers had been approached on the subject and were said to have signified their willingness to employ their extras direct from the proposed group, instead of from the agencies. One of the first approached was Lewis J. Selznick. He declared he was heartily in accord with the idea and that he would send a letter to all film producers in New York urging them to cooperate with him in the movement to pay the extras what they were worth and to eliminate the agencies from the business.[4]

Over the next few days the leaders of the movement to organize the film extras had several conferences with Hugh Frayne, general organizer of the American Federation of Labor (AFL), and Harry Mountford, leader of the White Rats Actors Union of America. As a result of those meetings it was arranged for the granting of a charter to the new union, tentatively formed and known as the Motion Picture Extra People's Association (MPEPA) of Greater New York, Local 30, White Rats Actors Union of America. Receiving a charter direct from the Rats meant the MPEPA was

1. Early Efforts and Equity's First Attempt, to 1923

a subordinate part of the Rats, whose members were mainly vaudeville players, but was also affiliated with the AFL. The Federation only allowed affiliation for a particular trade or occupation through one union. The White Rats controlled the AFL acting franchise. Thus, for another group of actors, regardless of which branch of the amusement field they acted in, affiliation with the Federation was possible only if the new group merged itself—gave up its identity—into the Rats or became a somewhat independent, but subordinate, part of the Rats. The extras chose the later. Another option, not used at the time, was for the AFL to redefine and restructure the acting franchise within itself. That would happen later in a clash between the White Rats and Actors' Equity Association, and later still, in a clash between Equity and the Screen Actors' Guild (SAG). With the news of the new extras' union, agents and contractor middlemen were reportedly perturbed and declared that any actor who joined this new union would be blacklisted by them. A representative of the William Sheer office spent most of a week telling every extra he could contact that there was no possibility that such an organization could survive and that they should keep away from the union agitators or they would be blacklisted.[5]

Endeavors had been made by the extras to ascertain the legal status of agents and contractors and perhaps shut them down that way. To that end they called on the Commissioner of Licenses, George H. Bell. But he told them that no provision was made in the city charter for such people and since no regulations covered their activities he, Bell, could do nothing to help the extras. A majority of film makers were reported to be in accord with the movement to eliminate agencies and William A. Brady (World Film Corp.), J. S. Blackton (Vitagraph), and W. L. Sherrill (Frohman Film Corp.) informed Isador Stern (interim president of MPEPA) that they would be glad to employ extras direct, as they were paying a hefty price for extras and believed the new movement would do away with a great evil in the industry. Fox film studio was one of the few producers that hired its extras direct instead of through agents or contractors. A journalist reported that directors at film studios were powerless to hire extras direct and though they could accept actors for employment who appealed to them directly, such people still had to obtain their employment from the agencies. For example, in August 1916, word came from the Rolfe studio that 20 men were needed for a scene. Men applied directly to the film's director and he informed them they could work for him on the picture, providing they accepted the employment through Ben Weiss, an agent, who was providing the extras for all of the Rolfe studio's production. B. A. Rolfe, president of the Rolfe Picture Corporation, told a *Variety* reporter that all extras receiving less than $5 a day were hired through Weiss because by using that method the studio saved a lot of time and trouble and also because they could get a more realistic type of character through the agency rather than if they hired their own people direct. As to the fee that Weiss got, Rolfe said he understood the agent got 50 cents from each $2.50 per day extra and he believed Weiss was entitled to that amount. At a meeting held by the White Rats that union — then the most powerful actors' union in existence, having been formed in 1900 — unanimously resolved to help the Motion Picture Extra People's Association in every manner possible.[6]

Yet just two months later it was reported that the affairs of the MPEPA were in a muddled condition owing to infighting among several rival factions within the group. Weekly meetings of the extras' union were held on Sunday nights in New York at the White Rats' clubhouse and on most occasions those meetings ended in what were described as "riots." Main trouble in the group centered on Isador Stern, MPEPA organizer and financial secretary. Stern had been charged by MPEPA president Joseph Scott with being incompetent to manage the affairs of the local owing to his being a minor; he would turn 19 years of age in a week. Acting under the advice of Rats' leader Harry Mountford, Stern submitted his resignation as organizer. That was voted on and accepted by the membership but he retained his position as financial secretary. Then the controversy came to a head at a meeting to decide if Stern should continue to hold any post in the union. He was voted out completely with a near fight erupting among the membership in attendance. Because of all the infighting the MPEPA was widely viewed as being on the brink of collapse. Stern was believed to have the backing of the Rats and it was felt that if he severed all his connections with the MPEPA he would immediately start a rival group that would have the support of the Rats. The journalist covering the events went on to state that the trouble in the MPEPA, ongoing since the formation of the union, was laid largely to agents and middlemen who, it was believed, were trying to break it up. "Members of the organization who are forced out are offered positions with agents to secure people for them, and have been making it a custom to work among the members of

1. Early Efforts and Equity's First Attempt, to 1923

the union in order to cause internal disorder in that body," wrote the reporter. After that the MPEPA was not heard from again.[7]

Actors' Equity Association (Equity) was the only other actors' union on the go in the 1910s, besides the White Rats. Equity, founded in 1913, covered mostly stage actors but was in a weak position all through the 1910s. After getting nowhere for some six years in trying to deal with theatrical producers — and being ignored — it called a strike in 1919 that Equity won resoundingly. It almost won a full union shop from the strike, something it would finally attain in the 1920s. On the other hand the White Rats had called a series of disastrous strikes in the period around 1917, and was crushed. While it continued to exist on paper for some time it was effectively dead from then onward. Equity wanted to affiliate with the AFL but because the Rats had the AFL acting charter, affiliation by Equity was possible only if Equity went through the Rats. Because of the pariah status the Rats had picked up during their disastrous negotiations and strikes, Equity refused to have any affiliation with the Rats. Vaudeville producers, having beaten their actors' union, were active in advising and counseling theatrical producers in their dealings with Equity. A logical step would have been for the AFL to redefine the Rats charter but to save face it did so indirectly by forming the 4As (Association of Actors and Artistes of America). That was a skeletal organization, a housekeeping move only. No individual player joined the 4As. Rather, the 4As was given the acting franchise for the AFL, with the Rats' original charter disappearing. Then the 4As chartered what remained of the Rats to represent vaudeville actors only; all other actors were put under the jurisdiction of Equity, chartered also by the 4As at the same time. The 4As never actually did anything, with the rare exception being when it refereed disputes within the acting community as to who belonged to what type of acting group. The other two branches of the 4As were tiny and insignificant, being a chorus union and a Hebrew actors' union. By setting up such a structure the AFL hoped it had saved face for everybody and yet was not perceived as deliberately doing the bidding of the producers by somehow punishing or emasculating the Rats, at least any more than they had suffered at the hands of vaudeville producers. During the 1910s both the Rats and Equity stood ready to accept film players as members. Both had some members from the film community but not many, and most of those were from actors active in two or more of the acting branches of film, legitimate stage,

Film Actors Organize

and vaudeville. Equity was far too weak to make any substantial efforts to organize film actors; the Rats were much stronger, for a brief period, but also involved in a vicious, protracted, and ultimately unsuccessful struggle for their own survival. What was true of actors' unions was that none had much success in cross-organizing. That is, the Rats could only organize vaudeville players successfully, Equity could only organize stage actors; and SAG would only organize movie actors. However, Equity would go on to enjoy some limited success in cross-organizing in the late 1920s, but not to the point of being recognized as the film players' bargaining agent.

Late in 1917, one news story related that film players were being admitted then to Equity, but only upon meeting a certain condition that had earlier been imposed by Equity's executive board. The condition was that the applicant had to have had at least two years' experience in individual acting on the stage of the spoken drama. Howard Kyle, Equity secretary, remarked that within the past year the legal department of Equity had disposed of numerous cases wherein film players, members of Equity, had been saved thousands of dollars by the union's legal department's action on their behalf. Still, it was not an active recruitment with open arms.[8]

Meanwhile, by 1916, most of the film production business had relocated to the Los Angeles area. Unionization efforts were then underway among the craft and technical people involved in filmmaking, but not among any of the artistic people. Those efforts caused the virulently anti-union *Los Angeles Times* to bluster in August 1916, "Efforts of union-labor agitators to unionize the film industry of Los Angeles and vicinity are a failure. Seventeen of the largest concerns operating here have emphatically affirmed their intention of continuing to operate open-shop plants.... The attempt to organize is a dismal failure." Studios pledging themselves to an open shop policy were: Majestic, Universal, New York, Fine Arts, Bosworth, Morosco, Keystone, Lasky, Balboa, Selig, American Film Company, National Drama, Fox, Lubin, Rollin, L.K.O., and Christie. According to the Los Angeles newspaper, under the open shop conditions the motion picture industry there had developed to "mammoth" proportions within six years. It was conservatively estimated that the total expenditures of the industry in a year ranged from $10 million to $15 million and that during the course of a year some 15,000 people were given employment in the various branches of the film industry. It was reported that 75 percent of all films produced in the United States were made in Los Ange-

1. Early Efforts and Equity's First Attempt, to 1923

les and vicinity. "Union-labor agitators have looked with greedy eyes upon the great motion-picture industry, our richest single field, and they have been reaching out their tentacles to seize and shackle it," declared the account. Then the *Times* went on to sneer at any effect unionists would have if they went so far as to try and boycott cinemas: "As a matter of fact, if every union-labor man and woman in Los Angeles should cease to visit the picture shows here the loss would be scarcely felt. The unions themselves claim not more than 12,000 members in Los Angeles County, and that figure is grossly exaggerated. They are so few in number now that they do not even dare to try to have a Labor Day parade." A very smug newspaper went on to conclude, "In order to generally advance their interests, seventeen of the largest motion-picture concerns of Los Angeles have banded together as the Film Producers' Association. It is this body that stands firmly committed to the open-shop policy. Workmen and women are employed by these concerns solely on their merit and ability to perform certain lines of work, and the union card is not new and never will be a necessity here." While the paper's remarks were directed at the craftspeople then trying to organize, they applied to anyone in Los Angeles — a notoriously anti-union city — trying to unionize. The irony of the newspaper praising the producers for forming a cartel, a monopoly, or, if you will, a union, to prevent the employees from organizing a union of their own, was ignored by the publication.[9]

Six months later, in February 1917, the same newspaper reported that union organizers, chagrined by the failure of their repeated attempts to unionize the film business in Los Angeles had finally made an appeal to the building trades department of the American Federation of Labor. That report, not meant for the public, said, in part, "with possibly one exception ... the [film] managements are not favorable to unionism as we understand it, and the task before us seems to be that of changing this adverse sentiment towards union men." A possible boycott of cinemas was mention in the plea but the *Times* declared the studios had little to fear on that point because "there are not more than 15,000 union labor members in the entire Los Angeles County, out of its more than 800,000 inhabitants, and their influence upon the crowds that attend moving picture shows would be negligible." As well, the report detailed numerous attempts that had been unsuccessfully tried in order to unionize the major studios, which caused the newspaper to boast, "With refreshing frankness the report chronicles the failure of these attempts. The document itself is enough to show the firm and staunch stand which the largest producers here have taken and are maintaining in support of the open shop and industrial freedom." With respect to the likelihood of unionization in the film industry taking place the article asserted; "the prospect is not brilliant that headway will be made in their attempt to put the yoke of union tyranny on the necks of local film producers, and the implied threat of boycott undoubtedly will not sit well with the producers."[10]

A year and a half later the *Times* declared again that the open shop plan would be adhered to in the film industry, adding that the idea of paying people time and a half for overtime was "inconsistent with the nature of the film industry and therefore irreconcilable." Such had been the decision made a day earlier by a special committee of representatives of the various film studios of Los Angeles, in the face of a walkout by some of the technical people. The International Association of Theatrical Stage Employees and Motion Picture Operators then had 1,100 members out on strike; one of their demands was for time and a half after eight hours on the job. Several studios had already agreed to the strikers' demands including Universal, Fox, Griffith, Metro, Ince, Sennett, and Chaplin. Studios holding out included Lasky, Triangle, Vitagraph, Morosco, and Christie. Despite the boasts of the *Los Angeles Times*, the open shop was starting to crumble and erode, although the actors remained largely on the sidelines.[11]

Still, all the union activity by the technical people in the film industry did seem to be a catalyst for some organizing activity on the part of the actors. Union organizer A. B. Dale called a meeting on September 15, 1918, to discuss his proposed Motion Picture Players' Union. Meeting chairman J. B. Lafflan announced that he was ready to "tear to pieces" any spies of the producers who were in attendance while one Seymour Hastings stated he stood for a flat $5-a-day wage for film extras and if an extra emerged from the crowd his pay was to be raised to $7.50 a day.[12]

Two months later a report datelined Laredo, Texas, stated the executive council of the American Federation of Labor had granted a charter on November 12 to the Motion Picture Players' Union of California. Reportedly it was the first recognition given film actors by the AFL. In announcing the charter the council said the Los Angeles union had more than 2,000 members. However, the account was at least partially wrong.

1. Early Efforts and Equity's First Attempt, to 1923

At the time the White Rats still held the AFL acting franchise. Any affiliation to the Federation by the Los Angeles union would have to have come from the Rats, and not directly from the AFL.[13]

Early in February 1920 Frank Gillmore (Equity) and Harry Mountford (Rats) were in Los Angeles for meetings and recruitments. By this time the 4As had been set up and both Equity and the Rats (no longer using the name White Rats) had been affiliated with the AFL by receiving a charter directly from the 4As, thus becoming separate but equal unions representing actors. The old Rats represented vaudeville actors; Equity represented all other actors. While in Los Angeles the two men arranged to issue a separate charter from the 4As to the Motion Picture Players' Union, having jurisdiction in Los Angeles County over what were called "atmosphere" (extras) players and bit players. By doing so Equity planned to remove a possible thorn in its side with respect to its future activity of organizing Hollywood actors by bringing the Los Angeles union into the same body as itself. However, before that charter was issued, and after a couple more conferences with the Motion Picture Players' Union it was decided that the latter body would, instead, enter the Actors Equity Association as a whole, thus eliminating it as an organization. With the housekeeping measures out of the way Equity began the real work of its western visit; it was Equity's first real try to organize the film players. In Los Angeles on February 1, 1920, there was a well attended meeting. It was called for actors to hear about Equity and for the union to gain new members. Both Gillmore and Mountford spoke. As the last speaker Mountford urged all actors to join Equity. Reportedly, he received a standing ovation at the end of his speech and then "hundreds" of applications for membership in Equity were filled out.[14]

Late in March 1920 the Motion Picture Players' Association (New York City) held a membership meeting and voted to merge itself into Equity, becoming a department of Equity. Membership in that union, some 400, was said to consist mainly of film actors who played small parts, extras not being eligible for membership. Thus by around the middle of 1920 Equity had established a motion picture branch within itself and was set to continue its first major push to organize Hollywood's actors.[15]

At the end of October 1920, talk of a strike by the motion picture section of Equity was minimized by Equity president John Emerson. Speaking in New York City, Emerson declared that while actors had grievances those could be taken care of, in his opinion, without resorting to drastic measures. In the course of a few weeks Equity would have ready a contract that the majority of film studios would sign, he insisted, and the one or two other studios from whom he might expect continued resistance "will be forced to" sign the Equity standard contract. One of the most serious grievances, he said, was double time work. If a movie would ordinarily take four weeks to produce, some directors worked the actors day and night to finish it in two weeks. "This sort of thing must be remedied," said Emerson, "and I believe I will have very little trouble getting the heads of the motion picture industry to sign the contract which would state that the men and women work only a certain number of hours during the week." Another evil for the actors was said to be the "grafting agents" who secured employment for them. Gouging by those private agencies had to stop, Emerson said, and as a first step taken to put them out of business, Equity had recently established its own employment bureau. Kempton Green, chairman of the Equity executive committee, urged the 500 people listening to Emerson not to talk about a closed shop. "While we are relying on the producers to give us work and since they are the ones who are putting the bread and butter in our mouths, please don't mention 'closed ship,'" he explained.[16]

At a meeting in Los Angeles on January 19, 1921, Fraser Hall, Equity organizer, reported that the Los Angeles Actors' Association would be absorbed into Equity. It had been formed to combat the agents in Los Angeles who were charging 10 percent. Within the Actors' Association dues were $10 a year with a five percent commission charged on income earned from engagements arranged through the group's own agency. However, a short time earlier the group had got into financial difficulty and its commission rate was raised from five percent to seven percent. There was a reported membership of about 800 in the Actors' Association. Also, in his speech, Hall explained the "Equity shop"—it meant no Equity members would work with those who were not members of the association but the membership rolls would remain open to all those having the necessary qualifications who wished to join. None of the film stars were at the meeting, though; those attending being mostly players from the supporting casts. One of the points most strongly made by Hall as he pitched for members was that certain studios were in the habit of working the players overtime without extra pay. Hall pledged that once Equity represented

1. Early Efforts and Equity's First Attempt, to 1923

the players it would make an immediate move to enter into an agreement whereby 48 hours would constitute a week's work.[17]

Even then as Equity made its first major pitch to represent the actors in 1920–1921, there was internal friction. Film players in New York belonging to Equity, in early 1921, wanted an AFL affiliated charter of their own, from the 4As. That was the consensus of a meeting of the Motion Picture Department of Equity, held at the Hotel Astor in New York City. After the desire of the gathering was made known, Equity representatives spoke against the proposal. They told those in attendance it was through the efforts of Equity that the film section had been formed and whatever benefits may have accrued to the members could also be traced to the same source. At the end of that meeting the decision on separation was deferred. Benefits of separation were seen to be that the film section, under a 4As charter, would be absolute in its field, under its own domination, and not subordinate to Equity, and under its direction, as it was as a department of Actors' Equity Association. It was reported the Equity Motion Picture Department then had about 2,000 members, all located in the East.[18]

In March 1921 movie producers were said to be worried that Equity intended to take steps to enforce the closed shop rule in regard to picture casts. Rumor had it that there was going to be an attempt in Los Angeles to compel the use of 100 percent Equity casts in films, with that rumor apparently coming from those who held Equity memberships. The recent merging into Equity of the Actors' Association and the Motion Picture Players' Union (both Los Angeles–based) was said to have had much to do with the recent cuts in salaries imposed by various studios. Since the Actors' Association had voted to merge into Equity the film producers had banded together and all had refused to do any business with the employment agency arm of that group.[19]

Late in April 1921 Equity held a mass meeting in Los Angeles at the Ambassador Hotel, led by Frank Gillmore, Equity executive secretary. Abut 1,000 attended with half of the crowd being members of the union. At the end of the meeting 248 applications for membership were reported to have been turned in, with the majority of those being from "small part and atmosphere people." Gillmore directed his talk to the benefits to be derived from Equity membership, repeating the argument that the Equity shop was not a closed shop because the association's books would always be open to membership from any actor who wished to join. As well, Gillmore asserted the film producers would have to meet Equity shop conditions once the group was recognized in Los Angeles. Taking a conservative position he carefully avoided talk of a strike but inferred that negotiations between players and producers conducted in a spirit of good fellowship would be sufficient to bring about a betterment of conditions. Among the other speakers was performer Will Rogers. Gillmore arrived in Los Angeles about one week before the meeting and worked with Frazer Short, the local organizer for the union. Advance publicity for the meeting said that an attempt would be made to enlighten the profession as to the aims and purposes of the union, as related to the motion picture industry.[20]

A general film studio strike took place in the middle of July 1921, when the mechanical trades walked out after they had refused to take the salary cut proposed by the producers. Studios affected by the strike included Goldwyn, Lasky, Metro, Fox, Realart, Hal Roach, Buster Keaton, Universal, and Christie. During the three weeks prior to the strike, Frank Gillmore had been in Los Angeles incognito and persuaded the local Labor Council that it would be a "general detriment to labor" if the actors were called upon to walk out and support the technical personnel. He stated Equity was in such condition that the actors did not understand what was expected of them and therefore they could not be expected to walk out when they held $1,000 a week contracts, for men who were only getting $7 a day. A call to walk out in support of the striking craftsmen, according to Gillmore, would entirely disrupt the actors' union organization and "put it on the rocks." On the pleas that the association was in peril of being disrupted and because the allied trades figured they could beat the producers without the aid of the actors' body, it was generally understood the Equity membership would not be called on to help in the battle. After receiving that assurance from the Los Angeles Labor Council, Gillmore left Los Angeles immediately for New York.[21]

That technical dispute started when the producers tried to impose a 12.5 percent wage cut and, according to the union, impose a 10-hour day—it had been eight hours. Working through their cartel, the Motion Picture Producers and Distributors Association (MPPDA), the producers denied the 10-hour day claim but a copy of an order posted at the Goldwyn studio at the start of the dispute listed a 10-hour day as one of the new working conditions. Unions on strike included the International

1. Early Efforts and Equity's First Attempt, to 1923

Alliance of Theatrical Stage Employees (IATSE) and 15 other unions. Producers argued they would be happy to close completely for part of the summer (given a general business depression) but only stayed open to live up to their contracts with the expensive stars. Further, they claimed, about 25 percent of the cinemas in America were then closed while those remaining open were demanding reduced film costs from the studios.[22]

Likely Gillmore had been right in seeing Equity's film actor section as being fragile and not ready, because the union's first try at organizing Hollywood, tentative, hesitant and weak, had failed and was over in the summer of 1921. In February 1922 it was reported that the Film Players' Club (FPC), a New York organization of film players ranging from extras to bit players to principal players who were paid as much as $50 a day, had tripled in membership in the previous two months, with half of the new membership coming from the Motion Picture Department of Equity. One of the reasons was that Equity charged a commission of five percent for securing work for its members, with the FPC charging no fee for the same service. FPC had dues of 25 cents per week and an initiation fee of $2; Equity's Motion Picture Department had an initiation fee of $12, annual dues of $12, plus charging the five percent commission. Another benefit in the FPC's favor was the large club rooms in its New York City office with its members encouraged to come and use the rooms to rest in, and so on. On the other hand, Equity did not encourage its members to use the office as a club room. It was estimated the FPC, an unaffiliated organization, had a membership of 300, and was six years old. Although it was touted in this account as a possible rival to Equity, the FPC was not heard from again.[23]

In November 1922 the New York City office of the Motion Picture Department of Equity closed. No official reason was given but rumor had it that the office was steadily losing money. William Cohill had been in charge of the office, at a salary of $100 weekly plus five percent of the commissions paid by the members for work; that is, five percent of the five percent. On the west coast, in Los Angeles, Equity's coast film branch remained in operation but rumor had it that it had to be supported by funds from Equity's New York headquarters from time to time.[24]

2
A Brief Lull, 1924–1927

Equity's first attempt had led to a quick failure with the union perceiving that Hollywood's players were in no frame of mind to unionize, as evidenced from the brief 1921 craft workers' walkout during which Gillmore had suffered the humiliation of going to the Los Angeles Labor Council and begging to have his people excused from any participation or support because they were not "ready." It must have been particularly difficult to bear because craft unions had come to the aid of Equity during its 1919 stage actor strike and had been of immeasurable support and assistance in bringing about a swift and successful result for the actors. What membership Equity had in the film acting community up to 1923 had come almost entirely from the lowest paid players. Hollywood's film stars were notable by their absence from Equity's membership rolls. Any union trying to organize Hollywood film actors understood support from the major players was essential if successful organization was to occur. Yet, of all the workers in America, those least in need of protection, those least in need of collective bargaining were the major film players. However, Equity was not ready to give up and remained active in its pursuit of the Hollywood player, but only sporadically over the coming few years as organization efforts stagnated.

Around June 1924 it came to light that Equity had been active in the studios in Los Angeles. It was reported then to have added something like 1,000 members to its Motion Picture Department. Numerous meetings of actors had been held in Los Angeles, some secret and others rather open. All were held for the purpose of preaching the virtues of the association and the influence it could have in the motion picture field. Speculation

2. A Brief Lull, 1923–1927

was that Frank Gillmore would be in Los Angeles soon to launch a full campaign to organize the actors and to achieve the closed shop. Wedgewood Nowell, in charge of Equity's Hollywood office, declined to comment on any of the speculation. Another round of salary cuts was also rumored to be in the works by the producers. Although the Hollywood major studios had a solid cartel, the MPPDA, and though they appeared united and solid on all items, and though they almost never let internal disagreements become public, there was one major problem. Studios constantly stole, and tried to steal, stars from each other. Poaching and the offering of lucrative deals to stars under contract to other studios were rampant. Due to escalating costs from such behaviors the studios developed the long-term contract, ranging from a few years duration initially to the later more well known seven-year contract. While such contracts helped slightly to control poaching they were not especially successful at curbing costs. Stars under long term contracts got paid every week (actually mostly 40 weeks out of 52 each year) and that also tended to push up costs. And poaching continued. Studios often came to "gentlemen's agreements" not to poach but no sooner had the hands dropped from the binding shake than one or more of the producers was off on a poaching expedition. Regularly the studios blamed the actors — who benefited enormously from the poaching, at least at the star level — for the obscenely high costs borne by the Hollywood studios. In reality, though, it was the greed of the studios that prevented them from controlling their own inappropriate behavior.[1]

A few weeks later it was reported that an unnamed featured player asking for a raise had been told by one of the producers that he could not give him an increase because at a recent meeting of the Hollywood studios' cartel, the MPPDA, it had been agreed that no salaries were to be raised for three months. That actor went on to see a second producer, who confirmed what the first producer had said.[2]

One month later an article appeared that outlined the speed-up efforts then underway at Hollywood studios — efficiency campaigns aimed at cutting the cost of film production. As a result, whereas in the past it had taken from 10 weeks to four months to turn out a feature, the directors had cut the time down to from four to six weeks. To do that the directors had been working their people day and night, seven days a week. Actors were told to be on the set or on location at 7:30 A.M. or 8:00 A.M. and required to stay into the late evening. It was hard on a large number of the players who were kept on their feet for almost the entire time, with rehearsals and retakes along with the regular filming. "Many of the women [players] have been prostrated as a result and left the set ill," noted a journalist. One featured female player told of being able to sit down for no more than 20 minutes total in a working day of from 12 to 15 hours and "there have been numerous cases of both women and men having keeled over either on the set or while off as a result of the speeding up program." People who ordinarily got from eight to 15 days on a film as extras then were fortunate if they got from three to five days; folks on the weekly wage scale got about half the work they did in the past.[3]

Whenever actors were threatened with pay cuts or subjected to speed-ups, or faced other abuses from the studios, the likelihood of union activity occurring increased. This time was no different and in July 1924 Wedgewood Nowell, still Equity's Los Angeles representatives met in conference with Will Hays, the "czar" of the motion picture industry. Producers back in 1922 had hired Hays to head the majors' cartel, the Motion Picture Producers and Distributors Association, and to give the appearance that he would clean up Hollywood abuses, improve morality among the players, and to ensure the studios presented a "clean" product on the screen, and so forth. Often the MPPDA was referred to simply as the Hays office and the production code of dos and don'ts — forerunner of our current film rating system — was often called the Hays Code. When Hays met Nowell in Los Angeles he received a tentative form of contract that Equity wanted the members of the MPPDA to use with the actors they engaged. Hays said he would give the matter some thought on his way back east — he was based in New York — and then go into the matter with both producers and Equity that fall. That conference between Hays and Nowell was actually the second one held on a visit to Los Angeles by the czar, with the first one having been held at the home of producer Jesse Lasky on July 27, 1922. At that time Hays and Lasky received an actors' committee that consisted of Mrs. Theodore Roberts, Nowell, J. Frank Glendon, Tully Marshall, Ralph Lewis, and De Witt C. Jennings. During that meeting various suggestions with respect to working conditions were put forward by the actors. At the conclusion of the meeting Hays declared he would see that certain changes were brought about.[4]

Among the items raised at the first meeting with Hays and brought up again at the second was the problem of calling actors to be on the set

2. A Brief Lull, 1923–1927

at 9:00 A.M. regardless of whether they were needed then or not. Sometimes they were not used until late afternoon, or for days. Another matter was the hazardous conditions actors sometimes faced. For example, an actor had an unlimited amount of water poured on him; explosions were set off behind players, scaring them (they had no foreknowledge of the detonations). Actors felt compelled to do the hazardous stunts because they feared if they did not they would not be used again. Some directors only allowed their people 15 to 20 minutes for a meal break and not at any regular time but only when the director felt like it. Sometimes an actor's work day ran to 17 hours. Another issue was that each studio used its own contract form — all were different. Equity wanted to see a single, standard form in use. One common feature in all contracts was that seven days constituted a work week; there was no overtime and no extra pay for holidays and Sundays. Also, keys were not supplied to actors for dressing rooms yet the studios took no responsibility when thefts occurred from those dressing rooms during an actor's absence. Producers often engaged players at reduced salaries with a promise they would be used for another picture in the future, in a bigger role, and so on. Such promises were never kept.[5]

At both of those meetings with Hays actors raised allegations that studios made a habit of obtaining people for parts through agencies that charged players 10 percent commission, despite the fact the studios had their own casting directors and knew the work and ability of most of the people engaged through the contractors. It was asked that the studios do their own casting directly, without subjecting the players to agents. While Equity wanted actors known at studios not to be compelled to apply for work through agencies, the union said it had no objection to agencies getting work for people unknown at the studios. The contract handed to Hays at the 1924 meeting requested a 48-hour week be the norm. However, it was reported that Equity did not expect to achieve a 48-hour week, but would be willing to accept a 54-hour week. As well, the union wanted a clause in the contract stipulating a producer or director must notify an actor he would be needed the next day, if such were the case, no later than midnight of the day before. Further, the union wanted pay to start when the actor left the studio for a location and continue until the time he arrived back at the studio, instead of the method then in place whereby the actor started to be paid only when he began work and stopped being paid when he ceased to work on location.[6]

Film Actors Organize

Complaints about the railroading of actors, as noted above, brought a response from Joseph Schenck, president of the Association of Motion Picture Directors. He said, in September 1924, that the practice of working actors unusually long hours without good reasons for doing so was a thing of the past. Explaining it had been brought to the attention of the association that quite a number of producers had been working their actors extremely long hours, he added that he and Fred W. Beetson, secretary of the MPPDA, acting on the complaints, "made an investigation and found that quite a number of them were true." Following the investigation Schenck made it known that any actors who felt producers had taken unfair advantage of them — by working players unusually long hours — should go to his association and register their grievances. Those grievances, he said, would be investigated with the name of the people making them held in confidence. Schenck did not explain how anonymity would be possible and if his hidden message was not clear enough he went on to declare that no actor need have any fear about lodging a complaint as Schenck would not tolerate the blacklisting of anyone who had a "legitimate cause" to complain. Noting there were 8,500 actors in Los Angeles, Schenck told a reporter it had been called to the attention of his association that a "pernicious practice" by some producers of working players too long at a time and then calling them to reappear at the studio after a short period of rest had been going on. "This is manifestly unjust, primarily to the actor and also to the public, for a tired player cannot give his best to the part," Schenck commented to the newsman. "I have heard where some pictures have been made in four and five days. That was through working the actors 18 to 20 hours a day. That was not fair to the actor, or to the public who will see the picture," he elaborated. "That condition must be eliminated immediately, for the good of all concerned. Sometimes the producer is at fault and sometimes the director. But whoever it is should have it brought to his attention he is doing wrong."[7]

According to an October 1924 account there were then about 8,000 film extras in the Los Angeles area. Most were said to be unhappy with the way Julius Bernheim, general manager of Universal studio, had treated them. A scene was to be shot for a film in which a circus was used. Those extras heard about the scene almost a month before it was to be shot and rumors spread throughout the agencies through which the extras would be booked that there would be a couple of days work for at least 1,000 of

2. A Brief Lull, 1923-1927

them in that movie. Then an advertisement appeared in the Los Angeles daily papers inviting readers to visit Universal City with their children on a Sunday afternoon to see the circus, admission free. No mention was made that a film was being shot or that they would be inadvertent and unpaid extras. In the ad children were especially sought, with the proviso they be accompanied by a guardian. Three of the extras who saw the ad wrote letters to the newspaper pointing out that those attending the free circus were taking bread and butter from the mouths of other children whose parents depended on film work for a livelihood. However, the public paid no attention to such appeals and on the appointed day there were more people on hand than the scene required.[8]

Early in 1925 it was estimated that $8 million a year was paid in the Los Angeles area for film extras and that 10 percent of that amount went to agents who secured employment for them. California State Labor Commissioner Mathewson felt those actors were being taken advantage of and said that he planned to ask the State Legislature to enact a law prohibiting the charging of large fees by the employment agencies. Mathewson explained that agencies got from seven to 10 percent commission on all the work they obtained for the extras and that most of the work obtained lasted only for two or three days. He felt the casting directors at each of the studios could handle the employment of extras without recourse to agencies, middlemen, or contractors, and if that happened then extras could retain the entire small amount of money they received for such short-term employment.[9]

Competition for Hollywood players by the studios was intense in 1925 and it was reported that more featured players would be put under long-term contract in 1925 (with terms ranging from one to five years) than ever before in any year of the industry's history. Signing players to long-term contracts was viewed by the majors as a protective measure, all of whom wanted to control an abundance of featured star talent. Even at that early time the studios contracted, or farmed, or loaned, out their contract players to other majors, usually at a premium of 25 percent over the contract salary. For example, if Metro had signed Jane Doe to a long-term contract at $800 a week but had no work for her at some point then Metro would loan her out to Fox for $1,000 a week. Doe, though, never received any part of the premium, still receiving the contract amount of $800. One of the ways the cartel retained its control over the business was through the practice whereby a major studio would only farm out one of its contract players to one of the other major studios, also a member of the MPPDA cartel. However, the ostensible reason given was that a star's value might be lowered if she appeared in an "inferior" vehicle — something said to be more likely to happen if the star was farmed out to a non-cartel studio. All that fighting over actors to sign them long-term meant that actors not already under contract in 1925, had offers that usually doubled or tripled their income of 1924.[10]

Such complaints over the treatment of actors could sometimes spur increased union activity, usually from Equity, but it sometimes caused the cartel to respond, all the way from empty rhetoric (in the example from Schenck as previously noted) to actual reform, however minor. Such reforms whenever undertaken by the cartel as preventive measures were put in place only to ward off feared intervention by government regulators and/or increased union incursions. In March 1925 it was reported the MPPDA had been working on reforms to improve the condition of movie extras. Under the proposed new system the agent and his commission would be entirely eliminated. At that point the MPPDA committee handling the issue had held two meetings. At the third meeting a central casting proposition was discussed with the plan being to have the MPPDA studios obtain their movie extras from that office. An estimated $40,000 was required to establish the office. As well, the plan called for regulating the working hours for the extras and the grading of their pay in accordance with the importance of the work done. Before such a plan could be put into effect, though, the MPPDA planned to make an attempt to minimize the list of available extras by culling that list and striking out the names of "undesirables."[11]

Meanwhile, on June 1, 1925, Equity held its annual meeting. Reelected was the official slate of officers that included John Emerson (president), Ethel Barrymore (first vice president), and Frank Gillmore (executive secretary and treasurer). At that meeting a recommendation was put forward urging a militant attitude be adopted to obtain for Equity members in the film section the benefits of a standard minimum contract. With respect to the motion picture situation Gillmore reported, "It may seem to some that this branch of our association has been overlooked but we were waiting until matters with the legitimate [stage] were settled. The interviews of your President and myself with Will H. Hays over a period of three years have been most unsatisfactory." Gillmore explained that

2. A Brief Lull, 1923–1927

when Hays had assumed the chairmanship of the film industry it was declared the interests of all those affected would be considered. However, the union leader added, actors had never been consulted about anything and as far as Equity was concerned no steps had ever been taken to remedy the abuses that the union had brought to the attention of the producers. "After exhausting every conciliatory method it will be up to us to adopt a more militant attitude to see that our members in the motion picture industry receive the benefits of a standard minimum contract," Gillmore concluded.[12]

By the fall of 1925 enough complaints had been received that women and children extras were being worked under unfavorable conditions in the Hollywood studios that Marian Mel, assistant secretary of the California Industrial Welfare Commission was making an investigation. Allegations had been made that women worked overtime without extra pay and that they were not paid for the full period of time they were present on the studio lots. Mel said other complaints included that extras told to report to the studio at 7:00 A.M. were compelled to wait around until 10:00 A.M., or even noon, before being taken to the set and that they were paid only starting from the time they reached the set. Many of the extras, especially women and children, were said to have worked 10 to 12 hours a day without receiving any overtime pay. Also brought to Mel's attention was a report that an extra was called from Hollywood early in the morning to work at a Culver City studio but that upon arrival at Culver City (over one hour later) the shoot had been called off and the extra got no work and no compensation.[13]

A little less than a year later, in January 1926, the California State Industrial Welfare Commission issued orders regulating the employment of women and minors in the film industry as extras. Defined as an extra by the Commission was a woman or minor who was employed on a daily basis in a film studio at a wage of $15 or less per day. Provided in the order was that all work of extra women in excess of a standard day of eight hours was to be compensated at a rate of not less than time and a quarter of the base wage, up to 10 hours; not less than time and a half after 10 hours and up to 12 hours; not less than time and three quarters after 12 hours and up to 14 hours; and not less than double time after 14 hours. Extras required to try on and fit costumes either at the studio or at the costumers were to be paid not less than a full day's wage even if not used after the fitting.

Film Actors Organize

Women called to work as extras at night were to be let off work in time to allow them to return to their homes by public transit, otherwise the studio had to furnish transportation. Employers had to pay in cash or negotiable paper at the end of the day's work, and carfare was to be paid on "weather permitting" calls. All those state labor rules regulating extra work applied only to women and minors; they did not apply to men.[14]

That investigation by the California State Industrial Welfare Commission was enough to spur the MPPDA into taking action. Plans to remedy conditions of employment for thousands of extras in film work were announced on December 11, 1925, by the Motion Picture Producers Association when it unveiled the formation of the Central Casting Corporation. Fred W. Beetson, western representative of Hays and the MPPDA, was announced as president of the new organization. It was planned the Central Casting Bureau would go into operation in January 1926. It was also noted that plans for the office had been worked out with the advice of the Industrial Welfare Commission. Reportedly, in this account, more than 30,000 extras representing a payroll of $3 million were utilized each year by the studios in Hollywood. Basically, the MPPDA adopted for its extras the regulations laid down in January 1926 by the Industrial Welfare Commission; however, the MPPDA's regulations applied to male and female extras. The Commission still imposed its rules despite the promised formation of the Central Casting Bureau in order to have all the independent film studios outside the cartel bound by similar regulations.[15]

On the occasion of the formal opening of the Central Casting Bureau in Hollywood on January 25, 1926, Will Hays declared the film industry would be purged of "movie vagrants" through the functioning of the new agency. "Good moral character and ability to act will be the first references necessary to listing by this free employment bureau which will be the only source of entry to film work," said a reporter. The MPPDA — it contained about 95 percent of the Hollywood film industry — pledged itself to obtain its film extras only through that bureau. All private employment agencies and contractors for extras, it was believed, would be eliminated. Extras would keep all of their film income as no commissions would be levied on them. Central Casting was the culmination of about one year's planning and thought by the major studios and was meant for all extras who were employed in motion pictures on a daily basis for $15 a day or less. All aspirants for extra work were to be classified and investigated

2. A Brief Lull, 1923–1927

before being listed on Central Casting's rolls. A full record of their film work would also be maintained.[16]

An account of the formal opening of the Central Casting Bureau in the *New York Times* remarked it came about as a result of the California State inquiry, would eliminate the $500,000 yearly that was lost by extras to agent commissions and it would establish "conditions that will make employment desirable and clean up and eliminate the misfit."[17]

Two weeks after Central Casting officially opened Hays was just about ready to head back east. He said the bureau was functioning well and that the extras were indeed receiving the full monetary benefit of their labor. Agents were out of the running entirely, claimed Hays. Among the other problems he planned to tackle, he told reporters, was the question of a uniform, standard contract to be used by MPPDA members. Central Casting was funded by a charge on the studios that operated it; each paid five percent of the total it spent on hiring extras, to run the Bureau.[18]

According to a June 1926 report there were 22,500 people who believed they belonged in movies. Included in that figure were 800 principal actors with about 500 of them continuously at work on films while, of the 25,000 movie extras, never more than 2,500 were in demand. "Not over an average of 10 extras a year are ever elevated to principal roles, permanently. Within the past 10 years the known names in filmdom today of those who entered pictures as extras will not reach 25, and those nearly all women," observed a journalist. Average earning capacity of the 2,500 extras looked upon as regulars did not exceed $75 weekly, at the highest, with from $40 to $50 a week being a closer average for the majority. Of that income, a portion had to go for the necessary wardrobe an extra in demand was required to keep in supply. Wardrobes included evening dress, uniforms, sports clothes, and so on, with modish shoes and hats. Studios required extras to supply the entire wardrobe necessary for a film — except, of course, for period pieces for which the studio supplied the period dress. Regular extras got to be among the tiny percentage who could claim regular status because they were able and willing to amass large, costly, elaborate, and varied wardrobes, paid for out of their own pockets.[19]

Despite the bleak outlook extras continued to arrive in Hollywood at the rate of 200 daily. Many of the 22,500 unemployed believed discrimination was in use against them, due to the steady call for the 2,500 regulars. Said a reporter, "Of the 25,000 extras there are not 40 of a type that could play a banker or preacher for atmosphere and these 40 are of course included in the available 2,500." Similarly, there was a reportedly low number to play "ladies and gentlemen" and all of them were also included in the favored 2,500, thanks to experience and a wardrobe. That extensive wardrobe was acknowledged to be the most important factor if an extra was to be able to answer a wide variety of calls. Idle extras were from all walks of life and were all waiting for the "big day." Their last chance had come when a call was sent out for 5,000 extras for *Ben Hur*, filmed about a year earlier. Those 5,000 people were engaged for one day only; the following day the number was reduced to 3,000; on the third day to 2,000; on the fourth day to 1,000; and thereafter to 500. Extras in *Ben Hur* received $6 a day for their work. Overtime was paid at the rate noted above, as set by the California State Industrial Welfare Commission and then imposed on, or adopted by, the MPPDA. A few extras earned additional money by working for one director for eight hours during the day and for another director for eight hours at night. However, a new rule had just been established whereby that practice was banned. At Central Casting (managed by Dave Allen) it was said the names of the 2,500 regular extras filling virtually all requirements were all known; that they supplied every extra need and that when more of a certain type were needed they were secured from the neighborhoods their types could be found in. In preference to taking people from the idle 22,500 and having them made up for types directors demanded those types be played by naturals. Allen had been in charge of the Central Casting Bureau (CCB) since it starting doing business on January 1, 1926. Previously, Allen had run his own casting agency for extras, a business he had operated for some years. He gave that up to be the general manager of the CCB. By this time it was said that no private agencies for extras then existed. To further discourage the star struck, Allen declared that outsiders were not wanted or needed in Hollywood and that it was impossible to "make it" in the movies. Allen pointed out the CCB had two clerks employed whose sole duties were to inform the incoming mob why they could not hope to land a spot in filmmaking. The CCB then went so far as to ask the aspirant his previous occupation and if it was something like bookkeeper, barber, clerk (for men) or waitress, seamstress, manicurist (for women) an effort was made by the CCB to find that person a job in their former occupation.[20]

Nor was the situation for extras in the New York area film produc-

2. A Brief Lull, 1923–1927

tion world any different. While film production continued to some extent in the east, it remained in decline. "Experts" in the film industry estimated that 2,300 of the 3,500 extras in New York did not belong. The situation was the same for extras in New York as it was in Hollywood.[21]

In the first six months of operation as a free placement organization for film extras, the CCB provided employment for 113,837 people who earned a total of $983,903, of which no portion went to agencies or middlemen. During those six months, January to June of 1926, average daily placements numbered 629. Of the total placements, 75,875 went to men extras; women received 34,795 placements; boys, 1,730; and girls, 1,336. During that half-year period not a single complaint was made against a studio member of the MPPDA, or the CCB, to the California State Labor Bureau, by an extra. Prior to the establishment of the bureau an average of from 12 to 20 complaints a day were registered either against studios or casting agencies by extras, usually over wages. In addition to the salaries paid out the producers paid an additional $49,195.15 (five percent) to the CCB, which was used to operate the bureau. Although 113,837 placements were made in total, it was split up in such a way that only about 4,500 people were actually used. That was because about 3,000 of the extras registered were known to all of the studios and casting directors and in most cases those studio officials in issuing orders to the CCB for people would request that certain of the people be obtained for them. That is, Fox, say, would not send an order to the CCB for an Italian woman in her early thirties, but ask specifically for Jane Doe. Most of the extras specifically requested were in the $7.50 a day and over class, due to their ability to "properly dress" and function and some of those extras found work for up to 200 days a year. On the other hand, another 20,000 extras on the books were rarely if ever used because casting directors or assistant directors who issued the call were not familiar with them and would not take a chance with them unless a general "mob scene" was to be shot. On file with the CCB for each applicant was a photo and general working history. Salary scales paid by the CCB to the extras fell into seven categories: $3 per day (just for the huge mob scenes); $5, $7.50, $10, $12.50, $15, and over $15 a day, in all cases for an eight-hour day. Of the 113, 837 placements made, just 1,616 fell into that last and highest pay category. The average daily earnings of an extra in that period were $8.64.[22]

In a statistical release in August 1926 the United States Department of Labor announced the theatrical profession was represented in the American Federation of Labor by the Associated Actors and Artistes of America, embracing all entertainers except musicians, with an enrollment of 14,000. Chartered separately by the AFL the American Federation of Musicians had a membership of 125,000 while the International Alliance of Theatrical Stage Employees (IATSE) had 22,000 members.[23]

Throughout this period the studios continued direct and indirect attacks on actors as they sought to control the players and find ways to limit their salaries, refusing all the while to recognize themselves as the main problem. Also in August 1926, the MPPDA announced it wanted to control the way actors' agents worked, by franchising them. That is, only allowing certain agents to do business with them, and barring all others. It was to involve licensing just the "reliable and responsible" agents, in a plan similar to one in use in vaudeville. Each of the approved agents would be required to furnish a performance bond to the MPPDA. Some of the producers wanted to eliminate agents entirely but were swayed by arguments that agents were effective in finding new talent and bringing it to the attention of studios, something the studios did not have the time to do. All of it was a further way to control talent and try to limit salary increases since the MPPDA majors would not do so themselves, just as they would not stop poaching. However, such plans and strategies were always presented by the majors as being benefit and boon to actors. For example, in this case the example was cited of some agents who had actors under contract (personal contract) for $x a week and then sold them to studios for up to $400x per week, keeping the premium for themselves. No details were provided.[24]

Several months later Will Hays claimed he had received numerous requests from film actors asking for the establishment of a franchise booking office — the plan outlined above — but nothing ever came of that idea.[25]

A few months later the Keith-Albee (a chain of vaudeville theaters) legal department had a clause drawn up and inserted in all its contracts giving it an option on all who played its vaudeville houses for the first rights to use them in motion pictures. Keith-Albee was then in the process of trying (ultimately unsuccessfully) to affiliate with one or another major film studio. Because of that clause an actor could have perhaps been blocked from accepting a film offer from an unaffiliated film studio, or need consent from Keith-Albee. Actors were incensed.[26]

2. A Brief Lull, 1923–1927

Since one of the reasons Hays had been hired by the film cartel was to be seen to be cleaning up the morality of Hollywood — both on-screen and off-screen in the players' private lives — the czar moved in that direction in the fall of 1926. At that time it was reported that easing a player out of the picture industry was the method adopted by the MPPDA, through Hays, if a player got involved in a scandal that made it into the press. "The Hays system has been in operation for some time. Nothing has been given out or printed about it. The Hays organization prefers no publicity and the picture colonies don't have to read to know," explained a reporter. "The 'silent system' passes up a Hays-marked person. No written notice is sent out to an 'undesirable.' It's just passed around that so-and-so isn't a credit to the film industry."[27]

Around the middle of November 1926, a December 1 strike by Hollywood's craft and technical people seemed likely. It had the potential to lead to a massive walkout if all AFL unions followed suit. Equity was not then affected but would be if a strike took place and the studios tried to produce movies using non-union technical personnel. None of the unions on the verge of taking strike action had asked Equity about its attitude to such potential action. Rumor had it that Frank Gillmore favored a sympathetic move while Equity president John Emerson was opposed to his union getting involved in any way. Membership in Equity on the west coast was then estimated at between 500 and 1,000, with none of the extras being unionized.[28]

As the December 1 strike date neared (it was averted at the last minute) film actors who were members of Equity held a secret meeting in Los Angeles, around November 23, and voted to remain neutral in case the technical unions went out on strike against the Hollywood studios. Reportedly, efforts were made by some of those unions and also by Gillmore to get the players to side with the craft people in case the latter walked out. But with Equity not being organized in the studios even to the 50 percent level, it was figured by the players that it would be an unwise thing at that time for Equity to assert itself in a situation that "had no particular significance to its members." Actors were said to have found they had no grievance against the producers with working conditions satisfactory and therefore, in fairness to themselves as a large number of the Equity members were under long-term contracts, it would be best to remain neutral.[29]

Film Actors Organize

Over the full 12 months of 1926, the CCB made 259,259 placements that paid a total of $2,195,395.65, with an average daily wage of $8.46. The average daily placement was as follows; 485 men, 205 women, and 20 children (710 total). Total placements were as follows; 177,226 men, 74,614 women, 4,188 boys, and 3,231 girls. Because there were 18,000 or more people in Hollywood ready to take those 710 daily placements, Fred Beetson, president of the CCB, had issued a ruling that under no conditions or circumstances should any more people be registered for work as extras with the CCB. That bureau had one of the largest telephone exchanges of any private industry with 42 trunk lines feeding the switchboard. Over eight million calls were cleared through it during 1926.[30]

A March 1927 directive from the United States War Department declared that American soldiers would no longer do double duty by appearing in Hollywood films as extras, as the producers had continued to take advantage of such a large source of free labor. Specifically the War Department refused to permit 3,000 of its soldiers to double as Germans in *The Patent Leather Kid*. When a *Variety* reporter followed up the story the War Department explained that such a prohibition would henceforth be its policy. The order, sent to each corps area commander, followed a protest from the AFL. It was argued by the labor body that with thousands of unemployed extras, soldiers on the United States payroll should not be used to save the film studios money.[31]

When the actors who were members of Equity had declared they had no grievances, in advance of a threatened December 1, 1926, technical strike, it was mostly a case of cold feet. And many of the actors then said to be in Equity were among the higher-paid players, those least in need of a union. No extras or bit players were in Equity. Plenty of grievances did exist, though, as the majors continued to try and chip away at the actors. Over the last seven months or so of 1927 there would be much activity as Equity made its second major attempt to organize Hollywood, a more vigorous attempt than its first effort. And that second attempt came in the wake of the majors trying to impose salary cuts. First, though, the majors, probably sensing their proposed but still secret salary cuts would generate pro-union activity, launched a pre-emptive move. It adopted an old tried and true capitalist initiative; it set up a company union.

3

AMPAS and Salary Cuts; Equity's Second Attempt, 1927

As March 1927 came to an end an editor with the *Los Angeles Times* lashed out with one of the newspaper's regular editorial rants and tirades against the union shop. Specifically it was about Equity and the stage but, of course, it was meant as an object lesson for the motion picture industry. Bemoaning Equity's closed shop on stage the editor grumbled, "It not only has closed a fruitful avenue of rewarded effort to the free worker — and this includes both white collar and shirt sleeves — but it threatens to slam the door shut entirely for the actor and audience alike." Then he complained about the supposed declining number of stage plays being produced, a hopeless situation that he deemed was becoming more hopeless every year. "Except in a few large cities the spoken drama in America is extinct.... Outside New York 75 per cent of the legitimate theaters had permanently closed their doors," he added, but he gave no data to support any of his contentions. "This condition is not due to the competition of the motion picture. It started from the day the actors' union was able to enforce the closed shop and kill the freedom of the stage." He did say that Los Angeles was "one of the conspicuous exceptions" to the decline in stage productions, but offered no reason as to why that was so. Since anyone living in Los Angeles could see the editor's rant was senseless with respect to the home city, the editor had to claim Los Angeles was an exception to his arguments. However, since his arguments were all without foundation he could not say why his city was an exception. When he continued his screed the editor warned that "the motion-picture industry is wise in putting up a stiff fight to prevent this ruinous dictation by labor-union leaders from fastening itself on Hollywood."[1]

Today the Academy of Motion Picture Arts and Sciences (AMPAS) is known as the sponsor of Hollywood's annual awards extravaganza, the Oscar ceremony, where awards are handed out for best picture of the year, actor, and so on. When it was set up there were more important and pressing reasons for its establishment. For one thing it was foreseen as becoming something of a general fan club. Just as, say, Joan Crawford had a fan club, then why not have a general fan club for Hollywood. It was one more effort from Will Hays to win over and/or deflect what was perceived as an increasing questioning of Hollywood and its values, lifestyles, and so on, both on- and off-screen. Perhaps the single most important reason for setting up AMPAS, though, was that the majors, who set it up, viewed it as a company union, hoping its existence would make it impossible for a true actors' union, such as Equity, to take hold in Hollywood. Company unions were a regular part of the American scene and ran parallel to all the actors' unions in America. In vaudeville the producers set up the National Vaudeville Artists (NVA) to counter the White Rats; in the legitimate stage world the producers set up the Actors Fidelity League (an organization that came to be quickly and derisively known in the trade as Fido) to run against Equity. AMPAS was put in operation to try and keep Equity out of Hollywood, and later the Screen Actors' Guild (SAG). Of course, AMPAS was never officially presented as a company union but even publications such as *Variety* and *Billboard* (both of which were far from being pro-union publications) quickly saw it for what it was and usually refused to play the game by pretending it was something that it was not.

And so AMPAS was launched in Hollywood on May 4, 1927, sponsored by leaders in the industry and embracing every branch of it and with the official approval of Will Hays, president of the MPPDA. Or so declared an account in the *Washington Post* as it credulously followed the official line. Officers of AMPAS were: Douglas Fairbanks, president; Fred Niblo, vice president; Frank Woods, secretary; M. C. Levee, treasurer. Set up with five separate branches—producers, actors, writers, directors, and technicians—the AMPAS directors were: Mary Pickford, Louis B. Mayer, Joseph M. Schenck (for the producers); Douglas Fairbanks, Milton Sills, Conrad Nagel (actors); Jeanie McPherson, Carey Wilson, Joseph M. Earn-

3. AMPAS and Salary Cuts; Equity's Second Attempt, 1927

ham (writers); Fred Niblo, Frank Lloyd, John Stahl (directors); Roy Pomeroy, Cedric Gibbons, J. A. Ball (technicians). With respect to the organization, said the piece, "Plans include the erection of an academy building bestowal of awards of merit for distinctive achievements, interchange of constructive ideas among members and cooperation with colleges and universities in their recognition of motion picture making as a distinct art."[2]

A couple of days later *Washington Post* reporter Felicia Pearson remarked that AMPAS had been formed in order to unite all branches of the film business into one body. "The purpose of the organization is to promote harmony and unity among the five creative branches of the industry, which, altogether, are producers, actors, writers, directors and technizcians," she explained. "If any differences arise between the different branches or their members, they are to be settled by the members of this organization."[3]

A lavish banquet was held in Los Angeles on May 17, 1927, at the Biltmore Hotel for the official kickoff of AMPAS with 275 of the most prominent people in all branches of the film industry being present. Each person in attendance, reportedly, subscribed to a membership, paying a $100 initiation fee, making a total of $27,500 collected that night. The keynote of "one for all and all for one" was struck by Mary Pickford. Douglas Fairbanks started the proceedings by explaining a few people had been working together behind the scenes for five months on a plan for the welfare, protection, and good of the industry; that the new group would be the militant combination to come to the fore for the protection of the profession as well as the industry He introduced Fred Niblo who explained the idea for AMPAS was conceived by Louis B. Mayer at his home five months earlier while he, Niblo, Mayer, Fred Beetson (the representative of Hays and the MPPDA in Los Angeles), and actor Conrad Nagel were talking about the misunderstandings existing in the industry. Following that initial gathering some 32 more meetings had been held until an agreed upon plan had been devised.[4]

At that banquet Nagel said AMPAS would not conflict with any other organization as each branch of the business had its own organization and "the object of this body was to get all the affairs together for the purpose of eliminating friction, which might arise among the combined forces." According to Niblo "the plan had as its foundation honest and clean principles and in no way conflicts with the individual rights of anyone in the profession, but would be beneficial to the entire industry." Nagel explained there would be an elimination of discord in the industry though a grievance procedure in AMPAS. Complaints would first be made to an executive committee of the appropriate Academy branch. If the grievance was not resolved there it would go on to another committee, with a representative on it from each of the five Academy branches. A final decision would be rendered there. AMPAS, said Nagel, would have no connection whatsoever with any other organization in the film industry, but that it would be affiliated with the Motion Picture Producers and Distributors of America (MPPDA). Joseph M. Schenck, in his speech at the banquet, said there was no reason for the film actor to be dissatisfied or to distrust the producer. Mary Pickford, in her speech, pointed out indirectly another reason for setting up AMPAS [besides a company union it was to be a PR front]. She spoke of the idea that Schenck had of using the millions of fan letters that poured into Hollywood from all parts of the world and of enrolling those sympathetic individuals as corresponding or lay members of AMPAS, and of publishing a weekly bulletin and sending it to those millions of people — a fan club for Hollywood, as it were. "We are capable of self-government, of defending ourselves and of protecting our good name against unjust accusations," said Pickford. "I do not mean that we should defend those things that should not be defended. When we are in the wrong and censure is justified we should undertake whatever corrective measures may be necessary, but this discipline should come from within." The speech by Hays and the entire tone of the article in *Variety* indicated a Hollywood that viewed itself under siege, with AMPAS being a response. *Variety*'s article on the banquet was unusually long, almost a full page (spread over three) yet not a single word was mentioned in it about AMPAS and awards of merit. All of which indicated the Academy Awards for which AMPAS would become so well known were very far down in the group's list of priorities, at its inaugural banquet. Though there were only 275 members then of AMPAS (all apparently taken in at the banquet) plans existed to take in another 175 members. AMPAS membership was always limited in number and perhaps always, or mostly, by invitation only. Plans were also underway, reportedly, for the organization to have a category for associate membership, in each of the five branches. People eligible for that category were to be drawn from the ranks of those "who have not as yet performed any distinguished service to the industry."[5]

3. AMPAS and Salary Cuts; Equity's Second Attempt, 1927

Less than one month after holding its opening banquet the AMPAS dispute settlement apparatus had the first matter brought to its attention by an actor against the cartel, a complaint by Conway Tearle alleging he had been frozen out of acting jobs by all the majors, because of his demand for a salary increase. About two years earlier Tearle had served notice on the producers that he wanted a raise from $2,500 to $3,500 a week. Since none of the major studios looked with favor on the request the actor was reduced to freelancing and appearing in productions of independent studios, receiving his higher price for short-term jobs. Tearle implied he might have to take civil action against the cartel if he did not receive satisfactory redress for his complaint. He said, in June 1927, that he had only three weeks of acting work since he had finished a movie in 1926. It was understood the producers felt Tearle was asking too much and even though the actor had appealed to AMPAS to intercede, "it is said that several producers are determined to prevent action being taken in his favor as it would establish a precedent," according to a reporter. Recently Tearle sensed he would not get anywhere unless he forced the issue, especially when Jesse Lasky declared that no individual could be allowed to dominate Paramount and that pictures were supreme. Tearle was one of the original 275 who had joined AMPAS at its inaugural banquet and had been on the legitimate stage and screen for 25 years. But Tearle got no satisfaction and within a couple of years was out of the film acting world.[6]

On June 9, 1927, a secret meeting attended by representatives of the majors was held in New York City. At that gathering the film men were said to have determined to take hold of the motion picture industry in order to "protect" it. Discussions centered on the overhead costs of the picture business with the film executives wanting to map out a general working plan to really "stabilize" their industry in both production and distribution costs. To that end the two main subjects discussed were salaries and studio bidding for actors in the open market. Supposedly not just the salaries of actors and directors but also the salaries of executives and all employees who received high pay were due for slashing. Also contemplated at the gathering was the morale of the industry, including scandals, undesirable publicity, and so on. When all the plans were drawn up it was expected they would be submitted to the U.S. Department of Justice for an opinion — in case any provisions of the proposed plans violated existing anti-trust measures such as the Sherman or Clayton acts. According to a reporter the film industry had grown so large "the former 'gentlemen's agreements' under which many have operated for different things will no longer be employed." A concerted effort was to be made by the studios to stabilize salaries and it was said the MPPDA studios were all prepared to release from contract any actor, director, or writer above a weekly salary of $1,000 when their contracts or options expired if they asked for more money than they had been receiving; "That is with the exception of outstanding money getters for the organization." Producers had pledged themselves at that meeting to aim at a salary reduction of 25 percent for players, writers, and directors.[7]

Ten days or so later, Frank Gillmore was on the west coast conferring with members of the local Los Angeles Equity council, with a view to getting Equity recognized by the producers. Conrad Nagel, an MGM contract player, had reportedly been recruiting in Hollywood for Equity over the previous year. Producers had adopted the attitude that with conditions and salaries as they were actors had no need of a union. Any protection the actors did need, declared the producers, could be obtained through membership in the newly formed AMPAS. Will Hays had been immediately informed about the latest Gillmore visit and was monitoring the situation.[8]

The first real shot in the 1927 skirmish between Equity and the MPPDA was fired on June 26, 1927, when Equity's motion picture branch announced that it would ask all contract actors, writers, and directors, to decline to sign a proposed salary cut agreement with film producers until Equity had made a study of the situation. Officials of Equity said the investigation would include questioning of producers regarding the purpose of the proposed 10 percent wage reduction. That announcement came following a meeting on June 25 of Equity with Nagel in the chair and Gillmore present. It was declared by Equity officials after the meeting that the actors were not definitely opposing the decrease but wanted to know the reason for the cut and would consent to it if the reason satisfied them. According to the article, Equity's motion picture branch "included but a small number of the film actors. But efforts were said to be underway to expand it."[9]

With definite opposition to the proposed salary reductions (from 10 to 25 percent in this account) freely expressed among actors and others affected, "signs of war" were apparent in the film industry on June 27 when

3. AMPAS and Salary Cuts; Equity's Second Attempt, 1927

the decreased pay envelopes were due to be first delivered. Principal opposition to the cuts came from the ranks of the contract players, who made up about 50 percent of the workers on the various movie lots. Both Equity and the actors' branch of AMPAS had scheduled meetings. Equity was following a policy of "watchful waiting" pending further developments. Paul Dullzell, the union's assistant executive secretary, said nothing definite could be done until the attitude of the Equity members in the movies was determined. "About the middle of May an organization known as the Academy of Motion Picture Arts and Sciences was formed in Hollywood," explained Dullzell. "Douglas Fairbanks was elected President. It is really a company union and the ink was hardly dry on the organization's papers when the producers announced salary cuts." He added that there were some 800 Equity members in Hollywood but they were not organized as a unit with an Equity shop policy and that most of the more influential actors belonged to AMPAS. "If the members of the so-called Academy, especially its Equity members, decline to accept the cuts, that will probably split the Academy and Equity will actively enter the situation," added Dullzell. "I can't say exactly what will be done, but I imagine we'd start a membership campaign, in cooperation with the American Federation of Labor and work for the Equity shop in the studios as it exists on the stage." Although about 45 percent of the film actors belonged to Equity Dullzell said they had been inactive as an organization because their leaders had not felt the need for attempting to unionize the studios; "Most of them belonged to Equity merely because they joined it when playing on the stage or approved of the union in principle and wished to ally themselves with it."[10]

Payrolls of the MPPDA-member film studios were reportedly due to be cut a combined total of $350,000 in the last week of June. Jesse L. Lasky, for the MPPDA, told the studio heads it was the most critical time in the history of the industry and that the producers had to cut the pay of everyone who was drawing a salary in excess of $50 a week, anywhere from 10 percent to 25 percent. A meeting of studio representatives had decided that all non-contract employees, and contracted employees, including stars, directors, actors, writers, and other artists be requested to reduce their salary according to the amounts requested by their particular studio (each studio selected its own percentage cut, from 10 to 25 percent). Cuts did not apply to people paid by the hour; that is, the craft and technical people—all of whom were unionized while none of the artists were unionized, at least not in unions recognized by the studios. As well, the pay of extras was not affected as it could not be lowered without the permission of the California Department of Labor.[11]

No salary cuts were actually implemented as the usual solidarity of the MPPDA cartel crumbled a bit. A few of the 14 major studios then members of the MPPDA failed to follow the proposal for cuts with the result the others, all intending to implement cuts, backed off. In a face-saving move at the end of June the MPPDA notified the board of directors of AMPAS that the hitherto ordered salary cuts of from 10 to 25 percent would be deferred to August 1, 1927. In the meantime the artists themselves, through the Academy promised to attempt to raise their efficiency to the point whereby wage reductions would be unnecessary. However, it was said, the apparent victory of the workers failed to make any change in the campaign for members launched by the motion picture section of Equity. Conrad Nagel, an executive with Equity's Los Angeles council, declared that virtually all the motion picture players were then Equity members, although the membership of the film section "had been negligible until but a few days ago."[12]

As early as July 5, 1927, it was reported from Hollywood there would be no sweeping salary cuts among the artists at that time; that is, proposed cuts were permanently dead and not deferred to August 1 or any other date. And that the deferral announcement was made simply to allow the MPPDA to save face. Those proposed cuts were cancelled, wrote a journalist, because due to "a seething storm of protest waged from every studio, with threats of contract cancellations, walkouts and strikes, the producers individually and collectively reached a decision to abandon any idea of reducing salaries." They decided instead to bring about "efficient economy reforms." To the recently formed Academy, he added, "is attributed the successful termination on the fight waged alike by actors, directors, writers, cameramen and other studio employees in protest against the salary reduction." AMPAS branches had gone on record as being against the proposed cuts, and perhaps gave the cartel pause to reflect. The actors,' writers,' and directors' branches had not functioned as the subservient company union the organization was set up to be. A message had been delivered to the MPPDA that perhaps AMPAS might turn out to be a Frankenstein monster.[13]

3. AMPAS and Salary Cuts; Equity's Second Attempt, 1927

Early in July a journalist with *Variety* speculated the move by the studios to try and cut salaries would probably result in an intensive membership drive by Equity on the west coast to bring in the unaffiliated players. It was said to be the opinion of many prominent players that a concerted movement among actors to join Equity was absolutely necessary to protect the artists against any future moves by the producers to control or slash salaries. Although AMPAS, said the report, "is receiving all of the credit for delaying any general cut in salaries by the producers, there are claims by many actors, directors, and writers that the Academy is fostered primarily by the producers and will in the end give the breaks to the latter." At the meeting of the actors' branch of AMPAS a week earlier all members of the Academy who were not members of Equity signified their intention of joining the latter immediately. Frank Gillmore announced he would stay on the west coast for "some time," adding that the plans of his organization were not yet framed but undoubtedly there would be an intensive membership campaign among the film players over the coming months.[14]

Although the purpose of AMPAS was ostensibly to unite in one body all branches of motion picture production, according to a July 6, 1927, report in *Variety* the group had only 294 members in its five regular branches (actors, directors, writers, technicians, producers) and one special branch (containing just three members) with the rank and file of those in the industry beginning to call it an "up stage" gathering. Those who were on the outside seemed to feel that unless they were able to become favorites of the "powers that be" in AMPAS or in the industry, that they had little chance of every becoming members of this "exclusive body." And much of that sentiment was due, they claimed, to the qualifications necessary for active membership in AMPAS. Section one, article 11, of the AMPAS constitution and by-laws read as follows: "Any person who has accomplished distinguished work or acquired distinguished standing in or made valuable contribution to the production branches of the motion picture industry, directly or indirectly, and who is of good moral or personal standing may become an active member of the Academy by vote of the Board of directors, or recommendation by the Committee on Membership." Fees for membership in each of the five branches consisted of a $100 initiation fee and $5 monthly in dues. By this account, as of June 20, 1927, there were only 86 actors shown on the membership rolls (out of thousands theoretically eligible). Of those 86, less than 25 percent were freelance players. Of the 60 directors on the rolls, just five were in the freelance category with the others all under contract to MPPDA studios. In the writers' branch were 55 members, of which eight were in the freelance category. In the producers' branch were 46 members, none of which were listed as freelancers. The actors' branch contained no Charlie Chaplin, no Fatty Arbuckle, no Theda Bara, no Marie Dressler, and no Eddie Cantor.[15]

At a mass meeting in Hollywood on July 7, 1927, 700 film actors voted to join the motion picture branch of Equity and drafted a list of proposed working conditions. Among the demands wanted in a basic agreement between players and producers were a standard form of contract and an eight-hour day. Conrad Nagel presided at that meeting with other speakers including Wallace Beery and Thomas Meighan. Paul Dullzell, speaking from New York, commented that in trying to impose salary cuts across the board, the producers were responsible for the 700 actors voting unanimously to join Equity. He added that the meeting was the culmination of five years of effort on the part of his union to organize the film folk.[16]

One observer remarked, with respect to the 700 actors voting to join Equity, that it was a case of the Hollywood actors dropping a "bombshell" on Hollywood when they made the first move in an attempt to win the closed ship from the producers. Using colorful prose the *Los Angeles Times* declared, "In a moment of exhilarated enthusiasm induced by the beautiful pictures of a Utopian existence under the so-called protecting palm of a motion picture actors' union, a resolution was passed amounting to a threat of a widespread strike if producers will not accede to the demands made on them" although the account acknowledged the main demands were limited to the relatively modest basic agreement, standard form contract and eight-hour day. That actors' meeting was held secretly with no printed announcement made of it in advance — the message was spread by word of mouth. With Nagel being a member of AMPAS and one of the people on the speakers' platform at the meeting, the newspaper was somewhat baffled by that situation because AMPAS, it insisted, "originally was formed to keep peace and understanding between all branches of the film industry." Trying to assess and understand that turn of events of a massive move to Equity, the *Los Angeles Times* remarked it was the first time the film section of the union had gained any standing in Hollywood. It

3. AMPAS and Salary Cuts; Equity's Second Attempt, 1927

had struggled along for some time trying to gain a foothold, "but has been considered weak and without any danger of gaining any power." The account added that the mass meeting apparently grew out of the recent attempt by producers to cut salaries "although they agreed, after holding conferences with all branches of the industry, to abandon any such plans for the time being." Unprepared for that sudden move to slash their incomes, actors moving in large numbers to Equity was seen as a precaution against any such producer proposal being made again without warning. All of the prominent Hollywood players, with the exception of half a dozen or so, it was admitted, were at the meeting, with all in attendance unanimously voting to join Equity.[17]

One day later the *Los Angeles Times* commented on the meeting again, drawing upon harmony in the film business that had never really existed. Sadly it declared, "For the first time since the motion-picture industry was founded in Hollywood nearly twenty years ago it last night found itself divided with producers on one side and the majority of actresses and actors in the new closed-shop aligned on the other side."[18]

Such a shocking move by the Hollywood actors called for another long-winded anti-union rant and tirade from the editorial staff of the *Los Angeles Times*. It was delivered in the July 11, 1927, edition of the paper. The rant began with the observation the present effort to establish the closed shop in the Los Angeles film industry through the affiliation of actors with Equity "is one fraught with danger to the industry, to the public and, most of all, to the players themselves." First, though, the editor issued a few positive words, admitting the group had done good work in promoting the legitimate interests of the profession such as by elevating the tone of the stage and by caring for the unfortunates in its ranks. "Latterly, however, the Equity has taken on many of the objectionable aspects which characterize other branches of the American Federation of Labor. It has identified itself with the principle of the closed shop, a principle opposed to the tenets of Americanism and of industrial liberty and justice." He went on to say, "It has set out to dominate not only the theatrical profession, but the theatrical industry as well, dictate to employees who shall and shall not work and where and when and how, and to employers how they shall run the businesses they own and which their capital makes possible."[19]

According to the editorial, Los Angeles was a city grown great in population, wealth, and industry on the cornerstone of the open shop and to force the closed shop on an industry that had gained unprecedented success by virtue of the very system under attack was to invite disaster. And, of course, the public had to be considered. "And the public will not stand for a system that foists upon it players who through affiliation with a union and not through individual merit are forced forward." Bizarrely, the editor went on to argue the players had less to gain and more to lose through union affiliation "than any other class of workers anywhere.... Under the union system of arbitrary wage scales, of achievement limited by the capacity of the least capable and of constant subjection to petty harassments by union agents ... the lot of unionized workers would prove intolerable to these freedom-loving players." For a long time leading film players had kept aloof from Equity, with good reason and good sense, asserted the editor, and if out of pique at the attempted imposition of salary cuts the players suddenly rushed headlong into an alliance with the unions hitherto spurned, they obviously did so with scant consideration of the facts because "in their Academy of Arts and Sciences they already have an organization capable of correcting any inequities in the industry through direct contact with the producers." As it was, the proposed salary cuts did not occur, but even if they had happened it was, concluded the editor, "no adequate reason for a precipitate rush by the players into a new alignment which will produce a far worse condition for them than would result from any minor reduction in salaries."[20]

In the wake of the meeting of the 700, a report stated that Conrad Nagel was the most active Equity booster on the west coast with Reginald Denny and William H. Crane also among the most active actors for the cause of Equity. Nagel had stirred up support by declaring that "the fact that the producers have their own organization is the strongest argument for us to have ours."[21]

Columnist Wood Soanes delivered a mocking column on the situation on July 13, 1927. Declaring that just a few weeks earlier there had been few actors in Equity, Soanes sneered, "The haughty cinema players would have none of their poorer legitimate brothers. Who are these vulgar people anyway?... Why, pray tell us, should we ally ourselves with the financial rag-tag of play-acting?" And, "the heads of the actors' union found the picture folk most unreceptive to their approaches for membership. They were told that the problems of the theater were not the prob-

3. AMPAS and Salary Cuts; Equity's Second Attempt, 1927

lems of the screen.... Only a few, and those old troupers, cast their lot with the actors' association." But that was a few weeks ago, explained Soanes and it became a different story when the studios tried to cut salaries. Suddenly the film players thought of Equity, and the mass meeting of the 700 soon followed, but "the picture players expect Equity to save the mortgages on all their fancy motor cars by forcing the producers to pay them the money they think they deserve. Equity certainly has no such aspirations knowing full well that it does well to insure the payment of a salary, not to set it." Still, Soanes acknowledged the union planned to regulate working conditions and he thought it would be helpful to the profession if Equity gained its demands.[22]

Equity's demand for the closed shop in Hollywood film studios was submitted in July to the producers in a communication from Gillmore to Fred Beetson, secretary of the MPPDA. In that communication Gillmore called the attention of the MPPDA to the meeting of the 700. His letter requested a joint meeting between the union and the cartel to discuss the resolution passed at the meeting of the 700, which included demands for uniform working conditions and for a 48-hour week, but without a demand for an eight-hour day. Gillmore said an entirely new form of contract had been prepared for film studios; that is, entirely different from the group's standard stage contract. Equity was on record as being agreeable to submit any contract clauses not agreeable to the producers to arbitration, either with AMPAS, or an outside disinterested party, and would abide by any decisions made in arbitration. Outwardly the producers assumed an attitude of indifference toward Equity and its demands. A bulletin issued by the union's New York City headquarters chided the film people and described AMPAS as a company union.[23]

It was a situation that called for another lengthy editorial rant from the *Los Angeles Times*, which appeared in the July 15, 1927, issue of the newspaper. When it became apparent that the "continued well-being" of the film industry would require a substantial reduction in production costs the fear that a salary cut would be involved created, wrote the editor, "a considerable and natural uneasiness among the players. Of this feeling of unrest the Actors' Equity Association, better known as the actors' union was quick to take advantage." For years Equity sought a foothold in Hollywood but, he continued, "Well aware that their own interests and those of motion pictures as a whole would be jeopardized — with no compensating advantages — by such union affiliations, the far-sighted leaders among the actors and actresses had rejected every overture of the Equity and by their example maintained the independence of their profession." When talk of a wage cut made a temporary breach in the players' united front (against the union), "the eager Equity rushed into the breach with extravagant promises of what it would accomplish for the players if they would only join the union and submit their future conduct to the dictation of the stage actors' union — an organization totally unfamiliar with film conditions and problems and naturally hostile to film players by reason of the high salaries and enormous prestige which the latter have received under open-shop conditions." After that first flurry of activity toward Equity, such activity quickly died down, according to the editor.[24]

Always preaching the benefit of the company union AMPAS, without identifying it as such, the *Times* editor pitched the Academy again. Pointing out it was incumbent on everyone in the motion picture industry to "join hands" in correcting problems the editor declared that therein lay the difference between the AMPAS program and that of the actors' union. "The former is an organization composed exclusively of representatives of the various elements of the film industry — players, directors, writers, producers, etc. It is an inside organization with exact, intimate, first-hand knowledge of the problems to be solved, of the conflicting interests to be reconciled in their solution and of what can and cannot be done for the maximum good of everyone involved." On the other hand, the "selfish" union would not take into consideration the producers' side and it would reduce the industry; "It would kill the goose that lays the golden egg." AMPAS proposed to solve the problem on the basis of mutual cooperation of all interests involved and with a balanced justice and advantages to each so that all could prosper with the continued prosperity of the industry as a whole, the editor insisted as he reiterated his belief AMPAS would dispense "even-handed justice to both players and producers." Most important of all, concluded the editor, was the spirit behind the Academy: "It is the concrete expression of one of the important qualities of good citizenship — the willingness and ability to see both sides of a question and to arbitrate them to the maximum benefit of both." And, "it is a recognition of the right of the worker to work and the producer to produce in harmonious co-operation, without outside dictation and with neither

3. AMPAS and Salary Cuts; Equity's Second Attempt, 1927

seeking an unfair advantage at the other's expense. It is the spirit of fairness of the American Plan, of the open shop."[25]

Producers continued to display indifference to the union with Equity's demands to receive no official attention from the cartel prior to the semiannual MPPDA meeting, scheduled to be held on August 10. At that time the letter sent by Gillmore to Beetson was to be read. Unofficially, producers had expressed themselves freely that they had no interest in Equity or its demands. As well, there was to be no cooperation on the part of AMPAS with Equity or any similar group of actors, writers, or directors. The Academy would ignore Equity in its conferences with actors since it was the belief of those sponsoring AMPAS that any and all wrongs then existing in the various film studios could be settled amicably without organized bodies outside of the Academy. A reporter admitted there was then a lull in Equity activity since the initial heat generated by the salary cut attempt. Second thoughts had set in "and sentiment in favor of the Equity shop in the local studios is not nearly as pronounced as immediately following" the proposal for cuts. As well, it was rumored in informed circles that one of the moves that would be undertaken by AMPAS would be the recommendation for a standard contract between players and producers. A move, it was felt, that might perhaps undercut Equity and eliminate it as a factor in the film business.[26]

At that time, July 1927, there were two male stars in films for every female one, with about 750 players on the west coast (excluding extras and bit players). Hollywood's weekly payroll for those people was about $800,000 for an average working year of 35 weeks. That represented an outlay of $26 million, or about 25 percent of the total cost of production for the coming year. Among the 750 were about 100 earning from $2,000 to $20,000 weekly; 150 were featured players averaging $2,000 per week; 500 were regular stock players earning an average of $100 a week. Of the $800,000 total, the stars drew about $450,000 a week, the featured players $300,000, and the stock players $50,000.[27]

A total of $1,385,100 was earned from 169,377 extras' placements made by the Central Casting Bureau from January 1 to June 30, 1927. Salaries earned ranged from $3 to $25 per day with the average daily earnings being $8.18. Average daily placements were as follows; men, 618; women, 281; children, 37; total, 936. A total of 111,843 (66.04 percent) placements of men were made; 50,886 (30.11 percent) women; 3,847 (2.23

47

Film Actors Organize

percent) boys; and 2,801 (1.62 percent) girls. While there were 37 daily placements of children made by the CCB, some 4,000 children in the Los Angeles area were ready to answer a call for child extras.[28]

Very suddenly and unexpectedly, Equity suffered what *Variety* termed a "bitter defeat" in its efforts to gain union recognition and bring the closed shop to Hollywood. Gillmore had been "repulsed" and returned almost immediately to New York while AMPAS had "supplanted Equity. Through it all future negotiations for a standard form of contract and working conditions will be ironed out." It all happened on the evening of Tuesday, July 26, 1927, in Los Angeles at a mass meeting of actors with 1,000 or more players in attendance. Observers were alerted to the fact that something dramatic was in the works earlier on that day when Conrad Nagel, on the local Equity council and a prime leader in the fight for Equity, issued a terse statement to the press that indicated a decided change of heart and a 100 percent alignment with AMPAS. At that crowded meeting Gillmore saw the work of several weeks crumble away as the bigger stars of the film world announced their allegiance to AMPAS and repudiated the recent activity by Equity in issuing its demand for the union shop in the studios. The resolution abandoning, temporarily at least, the effort to enforce acceptance of the Equity contract was presented at the meeting by Milton Sills and adopted virtually unanimously. In the resolution it was noted that the actors could not afford to make war at this time and that the demand for the union shop would split the industry. As a sop to Equity the meeting later adopted a resolution that any uniform contract entered into with the producers should come through Equity. Observed a journalist, "It was noticeable that the meeting was dominated by the stars and biggest names among the featured list [who were mostly against Equity], with the rank and file at first inclined to string along with Equity." Conrad Nagel, one of those on the speakers' platform, told the gathering that future steps called for most careful consideration. Explaining that the producers, through AMPAS, had agreed to present a uniform contract for actors and that practically every member of the executive council of the Los Angeles Equity branch was also a member of the actors' branch of AMPAS [including Nagel] he declared that it was all really a victory for the actors, even though the contract would come through a source other than Equity. Nagel pointed out the futility and impossibility of trying at that time to force the issue of an Equity contract and a union shop on the

3. AMPAS and Salary Cuts; Equity's Second Attempt, 1927

producers as it would not be right to advance the attack when the enemy had extended the hand of friendship. Further, he declared, Equity did not have the support and sympathy of people in its own ranks, which would add to the likelihood of the battle being lost. "Rather than advance to a crisis in which we would have the opposition of some of our own people, let us take the producers' word when they agree to meet and eliminate the abuses now common, and work toward a uniform contract for the good of all," said Nagel.[29]

Milton Sills told the meeting the actors were artists, the producers were industrialists, and blending the two was a hard problem. "If the producers cannot make pictures economically it will hurt all of us, individually and collectively. We must recognize the Academy of Arts and Sciences, and the sincere efforts of the producers to bring the industry back to a sound basis." Reportedly, the audience took the changed attitude of Nagel and other members of the Los Angeles Equity council "with astonishment." During the speeches of both Nagel and Sills "there was an air of disappointment manifest all over the hall. No applause and the general silence was a good gauge." Wallace Beery was called on to speak and he carried the audience by his comments that as far as he was concerned he was ready and willing to stick with Equity in its attempts to win its demands from the producers. After the Beery speech, which had wide audience support, Nagel tried to pacify the crowd by saying the local Equity council did not plan to abandon the union but for the good of all they should hold in abeyance the demand for an Equity shop. He further declared that Gillmore still had in mind the idea to achieve the Equity shop in film and, further, they had undoubtedly avoided a disastrous and costly war at a time when the organization "did not have the proper number of soldiers to fight with." Over the course of the meeting calls were made off and on for Gillmore to speak. Finally, he rose and spoke briefly. Pointing out the Hollywood branch of Equity had sent for him to lead the battle, he said he was sorry the local committee did not feel the present time was propitious to force the actors' demands. Gillmore advised the audience to follow the advice of the local committee at this time but hoped in the future he might be called to lead the local Equity in a fight for recognition of the organization by the producers.[30]

Further discussion at the meeting finally brought up the direct question as to the exact relationship of Equity to AMPAS. Nagel declared it was up to each individual to figure out for himself. He told the audience practically every member of the Los Angeles Equity local committee was a member of AMPAS and that at AMPAS meetings "Equity had been entirely eliminated from all discussions." He admitted that the organization "had been mentioned on various occasions, but it had been finally agreed that no reference would be made to it in the future." A journalist in attendance described the meeting by writing, "All through the meeting there was a tenseness and downcast spirit, entirely the reverse of the Equity meeting of two weeks previous. Members gathered in small groups to discuss the new turn of affairs, with a general accusation that the stars and high salaried players comprising the executive committee in going with the producers had given Gillmore the runaround. In many quarters it was said that the big stars and players will protect their own interests first and foremost, leaving the smaller actors and Equity to shift for themselves." Immediately after the meeting there was a movement to campaign for an entirely new local executive committee of Equity, one that would function fearlessly and independently in an attempt to establish the Equity shop in pictures. Although it was claimed that Equity would still continue to recruit members from among the Hollywood actors, a gloomy reporter commented, "the back down of the association on the issue of the Equity contract and closed shop at this time makes Equity practically a dead issue as far as the studios are concerned." And, he predicted, "It is doubtful if the local branch can hold the membership it has at present, rather than hope for an increase. The present difficulties on the coast presented Equity with the greatest opportunity for putting its demands through, and when the organization did not rise to the occasion, there is little hope that another such chance will present itself at any time in the near future."[31]

Reaction to the meeting of the 1,000 actors, and the defeat, from Equity's New York headquarters was a general belief that the film producers had again put one over on the players and the latter had lost a chance to gain self-protection under an organized structure that was independent of any influence from the producers, such as was found in AMPAS. Paul Dullzell, assistant executive secretary for Equity, and speaking from New York, insisted his union would continue to organize the film players but admitted that much of the interest in the project had, naturally, been lost. "The producers have only withdrawn their [salary cut] demands because of not knowing what Equity would do with the actor or what the

3. AMPAS and Salary Cuts; Equity's Second Attempt, 1927

actor would do with Equity. They have by these methods again succeeded in keeping the actor out of his organization. With regard to those actors who had helped to block Equity, Dullzell declared, "we say that we are convinced that the day is coming, maybe not far distant, when they will regret their attitude of today." He added, that it was understood that it took courage for the individual to make a sacrifice when called on, but if the film player is to be independent the sacrifice had to be made. "If there is no willingness to do this Equity does not feel that it should be called upon as a mater of convenience, and after it has brought up its heavy artillery find that there is no ammunition, the ammunition in this instance being the support when needed, backed up sincerely, in all that implies, by the battle cry of 'All for one and one for all,'" exclaimed Dullzell, speaking for an obviously bitter and frustrated New York executive staff of Equity.[32]

On July 28 in Los Angeles, a meeting was held by the actors' branch of AMPAS at which the players displayed the new spirit of cooperation and the joining of hands to solve problems, and so on. Speaking officially on behalf of his colleagues in the actors' branch of AMPAS, and unofficially on behalf of all the film players, Conrad Nagel pledged that temperament, long an actor's prerogative, was to be immediately sacrificed on the altar of economy in the film business. Stars and players would deny themselves the luxury of "blowing up" on the set or indulging in any other display of unreasonable or unnecessary type of temperament that made for filming delays and led to increased costs. Evidence of the producers' supposed gratitude for that and other pledges followed in the form of an announcement by Cecil B. DeMille that the proposal to cut salaries — still theoretically deferred and due to be imposed on August 1— would be definitely and finally abandoned. Of course, it had been finally abandoned much earlier with the rhetoric of "deferred" used merely to save face. Other pledges were made by other branches of AMPAS in the economy drive. Writers promised to achieve economies "by writing faster and shorter" while the directors, through Fred Niblo, promised a number of economy measures, with one of them being a promise to eliminate unnecessary retakes. Said a reporter; "The avoidance of scandal was lightly and indirectly touched upon in the actors' pledge to realize to the fullest extent the responsibility of their position, both in the industry and before the public."[33]

Film Actors Organize

Late in July, for the first time since the fracas over salary cuts began in Hollywood, the American Federation of Labor came out with an official opinion on AMPAS. In the group's bulletin, in a general discussion of the situation, AMPAS was described as "the producers' company union." Disapproval was expressed by the AFL toward the actors who had rushed to the labor camps only to develop cold feet and then back away after Gillmore offered them organization. Said a reporter, "As far as Equity officials are concerned, the issue is dead for the present."[34]

In the middle of August rumor had it that the new economies plan was to go into effect at the studios, although the producers vehemently denied it. Supposedly the new plan provided for the replacement of the current stars with players brought up from the film ranks to work at smaller salaries. It was a plan based on the premise that the attempt at salary cuts had failed and there was no other method left to try. All existing contracts with stars would be honored but as they expired the producers would not resign them at their old salaries, or higher, but only if they agreed to work for less money. When asked for comment on the rumored new plan, Frank Gillmore described it as "exceedingly unwise."[35]

Late in September 1927 the board of directors of AMPAS appointed a committee of five to work on the completion of the actors' standard form of contract. Conrad Nagel and Hallam Cooley were on the committee representing actors; M. C. Levee and B. P. Schulberg represented the producers, with John Stahl (director) being the fifth member of the committee. That proposed standard contract would apply only to freelance players as the contracted actors would continue to have varied forms of contract. After the proposed standard form contract was drawn up by the committee of five it would be submitted to the actors' branch and producers' branch of the Academy for approval. Then it would go on to the AMPAS board of directors for final approval.[36]

When the film industry held a trade conference in October 1927 a number of trade practices were adopted. And while some of those trade practices had a bearing on players, a reporter observed, "Actors, who are affected, have no representation. One proposal adopted was that when producers lent actors under contract to other producers they were to receive an amount equal to the weekly wage paid by the lender plus "a reasonable amount." Actors had no say in whether or not they received any of that premium paid by the borrowing studio and no say in whether or not they

3. AMPAS and Salary Cuts; Equity's Second Attempt, 1927

were loaned out at all. Another practice adopted was that producers should not bid for players, directors, and so forth, in competition with each other — a move that, arguably, clearly violated American restraint of trade laws. At that trade conference Louis B. Mayer, for the producers, presented a list of "don'ts" and "be carefuls" applying to film content — the forerunner of what would become known as the Hays Code, and direct ancestor of today's film rating system. A total of 11 don'ts were listed; such as no scenes of actual childbirth, no miscegenation, and no ridicule of the clergy. A total of 26 "be carefuls" were listed including arson; sympathy for criminals, and a man and woman shown in bed together.[37]

All seven resolutions proposed by the producers at the trade conference were unanimously adopted as fair trade practices. Most elements of the industry were in attendance, such as exhibitors, and so on. Ostensibly the conference was called to devise means of branding various restrictions of trade as unfair trade practices. The cartel seemed to believe that if it could get various parts of the industry to brand something that violated government anti-trust regulations as a fair trade practice it might somehow fool the government and delay or eliminate any federal government legal action against it. When the resolutions had been studied, two of them were said, by outside observers, to be unconstitutional and have little chance of standing up in any court of law, according to legal opinion. They were in themselves suppression of trade, it was said. One of those resolutions declared that producers could farm out actors, directors, and writers in their employ to other producers at higher prices without being obliged to pass a cut of the extra money on to the employee involved and without consulting or asking said employee whether he wanted to work for the borrowing producer at all, whether at the same salary or at a higher one. The other questionable resolution provided that none of the producers should bid for the services of players, and so on, with offers of higher salaries or other inducements. "It is, virtually, a declaration of closed shop for all workers under contract," said a reporter. "The actors were not represented at the conference. It is considered unfair that the measures have been adopted without asking to hear from those most concerned."[38]

A week later it was reported that studio-members of the MPPDA no longer loaned out their players or directors to each other at 25 percent or more profit. Rather, they had a new system they claimed worked more satisfactorily. Players were to be loaned out at no advance in salary but an additional three weeks' salary was to be added on to each loan out agreement for what the studios called "carrying charges." That charge was made whether a player was loaned out for one week or for 10 weeks. In that way the producers reasoned they did not profiteer on each other and gave each other a break as all made the same charge for farming a player out. Producers figured if they loaned a player out for five films a year (an average shoot was four weeks) they would only receive 35 weeks in salary from the borrower but still paid their contract people 40 weeks a year (standard payment for a long-term contracted actor was to be paid for 40 weeks, not 52, each year). But, noted a reporter, apparently sincerely, "they felt it was their duty to accommodate each other and not to profiteer."[39]

Of the total of 6,000 women and girls registered as extras at the Central Casting Bureau, late in 1927, only one had averaged as much as five days' work over the previous six months. There were two men who averaged six days' work each week in the same period, while two other men averaged five days each week. Registration of men at the CCB was about 5,000. Eight females averaged four days' work a week; 21 got three days a week; 20 males got four days; 36 males averaged three days' work a week. All of the above were paid $8 to $10 for each day's work as they were known as "dress extras" maintaining complete wardrobes enabling them to dress suitably for any occasion. A total of some 11,000 extras registered at the CCB drew a daily payroll of $6,556. Figures showed the majority of extras who worked at all got nothing more than an average of one day of work each week. Producers, through the CCB, hoped to cut down the total of registered extras to a number that would assure each one a living wage. No new registrations had been taken at the bureau for many months and, reportedly, no new names would be added to the lists until the total was reduced to less than half the current figure.[40]

Rumors of impending salary cuts continued to swirl around Hollywood. In the middle of November 1927 J. Robert Rubin, vice president of MGM, denied the latest speculation. Rubin denied "emphatically" there was a plan for an agreement among producers to hold actors and directors to the same terms as were then imposed upon professional baseball players — under baseball's waiver system when a player signed with a team he was their property for life, unless or until waived by that team. Also denied by Rubin was the idea the studios had any plans in the works for salary reductions. As far as Frank Gillmore was concerned, if the produc-

3. AMPAS and Salary Cuts; Equity's Second Attempt, 1927

ers were contemplating "any move which has for its aim the elimination of competition and the restriction of opportunity for actors and directors to sell their services to the highest bidder" it would be considered a combination in restraint of trade by Equity and that any such move by the producers would immediately "be brought to the attention of the proper authorities." According to Gillmore, Equity was well aware of the fact that it was not the higher salaries of actors that had brought the film industry to its present situation: "Actors' salaries comprise but 20 percent of the cost of the picture," he explained. "The great waste has been incompetence in management and the unwarranted promotion of relatives and favorites of producers."[41]

An investigation in Hollywood later that same month revealed there were 120 film directors in the various movie studios requiring, if all were actively engaged, a daily maximum of 1,200 players. In the entire film colony there were an estimated 4,000 principal players and since on average only 60 directors were at work at any one time that left 3,400 principals idle each day. Excluded from those figures were the 11,000 registered extras.[42]

At one of its meetings late in 1927 the MPPDA decided that Equity would not be dealt with directly in the negotiations and adoption of a standard form contract for actors to be used by the MPPDA studios. They agreed the producers' branch of AMPAS should negotiate the matter with the actors' branch of the Academy. It was believed the producers felt if the MPPDA were to handle the matter itself directly with Equity it would leave the door open for the latter body to come into the film industry and obtain official recognition. That if Equity were called upon to confer on the terms of the contract, in any way, the union might insist the resulting document was an official Equity contract, which would give them the official recognition in the movie field that Equity had been after for five years.[43]

Early in December 1927, in New York City, Equity's Council, after several special sessions devoted to allegedly unauthorized activities on the part of Equity's film section at Los Angeles, abolished the executive committee of that branch. The Council was the sole governing body of Equity as a whole. Without consulting the Council, went the allegation, the executive committee of the Los Angeles Equity branch voted to present a form of contract in which Equity did not figure, to film players. Thus, the committee was ruled out of existence. Henceforth the west coast Equity branch would be controlled by the designated deputy, under orders from New York headquarters at all times. The dispute dated to the previous June in the wake of the proposed salary cuts, when Equity moved in and made their demands, including one for a standard form contract. Then in November the decision was reached by the cartel to draft a standard form contract with AMPAS, but without Equity. That Conrad Nagel was chairman of both the executive committee of the Academy and Equity's Los Angeles branch committee was believed to have figured in the decision to dissolve the latter. Equity's governing Council agreed that Nagel and his supporters could not be loyal to both organizations. According to a journalist; "In light of recent events Equity has little chance of holding sway on the coast and last week's resolution [to dissolve] virtually means a let down in its coast activities."[44]

Among the members of that dissolved Equity Los Angeles branch committee were Nagel, Jack Mulhall, Vilma Banky, Richard Barthelmess, Wallace Beery, Marion Davies, Reginald Denny, Richard Dix, William Haines, Raymond Hatton, Jean Hersholt, Leatrice Joy, Rod La Rocque, and Adolphe Menjou. It was explained by Equity that the Council held nothing against those actors individually, only that in consenting to negotiate with the producers through a "company union" (as Equity viewed AMPAS) they acted contrary to Equity policy. The union would continue to maintain a branch office in Hollywood under the direction of the headquarters appointee Wedgewood Nowell.[45]

Working through AMPAS, producers and actors reached acceptance of a new standard form contract, in the middle of December 1927. It was to go into effect on January 1, 1928, and would be used by all Hollywood studios, both within and without the MPPDA, with the exception of a couple of minor independent studios. Prior to this point each producer had his own form of contract and, remarked a reporter, "all of them were unfavorable to the free-lance actor." The new contract eliminated the possibility of a producer firing an actor with the only explanation being "Unsatisfactory." As well, it provided for salary payment on the basis of a six-day week.[46]

A journalist with *Variety* observed that the new contract was the first standard one ever granted to film players and that it was said to give the players more protection than ever before provided. For example, there was

3. AMPAS and Salary Cuts; Equity's Second Attempt, 1927

a provision for salary to be paid to an actor when a film was delayed or postponed, unless notice was given 30 days in advance of the non-start of a film; compensation was to be paid actors for wardrobes damaged or destroyed; players who worked more than six days in any one week on a film got an extra payment of one-sixth of their listed weekly rate for working the seventh day. Prior to this contract a player got his listed weekly salary whether the producer worked him 40 hours over five days or 105 hours over seven days. Designed to prevent or forestall union activity the reporter for *Variety* commented, "The new contract form is a big step forward in coast picture circles, and it is said it will eliminate the continual unrest among the actors arising from the unfair contracts previously."[47]

This new contract did not apply to actors who held long-term contracts with the studios, which numbered probably about half of the players on the lots. For example, contract players would not be compensated extra for working more than a six-day week, but would continue to be paid every week (at least for 40 of the 52 weeks in a year) whether they worked or not. Long-term studio contracts remained unique items varying between studios and even within a studio.[48]

As 1927 ended it was reported that the working population of the west coast picture colony numbered 42,546, and that they produced 82 percent of the entire world's output of motion pictures. In Southern California were nine major and 45 minor studios producing pictures, employing a technical and office worker staff that numbered about 13,500. Larger studios were Paramount, First National, Warner Brothers, Pathé, Metro-Goldwyn-Mayer, Fox, Universal, United Artists, and Film Booking Offices. There were about 27,000 extras in the Los Angeles area, of which some 16,500 were registered with the CCB. On the freelance side the number of featured players and bit actors was about 3,000, in addition to the extras, and contract players. Equity had been beaten back convincingly in its second major attempt to unionize the players and seemed to be in disarray with respect to Hollywood and at a loss as to what strategy to employ and how to proceed. AMPAS had seemingly been strengthened as a company union and by coming up with a standard form contract and with extra pay for a seventh day of work the studios seemed to have seriously undercut any future union activity. Another brief lull followed but the studios could not resist more attacks, overt and covert on the actors.[49]

4
A Second Brief Lull, 1928–1929

Evidence of Equity's weakness in Hollywood and of the low point to which it had fallen came early in January 1928 when it was reported that an actors' organization to replace Equity in the film field was being formed by leading players on the west coast. It wanted to gain recognition from the producers as the actors' representative and to cut the number of film players down by more than half, from the existing total of about 4,000. Formation of the new group, discussed by various players for around two years gained momentum as a result of the Equity Council dissolving the Los Angeles branch executive committee. However, Conrad Nagel, Hallam Cooley and Douglas Maclean were all known to be against the formation of another organization to replace Equity in the film field but a canvas showed practically all the other members of that dissolved committee were willing to work with a new organization. One actor instrumental in forming the new association declared there should be no more than 1,500 players available to the studios and that the supply could be controlled by a series of eliminations such as was being carried out on the list of extras by the Central Casting Bureau. Nothing more was heard of this fledgling group.[1]

Meanwhile, Equity continued to stay active in the film field. An article in the January 1928 issue of *Equity*, the official organ of the union, was devoted to an exposure of the alleged weaknesses, from Equity's point of view, of the new contract. Whereas Equity contracts called for compulsory arbitration between actor and producer in case of dispute, noted the

4. A Second Brief Lull, 1928–1929

piece, the AMPAS contract made no such provision. Another weakness was the clause permitting a producer to "do anything he likes to a part" such as engaging an actor for a supposedly small part, paying him accordingly, and then building the part to any proportions he desired. As well, unfair leeway was allowed to producers on starting dates and retakes, being entitled under the contract to hold an actor for services without pay over a considerable period of time. The article chided the members of Equity in Hollywood for not standing together in order to obtain union recognition and an Equity contract from the studios.[2]

Studios' average pay scales, as of January 1928, were as follows; stars, $500 a week (low), $10,000 a week (top), $2,500 weekly (average); featured players, $150, $2,500, $750; extras, $5, $25, $8.30 (per day); typists (per week), $20, $30, $25; secretaries (per week), $30, $100, $50.[3]

Members of the MPPDA who obtained their extras through the Central Casting Bureau paid a total of $2,838,136 for 330,397 placements during 1927. Over that period the average daily wage earned, including overtime, was $8.59. Daily wage rates ranged from a low of $3 to a high of $25. On the CCB registration rolls there were three times the number of women registered for employment as men. However, there were twice as many placements for men during the year as there were for women. Some 35,000 people were reportedly registered with the CCB for employment as extras. Over the year four percent of the placements went to children. There were 220,345 placements for men; 97,908 for women; 7,070 for boys; and 5,074 for girls. Over the year $1,823,205 was paid to men; $801,747.50 was paid to women; average daily placements were as follows; men 603, women 269, children 33, total 905. Only 55 women averaged 2.5 days' work or more a week during the year; 12 women had 2.5 days, 23 had 3.0, 13 had 3.5, five had 4.0, one had 4.5, and one had 5.0. Of that group of 55 women, 84 percent were listed in the casting office as "dress women" who had extensive and expensive wardrobes. In the male division a total of 135 averaged 3.0 days' work or more a week, 74 had 3.0, 40 had 3.5, 13 had 4.0, four had 4.5, and four had 5.0. Sixty-five percent of that group of 135 of men was classified by the CCB in the dress group.[4]

That talk about the possible formation of a new actors' union to replace Equity led to a reaction in New York. Early in February the union announced that a general meeting of Equity would be held in Los Angeles in the coming couple of weeks, during which members of a newly created advisory board for the Los Angeles branch of Equity would be elected. That action was taken specifically in response to the talk of actors forming a new union. As well, Equity let it be known it would not object to the election to the new advisory board actors who had been members of the old, dissolved executive committee.[5]

MGM was negotiating with Universal in February 1928 to purchase the contract of actor Jean Hersholt for the two years it had left to run. Hersholt had been under long-term contract to Universal for several years and starred in a number of its pictures. On loan outs to other producers Universal had been charging $3,750 a week for his services and never had him idle. During those loan outs the actor had continued to draw his listed salary of $1,750 a week and Universal, as a reporter commented, "has shown a good profit for the contract." And so much for gentlemen's agreements, written pacts, and so on, wherein the majors pledged not to profiteer or loan outs and/or not to poach talent.[6]

Meanwhile, attacks from several quarters on the new standard contract for freelance actors adopted by AMPAS had resulted in the Academy's board of directors referring the contract back to the original committee at the end of February for clarification. Criticism leveled at the contract included the fact that producers would twist the wording of certain clauses to their own advantage. The AMPAS board "carefully" reviewed the criticism and the document itself, but could find no justification for complaint. Nevertheless, in order to silence critics the board referred it back to the committee with instructions that it be clarified to prevent any further misconstruction.[7]

A month later AMPAS announced the new contract, with language clarified, had been drawn up and accepted by all involved parties. An actor was engaged for a minimum of one week and the issue of pay and callback for retakes was clarified, to the benefit of players. Producers' liability to a player in case of the illness of any cast member was clearly defined. As well, a new paragraph was inserted that provided for the arbitration of any dispute over the contract between actor and producer. Either party could refer a dispute to AMPAS for arbitration, although no mention was made of the arbitration being binding.[8]

Around this time talking pictures were settling in to stay and that gave Equity a new burst of energy with respect to organizing Hollywood

4. A Second Brief Lull, 1928-1929

players. With the coming of sound Paul Dullzell, along with other Equity executives in New York, believed it was the psychological time to bring into their ranks at least 50 percent of the star and featured film players. Speculation had it that the renewed Equity drive would begin on July 1, 1928. Dullzell was in Hollywood in June and the producers were watching his every move. He was in Los Angeles to test the waters for a move to line up the players for his organization. A series of recruiting meetings were held at the Beverly Wilshire Hotel with a maximum of 150 potential members invited to each meeting, at which Dullzell expounded on the benefits gained from belonging to his union.[9]

Still in Hollywood in July, Dullzell declared AMPAS to be Will Hays' smoke screen attack of a year earlier against Equity and a flat failure currently. He predicted that between then and Labor Day Equity would be sufficiently strong on the west coast to demand a union shop for every cast in a talkie motion picture. What the rank and file player wanted, he declared, would prevail. Dullzell explained that Equity lost out a year earlier on the west coast because of a fast move by Hays and by stars who felt their fat salaries were secure. Since then, matters for AMPAS had changed. He then cited Conway Tearle as an example. A year earlier Tearle was a member of the actors' committee in AMPAS but now he was a 100 percent member of Equity and not even a film star. Tearle was "washed up" in pictures, said the union executive, and back in the legitimate theater. In explaining Gillmore's rapid return to New York from Los Angeles after getting the cold shoulder from AMPAS with a lot of "fast politics" at the time, Dullzell declared that Equity did not then want to see its house divided.[10]

It was the opinion of Equity officials that talking pictures would greatly aid in bringing the union shop to the screen because, commented a journalist, "The advent of talkies will bring hundreds of stage players to the screen and these will form the nucleus of an Equity screen group." Since the Equity shop existed in the theater world any stage player who moved over to films was already an Equity member. When sound films arrived there was for a short time a fairly strong and pervasive belief that most of the silent players would not make the transition to sound and would mostly be supplanted by actors from the legitimate theater who had experience in talking and emoting. For reasons never explained it was widely believed, for a time, that silent players would never be able to talk

Film Actors Organize

and emote at the same time. Obviously, such ideas were greatly exaggerated. Many stage players did move over to films, but they had always done so, even in the silent era. Players in silent films, for the most part, made an easy and successful transition to the talkies.[11]

Film extras in Hollywood had a new complaint in October 1928. They were protesting against the use by film studios of wealthy transient visitors to Southern California who wanted to be extras for a few days, just for the experience. Those visitors pulled strings, somehow, to end up cast as extras. Every time that occurred a real, and underworked, extra lost out on a day's pay. There were said to be hundreds of those visitors to Los Angeles every year, acquainted with somebody or who, through a mutual friend, secured the desired introduction to the studio casting executive. While the studios using the Central Casting Bureau were pledged to take no extras except through the CCB, nevertheless, the outsiders were slipped in continuously. Central Casting had, reportedly, tried to curb the practice, but with little success.[12]

Illustrating the idea that stage actors would come to dominate Hollywood films was a report that came out later in October. It was said the number of strictly film players available for principal roles, including stars and featured parts, would be reduced by one-third when the sound picture situation had settled down. That decrease was to be filled in by legitimate players, mainly drawn from Broadway. There were then said to be about 750 Hollywood players numbered among the available, heretofore in silent films. An estimate from an unnamed studio head was that no less than 250 players from the legitimate ranks would come west; some were there already. And that each one of them would supplant an existing silent film player. "It is further asserted by the same studio head that despite the reports strictly picture actors may be trained for dialog films, it is improbable except in special cases," observed the account. As an example it was said that First National studio was finding it difficult to get actors with voices to take part in the courtroom scenes for *Changelings*. Over 50 prospects had been given voice tests in the previous week but only one was found to meet the requirements. According to one of the best known producer/directors, regarding the arrival of sound films, "After all these years everything is swept away in a moment. It means that we all have to start from the beginning again. Past reputations count for nothing."[13]

Also in October 1928, Hollywood studios faced the possibility of

4. A Second Brief Lull, 1928–1929

being hauled before the California State Department of Industrial Relations as a result of their alleged frequent violations of regulations laid down the previous January, affecting extras. There were two state labor regulations said to be violated most frequently. One provided that if extras were called in to work and for some reason or other, even if the reason was beyond the studio's control, the company was unable to work that day, a notice had to be posted at the hour designated for the call stating the set would not work and instructing extras to collect carfare. If the extras were not dismissed immediately, they were to be paid their regular wages. Reportedly, three of the major studios violated that regulation consistently, keeping the extras on the lot and working them for an hour or two and then dismissing them with one-quarter time checks, instead of a full day's pay. The other regulation was the one that provided that when extras had completed eight hours of work on a set, and were held for at least another hour to turn in their wardrobe, they had to be paid an additional one-quarter time check for the overtime. One company, using several hundred specially costumed extras dismissed them from the set at 6:00 P.M. All had to turn in their costumes before they received their checks for their eight hours of work. Due to the length of wardrobe lines it was 1.5 hours before they were lined up in front of the cashier's window, and they were paid only up to 6:00 P.M. (All were legally entitled to two hours more pay.) One of the extras protested about the missing pay and threatened action. His name and address were taken and the next day he received his extra pay by mail. But he was the only one so treated. Supposedly, that practice was general among the studios that frequently used mob scenes (lots of extras). That the extras rarely if ever protested was said to be due to their fear of being blacklisted.[14]

Rumors that Equity would soon renew its drive for recognition and the union shop continued to surface off and on. Another such period came in late November 1928. A worried *Los Angeles Times* said the purported move would be their "most powerful" ever attempt and lead "to the enrichment of their pocketbooks and the extension of their iron ring of control over players and producers." This newspaper was one of the observers who feared a takeover of sound films by the Equity stage players. Also, a lot of silent players, who worried about their future in sound, had gone temporarily to stage work to be better prepared. And to play on the stage they had to join Equity. "This move will give Equity officials their first firm foothold in the film field. Extension of their power to domination will be easy from that advantage point," fretted the newspaper. Ultimately the *Times* worried the studios would bow little by little, without seeing the handwriting on the wall and "will yield the motion-picture industry to the same union domination in actor and craftsman fields which is blamed for so much of the low estate in which American theater today is wallowing."[15]

As this rumor of renewed Equity activity made the rounds it was reported the union was sending out questionnaires to its members and quietly tabulating results, to gauge player support for itself. Recipients of union questionnaires were being asked 1) Are you in favor of Equity protection for Equity members taking speaking parts in talking pictures? 2) Are you in favor of the Council passing a resolution prohibiting members from acting in speaking parts in talking pictures unless all speaking parts are held by Equity members? 3) Are you in favor of an Equity contract covering speaking parts in talking pictures? *Billboard* was another observer that pointed to the number of legitimate players moving to films and the number of silent movie players seeking stage work temporarily for speaking experience and then said, "In other words, Equity is gaining strength from both sources, and with its regular membership behind it the time to strike is considered at hand. The situation in Hollywood is understood to be favorable to Equity action. Reports have it that dissatisfaction has loomed over the Academy of Motion Picture Arts and that many members in that organization would be only too willing now to swing to Equity."[16]

With the coming of talkie films one result, at least in the beginning, was a decrease in the use of film extras. For 1928, the Central Casting Bureau reported, $2,469,711 was spent on extras (down from $2,838,136 in 1927) in 276,155 placements (330,397 in 1927). Average daily pay for an extra in 1928 was $8.94 ($8.59 in 1927). Based on 365 possible working days a year only one male and one female extra averaged 5.0 days of work each in 1928; two of each sex averaged 4.5 days each; 10 men and four women got 4.0 days; 35 males and 11 females received 3.5 days; 40 men and 15 women got 3.0 days; 94 men and 36 women got 2.5 days; 132 men and 87 women received 2.0 days' of work each week. Pay rates for extras ranged from $3 to $15 a day and, by this account, "some 45,000 people" around Hollywood were ready to do extra work. In the old silent

4. A Second Brief Lull, 1928–1929

days a group of 300 to 400 extras was called for a ballroom or courtroom scene. They were used for one day and pay ran from $3 to $10 a day. But at the dawn of the sound era, for the ballroom scene, perhaps 100 would be called; 75 for the courtroom scene. Instead of working just one day, though, they were kept working for perhaps several days. In 1928 there were 180,432 placements for men extras; 86,801 women; 5,473 boys; and 3,449 placements for girls. Average daily placements were as follows; 494 men, 237 women, 25 children, 46 veterans, 30 blacks. Of the total sum paid to extras, seven percent ($176,963) was given for overtime; that is, work running over eight hours in a day. Veterans were often given preference in the hiring of extras. The CCB was still not taking any new registrations unless, said a reporter, "requested by studio officials who have to give the parties registered work through the office sufficient to average two days a week." Of course, it was a loophole for favoritism and to allow new registration of extras even when the CCB, officially, was taking none. For example, if Jane Doe moved to Los Angeles from another state with the dream of making it in Hollywood chances were she would head first to the CCB. However, if they were taking no new registrations and if she had no pull or connections, she would be quickly refused registration and sent away. However, if the same Jane Doe was the friend of a friend, and so forth, of someone important in Hollywood then she got the studio to request Jane Doe from the CCB for extra work. Then when Doe turned up at the bureau's office she was quickly registered and sent off to work.[17]

Writing in the March 1929 issue of *The American Federationist* (the AFL organ), Alfred Harding said that film players were feeling a need to be unionized; not only the relatively low-paid extras but also the highly-paid stars were turning "wistful eyes" towards the Actors' Equity Association. It had tried for nine years to organize the players but had only met with "momentary" success. Only twice before had the actors felt the demands on them to be so unpleasant as to necessitate organized resistance. On both occasions, continued Harding, they gave indications of forming a union with Equity and each time the producers were quick to grant the contested demands. In the case of the salary cut dispute in 1927 the uproar was so great the producers, who had tried to impose those cuts, had a change of heart in less than two weeks. Harding argued that probably the most important single event leading to the possibility of the formation of a film actors' union was the arrival of talking pictures. "Many

Film Actors Organize

stage players are going to Hollywood. The movie magnates must have them, and in dealing with experienced Equity members they will find a strong feeling for standard contracts and a basic agreement uniform with the Equity regulations," declared the account. "Mr. Hays may yet be wise enough voluntarily to call a joint conference of leaders of the Association of Motion Picture Producers and Equity."[18]

With regard to renewed activity by Equity, little concrete action took place, only the rumors that came and went. One of the latter, in the middle of April 1929 had it that any efforts Equity might undertake to organize Hollywood would be directed from the group's New York headquarters, rather than from the west coast. Frank Gillmore was then in Hollywood but the New York office declared emphatically that no campaign would be launched.[19]

Equity had a standard form film contract prepared in Los Angeles in May 1929 by its attorney on the west coast, I. B. Kornblum, for the film industry, which was similar to the standard contract then in force for Equity members appearing on the stage. Later that month the contract was on its way to New York to obtain the approval of the Equity Council prior to June 1. At that time, June 1, Gillmore was due to return to the west coast to obtain recognition in the film field, or so the latest rumor went. It was understood that new contract provided that all Equity casts had to be used in talking pictures and that if the producers did not concede that point, Equity members would be pulled from the studios. Among the provisions in the new contract was one that required all disputes to be settled by binding arbitration.[20]

When the second annual AMPAS dinner was held in May 1929 it was called primarily to present the AMPAS awards of merit — the Oscars — for the year ending August 1, 1928. In his speech at that dinner Conrad Nagel told of a survey during the later period of the silent film era showing that at the peak of production there was employment for 600 actors of standing. Yet to fill those places 4,000 were available. With the coming of a "deluge" of players from New York in response to the talkies the situation was even worse. During the coming year, said Nagel, the actors' branch of the Academy would hold monthly meetings at which problems of the players would be discussed and solutions sought. The award for "most outstanding picture of the year" went to *Wings*. But action would commence much more quickly than Nagel had anticipated. So many rumors

4. A Second Brief Lull, 1928–1929

had come and gone with respect to renewed activity by Equity that nobody paid much attention to them anymore. However, the last one about the new contract and a June 1 date had been accurate. Equity was about to launch its third, and largest, effort to organize the Hollywood film players.[21]

5

Equity's Third Attempt, 1929

Suddenly and without previous announcement of its intentions, Equity declared for the union shop stating that on Wednesday, June 5, 1929, Equity members could appear in talking pictures only if the casts of such films were 100 percent Equity. The order was effective in both New York and in Los Angeles. Frank Gillmore — by that time he was president of Equity — was then in the California film capital. Among the provisions of that new contract was a demand for a 48-hour week, the minimum length of work was to be one week, all rehearsals were to be considered as actual work and to be paid for, disputes were to be settled by binding arbitration, all players' contracts signed after June 5 had to be the Equity standard form document. Equity anticipated it could be forced into a fight with the producers but believing that all players from the legitimate stage were a cardinal necessity in the talkies, it felt the time was right to organize. The resolution covering the Equity shop in films and the use of its contract was adopted by the Equity Council after considering the problem for six months. "It was stated that actors on the coast have not been treated fairly and conditions of their contracts not observed. The actors did not openly complain for fear of hurting their chances in future pictures, it is alleged by the Equity people," said a journalist. Contracts entered into prior to June 5, 1929, were to be honored, even if it meant a film's cast would not be all-Equity. In a letter to Equity members, Frank Gillmore gave the results of the questionnaire that had been mailed out earlier. In response to the query asking if the recipient was in favor of the

5. Equity's Third Attempt, 1929

Council passing a resolution prohibiting members from acting in speaking parts in the talkies unless all speaking parts were filled by Equity members the response was 1,087 votes in favor, and 98 votes against.[1]

Upon receiving the Equity demand the producers held a lengthy meeting throughout the night of June 5 and into the early morning hours of June 6. Then, on the 6th, they issued a dismissive comment and threw down the gauntlet to the union. Speaking for the producers, Cecil B. DeMille simply said that the producers would not agree to the demands made by Equity on the 5th. Said DeMille, "We will continue to engage artists for our productions only under the fair and just form of contract which was approved by representatives of both producers and motion picture actors [in AMPAS]. We decline to be restricted as to the source of our talent."[2]

The producers' move in Los Angeles was looked upon as an open defiance of Equity, though a *New York Times* journalist "with every indication that war will ensue" between the two sides. Several producers said that while there were some 2,000 players in films that belonged to Equity, there were 4,000 actors, ranging from bit players to featured actors who did not. They freely predicted there was not a chance there would be a shutdown of the studios. As well, they pointed out that most of the stars were under long-term contracts and thus, unaffected, at least until each individual contract expired. In his statement Gillmore said, "The official reply by the Association of Motion Picture Producers [MPPDA] is exactly what I expected.... But time is on our side and in the end sober second thoughts will prevail." He added that it was not just the terms of a contract that mattered but also its enforcement: "I regret to inform the producers that I have on record scores of instances where actors have pointed out their rights under this 'fair and just contract' [the AMPAS document] and have always received the reply: 'Well, what are you going to do about it?' And without an association behind the actor there was really nothing to do about it, since the warning glint in the eye of the person who said it had much significance. The motion picture producers are organized. Offend one and you may offend all." Morale of Equity members was excellent, asserted Gillmore, and they all expressed a feeling of happiness that the time had come when the motion picture actor "can prove to the world, as did his legitimate brother ten years ago, the falsity of the old saying 'Actors will not stick together.' The motion picture actor is just as loyal as his brother of the speaking stage, and there is not the slightest fear that he will every play false to his class. We believe that the trump cards are in our hands and we will play them at the proper time." In an informal discussion in Los Angeles with newsmen Gillmore said that at no time would a strike be called, arguing that the pressure of Equity members in refusing to sign anything but Equity contracts would be so great as to bring the producers into line. "We don't want any one to lose money. We have formed no alliance, except with the American Federation of Labor, and that will suffice, I think," he said. Also on June 6, AMPAS adopted a "hands off" policy with respect to the situation.³

In its summary of the sudden Equity move on June 5, *Billboard* called it the most wide-sweeping effort to organize the film business that had ever been attempted by the actors. The declaration by Equity was said to have come as a complete surprise to the studios, to Hays, to the MPPDA, to the general (not trade) press, and to the Equity membership. "Thus, Equity opens its fight to remedy working conditions in the picture field which has long been a thorn in its side. Overwork and underpay, evils against which the actors have had no weapons, are the chief bones of contention," said the account. Gillmore was quoted as saying, "Recently conditions in the studios, as far as the actors are concerned, have been going from bad to worse. Many producers have been working their people unconscionable hours and keeping it up day after day. Not a single person I met but complained of it." With respect to the poll results, Gillmore explained that the union's Council considered that a mandate and was acting on it as such. "Equity faces stiff opposition in that California, the seat of the motion picture industry, is notoriously antiunion," he added. "In any event, there is little likelihood that any drastic measures will be resorted to until all other means have failed. Equity, however, due to its affiliations with the American Federation of Labor, presents a strong front."⁴

Appalled by the move was the *Los Angeles Times*. An editor with the paper called the MPPDA decision to reject Equity's demands for a union shop to be "a matter for community congratulations.... If the Equity demand had been acceded to, the complete unionization of the film industry could have been compelled and the result would have been calamity." According to the editor, the motion picture industry had started open shop, reached prosperity open shop and could "remain prosperous only under open-shop conditions, with no discrimination for or against any-

5. Equity's Third Attempt, 1929

body because of membership or non-membership in a particular organization." If Equity was in a position to dictate to the industry, warned the editorial, "the industry will be stifled as the stage and vaudeville have been stifled." Arguing a union shop would lead to an increase in costs and admission prices the editor predicted there would be found some substitute for the pictures if ever it were unionized and a "gouge" of the public was started. The short-sighted view that some of the producers might have taken, that it would cost them nothing to accede to the Equity demands since all competitors would be in the same position and could raise their prices accordingly, "is precisely the theory on which all racketeering is based. It is a false theory, since the public can and will seek other forms of amusement. Racketeering cannot exist without the closed union shop, and the closed union shop leads inevitably to racketeering." In conclusion, thundered the editor; "There can be no compromise with the principle of the open shop; it is necessary to industrial peace and prosperity and has been demonstrated time and time again in other industries, here and elsewhere. It must be preserved in the nation and talking-picture industries."[5]

On June 9, actor Lionel Barrymore stepped forward to say the attempts by Equity to extend the union shop to film players was a move to cure ills that did not exist. He was then a director and actor with MGM and a member of Equity; his sister Ethel — equally renowned as an actor — was vice president of Equity. "I see no necessity of performing a major operation on a perfectly healthy child," said Lionel. "I do not see any fairness in having a small minority of people come into a new business and expect to change that business to conform with their own ideas. The stage is one thing and the motion picture industry is another proposition entirely." Lionel added that if there was a question of any injustice to the actor he would stand with Equity but that he had many friends among actors and he had heard of no grievance that would warrant such action as the union had undertaken. AMPAS had an arbitration board to adjust differences between actors and producers, he observed, and "I understand the board has had few, if any, cases since it was established."[6]

One day later, on June 10, actor Willard Mack added his voice to that of Lionel Barrymore in expressing anti–Equity sentiments. Declaring he had been a member of Equity for years he remarked he had never seen the union get work for the actor. As well, he claimed the stage and film industries were entirely different institutions and what might be good for one was apt to be bad for the other. "If Equity feels that there is any grievance — and I know of none — it could not expect to succeed by coming into another business with a club in its hand," he said. If Equity persisted in trying to organize the film players, Mack warned, the producers would stop using the services of the stage actors and develop their own talent exclusively. Thus, if the union persisted it would drive the stage actors out of the movies.[7]

All along Equity refused, of course, to give out a list of its members, or even to give the exact number of film players it had as members. Then, in its June 12, 1929, issue, *Variety* printed a list of names of all the members, more or less. There were a total of 528 names, 140 were under long-term contracts with the various studios while 388 were described as freelance players.[8]

Conrad Nagel, who had been active in the 1927 effort by Equity to organize and who had been one of the first to take up the union's cause, before switching to side with the producers and AMPAS, was said to be remaining neutral in the present situation. Nagel had talked with both Gillmore and Cecil B. DeMille, separately, to try and find some ground for conciliation but each man had reportedly told Nagel he was not interested.[9]

When production was at its peak it was estimated by producers that about 700 actors (those receiving screen credit) were used in filmmaking. When production was at its low ebb about 150 to 200 actors were used, mostly being long-term contract people. At the time of the Equity move it was estimated that about 500 players would be required to get out all the films planned. Besides those, another 300 to 400 players would be needed for parts that did not get screen credit. As well, an average of around 600 a day would be used for crowd scenes and atmosphere, with those extras all obtained through the CCB.[10]

Over the course of the first week after Equity's demands were announced rumors circulated about one thing or another. One had it there had been a secret meeting between Gillmore and the business agents of the various craft unions in the film industry. But no decisions had been reached at that meeting with action deferred. Producers had decided to refrain from any form of public discussion or controversy with Gillmore and officially remained silent. In the matter of actors, it was understood producers had agreed among themselves to loan each other contract play-

5. Equity's Third Attempt, 1929

ers who were deemed necessary to a film, in the advent of a shortage of talent. Producers claimed they could carry on for two years without being worried by Equity or the freelance players' union activities. Charles Miller, west coast Equity representative, claimed over 500 applications for membership had been received in that first week. Publicly, Gillmore said that 40 members of the union, offered jobs under non–Equity deals, had turned them down. No details were given. One major studio said it had signed five Equity members to non–Equity contracts since June 5. But here, as well, no names were given. Other studios were reported to be signing up actors secretly, holding off any announcements until the trouble had passed.[11]

A *Variety* reporter observed at the end of the first week that the freelance actors were practically solid for Equity but there was much less proportional support for the union among the stars. Gillmore then was claiming Equity had 2,800 members on the west coast. He further said that although they may not all be paid up in their dues they were still members of the organization and that under no circumstances would their resignations be accepted at this time. Some Equity members had resigned, or tried to, and then signed producer contracts after June 5 as non–Equity players. That allowed them to escape the union mandated punishment for an Equity member who signed a non–Equity contract — banishment from the legitimate stage — or so they hoped. The union president's obviously inflated membership count came from the fact his counting method involved the premise that once a member, always a member. On the two days following his June 5 declarations, said Gillmore, at least 12 Equity members had refused contracts from studios and at least two of them were "players of note." And during those two days 112 applications for new Equity membership had been received. He admitted to *Variety* there was a weakness in the union's position because there were so many actors on long-term option contracts. Thus, they could legally stay out of Equity for a long time and the union could do nothing about it and due to that fact he feared the battle to organize would be longer and harder than it would have been otherwise. Gillmore emphasized that Equity members in arrears on their dues were not free to accept producer contracts because of that delinquency.[12]

With respect to new contracts, Gillmore said considerable confusion existed among bit players and day workers. Because the union contract

Film Actors Organize

referred to weekly salaries and to a minimum employment period of one week the others thought they had been left out. Gillmore said that was not true and that special contracts would be available early the next week that applied directly to day and bit players. Said a reporter, "Equity figures that some actors may desert the organization, but because any actor who walks out at present could never work on the legit stage again, or even in pictures, should Equity win the fight, these factors straighten out any tendencies to fly away." Equity received no support in Los Angeles from the two leading morning newspapers. The *Los Angeles Times* remained virulently opposed to unionization of any sort while the *Los Angeles Examiner* came out with a strong editorial on June 8 saying that it, and all the other papers owned by William Hearst, were against Equity entering the picture field, even though they had supported the same union in its legitimate theater battle 10 years earlier. The same policy applied to the *Los Angeles Herald*, the Hearst afternoon newspaper in Los Angeles. Anticipating no drastic action and no strike right away, Gillmore explained that union actors would simply refuse to answer studio calls unless they got the official Equity contract signed. However, even then, the union president was worried the end result would be a repeat of what happened in the 1927 attempted organization. [13]

At the end of the first week each side was adamant in its position and each insisted the next move had to come from the other side. Hays and the MPPDA remained silent from New York, having earlier said the matter would be handled from California rather than from the east coast. *Billboard* declared the general run of motion picture actors was in favor of the Equity shop in films and that those that pledged themselves to support the union included many of the big stars, at least according to Paul Dullzell. Herein it said that Milton Sills and Conrad Nagel were once again supporting the union. [14]

On June 12 in Los Angeles Gillmore announced that 10 "prominent actors" had refused to sign new contracts unless they were Equity documents. However, he did not name any of the players. As well, the union president made public a letter from Pat. D. Powers, an independent producer, who pledged his support to the Equity movement. On the other hand, adding his voice to those of Lionel Barrymore, Willard Mack, Louise Dresser, and Marie Dressler, Equity member John Gilbert issued a statement on the 12th protesting against the union's entrance into Hollywood.

5. *Equity's Third Attempt, 1929*

Remarking that he did not see where "control" by Equity would benefit any one connected with the motion picture business, he went on to say that his principal worry at the time was to successfully make the transition to sound films; "I would hate to have my desire to improve my work disturbed by any concentrated move on the part of the Actors' Equity, of which I am a member. I feel my sense of loyalty to the men who have assisted me so greatly would direct my course of action."[15]

When he denounced Equity's move Gilbert's statement also included this comment: "Great stars rise from obscurity overnight into unheard of and undreamed of position and prestige. Such a condition is most certainly not the result of group control, therefore I do not see how control by Equity could benefit anyone in or connected with the motion-picture business." He added that throughout his 15-year career as an actor he had managed to solve "all my problems by myself without the assistance of any group agency. I have been broke and hungry on many occasions. No one rushed to my assistance.... My statement is entirely unbiased."[16]

Star after star turned up in print to denounce Equity and its demands. Adding their voices to the growing number were Norma Talmadge and Charles (Buddy) Rogers, who issued separate statements on June 14 protesting the entrance of Equity into Hollywood. Talmadge said she could see no reason for the recent action of the union, while Rogers believed the union wanted to enter the film industry because many stage players had deserted New York and the stage and, therefore, the union was looking for new fields for its "powers."[17]

Clara Bow added her name to the long list of prominent screen players protesting against Equity activities, on June 15. Said Bow, "I think it is quite wrong for Equity to attempt to invade Hollywood. We have absolutely no need for it here. It is a slight on the intelligence of screen players when an effort is made to make us believe that we have suffered indignities, grievances and hardships that Equity alone can remedy." Bow added, "Under Equity we would begin work in the morning and quit in the evening like workmen in a factory. I want none of it. I have a certain work to do. I do not want Equity telling me what to do and how to do it." Pointing out that she was a Brooklyn schoolgirl without a friend in the business to help her, that she had started her climb to stardom on the lowest rung of the ladder and that she worked her way up through her own efforts, Bow explained that not once along the way did she ever have need for the aid Equity purported to be able to offer. "I got along very well without Equity and I still can continue to do so," she said. "Equity wants to add a fifth wheel to a perfect-running motor car, and to me that fifth wheel has a flat tire."[18]

One of the few successes Equity managed in the first two weeks it tried to gain recognition and a first contract came not in California but in New York. A statement from the union's headquarters on June 17 announced that Pedro de Cordoba, a legitimate stage star, had prevented the filming of the Pathe production *On the Stairs* by refusing to report for work under open shop conditions. Pedro, though, was the only actor to walk out. He was a member of the Equity Council. Two union staff members went to the New York studio of Pathe and informed Hamilton McFadden, the movie's director, Pedro would have to have an Equity contract. He was referred to Pathe president Robert Kane who said he had orders from the Hays organization (MPPDA) not to recognize Equity or to issue one of its contracts. Kane was told Pedro would not report for the first rehearsal at 2:00 P.M. and when that was confirmed the production was called off; Pedro had the lead part.[19]

In its June 19 issue, *Variety* listed by name 100 reputed Equity members who had signed for movies on or after June 5. For 24 of them, negotiations had been entered into prior to June 1. All of them signed contracts for one picture deals, except for two who signed long-term contracts. Meanwhile, IATSE and the other film industry craft unions, it was reliably reported, would stay aloof from the Equity struggle. Union craftspeople in the Los Angeles studios would lend their moral support to the actors' union but would not walk off the job in support of any future player strike action. Gillmore had been so informed.[20]

In Los Angeles on June 18, Charles Quartermaine, an English actor, was the first film player on the west coast to be suspended by Equity for signing a non–Equity contract after June 5, when he inked with Fox. Attempting to strengthen the demands it had made on June 5, Equity declared, almost two weeks later, that while it acknowledged a player on a long-term non–Equity contract signed prior to June 5 had a valid document that the union would honor, Equity declared it was against any player on such a contract being farmed out to other studios during the life of the contract. Otherwise producers would shift actors from one studio to another as needed to meet any talent shortage and thus weaken Equity's

5. Equity's Third Attempt, 1929

position. Thus, if Jane Doe had singed a five-year non–Equity contract with Fox in April 1929 she could continue to appear in Fox films for the duration of the contract and without being a union member but Equity would respond against Fox if the studio loaned her out in that time period for a picture at, say, Universal. At least it would respond if Fox's contract with Doe was silent on the question of loan outs. However, if a long-term contract had a clause that specifically mentioned loan outs were possible then Equity would not challenge it. The vast majority of long-term contracts did not mention loan outs; studios just went ahead and farmed players out when it suited them.[21]

Before a crowd of almost 700 actors at a mass meeting on Monday, June 17, 1929, in Los Angeles, Frank Gillmore opened the more public part of his campaign against the producers. He read to his audience a telegram received at the union's New York headquarters from William Green, president of the American Federation of Labor. It read, in part, "The American Federation of Labor will give Equity its heartiest support." With Gillmore on the rostrum were Charles Miller, Equity west coast representative, and George Arliss, a Council member. One reporter present at the meeting declared "Screen credit actors were notable among the gathering by their absence. Few of the new eastern recruits to films via legit made an appearance in the flesh.' Among the subjects Gillmore touched on during his 53-minute address was the following: "I am not going to attack the Academy of Motion Picture Arts and Sciences. I believe, indeed I know, that there were many sincere men who started it, but the result as far as we are concerned is that no actor dares take his complaint to them because he fears the blacklist. It must be so, otherwise the Academy would be flooded with complaints." And, "Some of you do not love Equity because you do not know us. But I can assure you that for years we have been the silent policeman on the beat that has protected your pocketbooks from depredations." He stated that at the moment many big stars, on contracts, were in sympathy with the union but were on the sidelines unable to help because of those long-term contracts and due to Equity's unwillingness to ask them to jeopardize themselves by an illegal act. It was the union's first mass meeting since the June 5 demands and a journalist concluded that the "first meeting revealed some enthusiasm at start but absence of fireworks prevented demonstrations."[22]

During the second week of Equity's action there was little activity from the union, except for the mass meeting of members. Nothing whatsoever came from the MPPDA officially with the film men giving no public acknowledgment or recognition of either the union or of Gillmore. On Friday June 14, Equity was admitted into the ranks of the Los Angeles Central Labor Council, which was made up of all the unions in the Los Angeles area that were affiliated with the AFL and thus assured the actors' union of the moral support of that body. Gillmore admitted the producers had made no effort to talk to him and had shunned him completely in the two weeks since Equity action commenced. Except for the brief statement made by DeMille on June 6, the day after the ultimatum, not a single word had been said for publication by any member of the MPPDA. After the second day following the June 5 action statement by Gillmore the local daily papers in Los Angeles had blacklisted the union and carried nothing further from Equity or statements from its chief. Of course, they continued to carry attack pieces on the union on a regular basis but Equity and Gillmore were given no right of response, and so on. Local papers continued to regularly carry pieces on actors, union members and non-members, who protested against the Equity action. Among those so featured, and not mentioned previously herein, were Lewis S. Stone, and Monte Blue. Finding itself denied access to the columns of the daily press in Los Angeles; the union was then producing a four-page news sheet twice weekly to get out its position. It sold for five cents a copy. According to a *Variety* reporter studios reported that since June 5 they had signed some 200 players to either term or one-picture contracts, and that a majority of those actors were Equity members. Some of those engagements involved negotiations that began prior to June 5. (Equity ultimately ruled that if negotiations had been honestly entered into prior to June 5, and a contract resulting directly from those negotiations entered into after June 5 then the document did not violate Equity rules.) Producers also claimed that where contracts had been offered to Equity members, few had been refused. However, Equity stated that only about 25 of its members signed contracts and that the majority of those people had opened negotiations prior to June 5 and were, therefore, permitted to accept. Gillmore said that to his knowledge, only two or three union members had violated the rules by signing non-union contracts after June 5, with no negotiations opened prior to that date. Film extras had been almost completely forgotten by Equity but a report at this time had it that efforts were being made to

5. Equity's Third Attempt, 1929

organize the extras as an auxiliary of Equity. Supposedly that was being done on film sets by Equity members who worked in the background ranks.[23]

Also on June 19, Equity received another communication from AFL president William Green. In the letter Green said his organization stood squarely behind Equity's attempt to organize the film players. Some observers interpreted the letter to mean that in the event of a strike by actors in the studios the AFL would support the actors' union by calling out musicians, studio employees, and union men employed in cinemas all over the country. Studio indifference caused Paul Dullzell to say that day, from New York, "By their indifference to Equity's fair request and by their attempt to continue their arbitrary rule over players in sound and talking pictures the motion picture producers are forcing Equity into the necessity of availing itself of the help of the American Federation of Labor, which Equity has so far refrained from asking."[24]

At the end of that second week *Billboard* stated, "Equity has not yet been permitted freedom of the local press and the association is getting out its own special organ, *Actors' Equity News*, selling at a nickel, to disseminate facts which the dailies will not print." The lead editorial in the first issue of that sheet was a scorching condemnation of Lionel Barrymore for his attitude toward the union. It was observed that during the actors' theatrical stage strike in New York in 1919 the entire Barrymore family supported the Equity cause but Lionel, then sitting comfortably in a director's chair, had reversed his attitude. Since that time, continued the story, Lionel had been regularly delinquent in paying his union dues. At a meeting held on December 9, 1924, the Equity Council passed a motion that unless Lionel's indebtedness was paid by December 1925, Equity members would not be allowed to rehearse with him or to play with him; the actor was so informed. As a result of the motion Lionel paid his dues up to May 1925 but was again suspended for nonpayment of dues in December 1927. In January 1928 he was reinstated after he paid his dues up to May 1928. As of June 1929 he was $30 in arrears on his dues. Of the three prominent actors in the Barrymore family only Lionel had come out publicly against Equity. John Barrymore (brother) came out publicly in support of the 1929 Equity movement and sister to the pair, Ethel, continued to hold an "exalted" position in the union due to her work in the 1919 strike, although she continued to play mainly in legitimate theater. Louise

79

Film Actors Organize

Dresser was also cited by the Equity sheet as having been all in favor of the union shop during her earlier years in films, before she became a star "under a fat, long contract." She was then also the wife of the casting director at Fox studio. William Hearst had supported Equity in its 1919 strike, through the newspapers he owned, but was against the union action in 1929, it was claimed, because Hearst had an interest in film production. As far as Equity was concerned it was significant that almost without exception the actors publicly condemning the union had fat contracts with the producers and were interested solely in their own gains instead of the welfare of actors in general.[25]

With the AFL "squarely behind" Equity in its campaign to unionize Hollywood, an editor with the *Washington Post* was moved to remark that it seemed inevitable that producers had to agree to a closed shop. "It seems incredible that producers should try to fight. Practically all the artisans that labor on the Hollywood motion picture lots are members of unions affiliated with the federation," observed the editor. Along with the fact that employees in cinemas were unionized, "the federation's support of Equity means, in effect, that if Equity's demands are not met, work on every producing lot will be halted and the theaters of the country darkened. Equity will not hesitate to invoke a general strike if its end can be attained in no other way."[26]

A report from Los Angeles on June 21 indicated that, in defiance of Equity's edict that none of its members sign a non–Equity film contract after June 5, 164 actors had done just that, at least according to Fred Datig, chairman of the casting directors' committee, which represented all the major studios. Union members were to sign only Equity contracts and to refrain from signing at all unless the entire cast of the production consisted of Equity members in good standing. In response to that report from Datig, the union announced the suspension of two more actors, and the possible suspension of many more. Placed on the union blacklist with Charles Quartermaine were Albert Gran and Ilka Chase. All three were named by the producers on the list of 164; Equity deserters who had signed a studio contract after June 5. As well, the union promised it would investigate all the other players whose names were on the list.[27]

Illustrating the visceral hatred the *Los Angeles Times* harbored toward Equity, and unions in general, was a piece that appeared in the newspaper on June 23, supposedly authored by Lillian Albertson. She was then

5. Equity's Third Attempt, 1929

a prominent Los Angeles and San Francisco theatrical producer, and herself a member of Equity. She wrote, "For the first time since Frank Gillmore began his attack on the picture industry I now am free to join the constantly growing chorus of censure he has brought down upon himself and his union by attempting to force the picture producers to turn over to him and his fellow union leaders the control of the film industry." Supposedly she had been compelled to stay silent until then for fear Gillmore would call a strike against her theatrical production *Desert Song*. However, as it was ending its run that week she felt free to speak out. Albertson then went on a long, emotional tirade against Gillmore and Equity about how they had allegedly mistreated her as a legitimate producer — there was no mention of the film industry. Such unsupported allegations, bordering on slander, were not refuted by Gillmore and the union because they were denied access to the local papers, which continued to publish unwarranted attacks.[28]

Three weeks after Equity began its action there was still not much that had happened. Producers continued to hold daily meetings regarding the situation but maintained a strict policy of no comment, officially. Equity refused to say what strategy it was pursuing, and so on. More publicity was given by the media to stars denouncing Equity. Among the most recent additions to that list were George Jessel, Noah Beery (brother of Wallace), Edmund Lowe, and Lenore Ulric. Another contingent of players declared the so-called referendum ballot asking the actors if they wanted Equity in films, which Gillmore had mailed out the previous fall, was never received by them. Those who said they were never given a chance to vote were: John Barrymore, Louise Fazenda, Patsy Ruth Miller, Hobart Bosworth, Evelyn Brent, James Hall, Jack Oakie, Louise Dresser, Norma Talmadge, Glen Tyron, Edward Nugent, William Haines, John Boles, Bert Roach, Lowell Sherman, Claude Gillingwater, Clive Brooke, Neil Hamilton, Warner Oland, Lionel Barrymore, John Gilbert, Lilyan Tashman, Robert Ober, and Mary Doran. At that time Equity had no contract drafted for actors who accepted long-term engagements. However, Gillmore, in a letter sent to producers and agents, pointed out that long-term contracts had to include the working conditions specified in the Equity basic agreement and that all long-term agreements had to be approved by the union. Nothing had been said about extras, by the union, except that a day-worker contract was being prepared.[29]

Film Actors Organize

Variety published a list of names, supposedly more or less complete, of all actors who were members of Equity and who had signed studio contracts since June 5. Its first list held about 100 names while its second list (those who signed since June 18) contained 75 names.[30]

Equity's second mass meeting of actors was held on June 20. Big names from the ranks of the actors were expected but none showed up. The crowd was said to be only 100. A little later Conrad Nagel, Lois Wilson, Rod La Rocque, Basil Rathbone, and Ralph Forbes, constituting themselves a committee of five, called a meeting to be held at the Beverly Wilshire Hotel on Tuesday, June 25. All featured and principal actors, whether members of Equity or not were invited. That committee had called upon Gillmore asking him to call a meeting at which a vote could be taken publicly as to whether or not the actors favored the entrance of Equity into the film field. Gillmore declined to call such a meeting on the ground the union membership had already voted by a 10–1 margin for Equity intervention — based on the mailed-in questionnaire from the previous fall. In the view of the committee the freelance players were being made the goats in the present situation. According to a reporter, "Producers are behind tonight's meeting and have requested all their contract players to arrange to be present." Also, it was speculated that the committee of five would try to have a resolution passed at the meeting asking Gillmore and Equity to retire from the film field and stick to the legitimate theater. During their call on the union president the committee stated that at the last Equity open meeting in Los Angeles the attendance was conspicuous by the number of union members whose dues were in arrears.[31]

One day before that meeting, on Monday, June 24, Equity held its third mass meeting with some 900 members of the film colony present, including more prominent stars than had appeared at such gatherings in the past. Thus, that meting had the largest turnout of the three. During his speech Gillmore said he would soon announce what punishments would be handed out to union members who violated Equity's dictates. But, beyond that, the union president had no other strategy to outline, despite the fact that the meeting called by the committee of five for a day later was then well known. One of the other speakers remarked that Conrad Nagel had called an anti–Equity meeting for the next evening at which "traitors will show their colors."[32]

Finally, around June 23, Equity came up with a day workers' form of

5. Equity's Third Attempt, 1929

contract. It amounted to a tiny piece of paper that formed a sort of addendum to the main Equity basic agreement. It was not available (printed) on June 21 but was as of June 25. Starting on June 25, Equity had a daily Los Angeles newspaper that was prepared to allow it print space in order to respond to allegations, make press statements, and so on. That publication was the *Los Angeles Record*, a Scripps-Howard newspaper. It began that date by running serially on its front page a probe into studio conditions giving the Equity side of the case. "Producers have had it all their own way in the other Los Angeles dailies with the exception of the *Hollywood Citizen*, which has been favorably inclined toward Equity," said a journalist.[33]

The anti–Equity meeting was thrown into an uproar when a crowd of people said to be Equity members appeared at the meeting and heckled the speakers. "The proceedings approached the riot stage several times," commented an observer. Nagel and the others in the committee declared that since Gillmore had arbitrarily dissolved the Los Angeles branch advisory board a few weeks earlier the Hollywood actors thus had no representatives on the Equity Council. Thus, the Nagel petition requested that Gillmore call a meeting of only paid-up members in California to consider the present situation and vote on whether or not they supported the present policies of the New York Council and the president, and also to elect an executive committee in Los Angeles to work with Gillmore during the emergency, thereby giving the film player a definite voice in things concerning his welfare. Days before the meeting, when the committee had spoken to Gillmore he had told them, according to the committee, that such a resolution as they proposed would be given consideration if it was presented to him in the form of a petition signed by at least 30 members of the association. That goal was met at the meeting when slightly more than 30 names were affixed to the petition.[34]

During that raucous meeting Nagel tried to quiet the pro-Equity people in the crowd by saying the meeting had not been called as a protest against Equity but, "many of us feel that the way the situation is being handled by President Frank Gillmore, is not as it should be."[35]

Another account of the June 25 Nagel meeting described it as follows; "For more than two hours cries of 'traitor' and 'betrayer' were hurled across the floor at various players during this turbulent session called by Conrad Nagel and his committee of five." Some 450 people tried to fit into a space designed to hold 200.[36]

Film Actors Organize

On the night of July 1, 1929, Equity held its fourth mass meeting; it was a rally that attracted the largest crowd to date — about 1,500 — but was also called the dullest to date: "Many of those who spoke alluded to the lack of a definite campaign plan which they stated was placing everyone in a tough spot." Surprise of the evening was the appearance on the rostrum of George Jessel, the first actor who had made an anti–Equity statement in the press to then later have returned to the association to be forgiven and accepted back by the union.[37]

Near the end of June local merchants in Los Angeles were asked to place a "We are for Equity" sign in their windows. A number of stores were said to be displaying those cards. As well, the Equity Los Angeles office was listing markets where actors could buy foodstuffs at discounts ranging from seven to 10 percent. Nine restaurants were listed that were giving discounts of from 10 to 20 percent. One service station gave players a 10-percent reduction on gasoline purchases. In all cases an Equity membership card had to be shown before the discount was applied.[38]

The deadlock between Equity and the producers completed its fourth week and started its fifth week at the beginning of July with little sign of change on the part of either side. Reportedly, of the players reputed to have signed the studio contracts after June 5 in defiance of Equity, about 30 percent were not members of the union. Others were alleged to be in arrears on dues or already suspended. In the event that Equity won its demands it was admitted that non-member actors who had been signed to studio contracts since June 5 would not be punished. Paul Dullzell, the union's executive secretary, said from New York that his organization had sent letters to all New York casting agents requesting them to refrain from placing people in studios within the metropolitan New York district, unless the Equity contract was used.[39]

Hollywood studios did admit that many Equity members had declined offers from them, but insisted that many other members of the association had signed up with them, in spite of the union's edicts. According to the studios, in the month of July they expected to accomplish about 75 percent of their planned production; that is, Equity's action was expected to disrupt through shut down or delay some 25 percent of the industry's planned filmmaking. Tightening up even more, Equity imposed a rule on June 28 that every union member not under contract to a producer prior to that date was prohibited from setting foot on any set, stage,

5. Equity's Third Attempt, 1929

or location in any and every capacity until the situation was resolved. That was reportedly done to cover those members who had received or expected to receive offers for work as extras. It was figured that some members who had refused to sign the studio form of contract might, without impairing their standing, take jobs as extras as there was no ruling against it prior to the order of June 28. Many Equity members functioned also as directors, writers, and advisors, and it was understood the ruling would apply to them as well, keeping them away from the studios. Gillmore informed a *Variety* reporter that the union expected to win the "strike" on its own and that he thought it would all be over within two weeks. According to Equity headquarters in New York, since June 5, 725 new members had joined the association.[40]

Another new, more stringent measure, was adopted by the union at the start of July. A verification was necessary from actors who signed studio contracts after June 5 but wherein negotiations for that contract began prior to June 5. Equity then demanded a written statement from the studio casting director involved that the agreement for the player's services was reached prior to June 5.[41]

Claiming threats had been made against Conrad Nagel, MGM furnished personal protection for its star while he was in the studio. Paramount was reported to have suffered many annoyances on its lot since the anti–Equity meeting called by Nagel and the others. Sudden coughing and dropped light bulbs on Paramount sound stages were understood to have allowed the shooting of only two scenes in two days on the film *Kibitzer*. On the MGM lot similar interruptions took place during the shooting of *The Thirteenth Chair*, especially in scenes involving Charles Quartermaine; he was the first actor suspended by Equity for signing a studio contract after June 5. Albert Gran in *Kibitzer* was the second to be suspended.[42]

In its July 3, 1929, issue, *Variety* published its third list of names of union-member actors who had signed studio contracts That one contained 39 names of players who had signed the banned contracts since June 25.[43]

When Equity held its fourth rally, on Thursday, June 28, speakers attacked Nagel and the others responsible for the anti-union meeting, calling them "secessionists" and "scabs." Most active for Equity were said to be the players who came to film from the stage in the previous year or so.

85

Film Actors Organize

Gillmore declared it was time for agents and other actor representatives to show their colors, that they should not handle Equity and non–Equity actors. At the meeting all Equity members who were working were called upon by union officials to donate 10 percent of their weekly salaries to the Equity relief fund. Frank Gillmore read out a letter at the meeting from Lewis Stone in which Stone denied a statement in the local papers attributed to him that "Equity Must Fail." The union head told his audience that he was still working on a strategy plan. Gillmore spoke of his trip to Los Angeles at the end of April to sound out folks on the question of a strike. He said he had dinner at the home of Nagel where a lot of the latter's friends were gathered and told them of his plan and declared they were heartily in accord with his line of action. Then he attacked the petition signed by 32 actors at the Nagel anti-union meeting. He said he never officially received the petition and that anyway it was no good because only 11 of those who signed it were in good standing, that is, paid-up members. While Gillmore in the past had insisted in counting members in arrears as members when it suited his needs, he was just as quick to declare them not to be members, if that better suited his purposes.[44]

Also at that meeting, Gillmore said that only 111 stage actors had come from New York to Los Angeles from January 1 to May 31, 1929, on film contracts. Lenore Ulric also sent word to the meeting—saying she had not made the anti–Equity newspaper statement that was attributed to her. *Billboard* noted a change in local newspaper coverage of the situation at the start of July, and that it was starting to change in favor of the union. Noted was that the *Los Angeles Record* had stated it would start to present both sides of the story "and other papers appear to be disposed to give some space to the Equity side of the matter." Given that and the support from organized labor, all the way from city labor councils to the AFL, led this reporter to conclude "that the position of Equity, through its labor union affiliations, is much stronger than the producers care to admit is evident."[45]

The cartel's self-imposed silence was broken on July 5 when Cecil B. DeMille, for the MPPDA, said he had no trouble casting films, despite Equity's action of June 5, and he anticipated no trouble in the future. Producers, he added, needed no sympathy: "It would seem to us that if any sympathy is to be extended it should be extended to those actors who are harassed and distressed by the unreasonable demands of the Equity Asso-

5. Equity's Third Attempt, 1929

ciation and whose livelihood is interfered with by the extractions of that association." He added that their disposition as producers was to use those who cast their lot with them "to the utmost limits of possibility. There are plenty of new faces available, plenty of new talent at hand, and the public is not averse to new faces and talent. But we naturally will stand firmly behind the artists who are now working in our studios or applying for work there. We shall proceed on that basis."[46]

One day later, on June 6, an editor with the *Los Angeles Times* heaped scorn on AFL president William Green, who had on a number of occasions pledged the support of his federation in Equity's fight to organize Hollywood. Such declarations of support were delivered in such a way that everyone involved knew what they really said — that the AFL would not call out any unions in the event Equity called a strike, and that the pledged support from the AFL was to be limited to moral support only. Nevertheless, the *Times* went on the attack declaring most of the unions "under President Green's headship are organizations whose officials make it their business to foment illegality, to take unfair advantage, and to try to protect their members from the consequences of criminal and quasi-criminal acts." Agreeing with a Green comment that the actors needed an organization the editor said that declaration "is, of course, measurably true, but they already have the kind of an organization they really need in the Motion Picture Academy of Arts and Sciences, which is as different from a labor union of the Equity type as day is from night." Readily conceding the right to organize and the value of organization the editor smugly declared that did not include the "loss of the right to object to the wrong kind of an organization." Working himself into a state of furious indignation the editor said an organization to promote "industrial warfare" was the wrong kind of organization, always and everywhere, in the motion picture business and outside of it: "Equity is such an organization. An organization to promote industrial peace is the right kind of an organization; the Motion Picture Academy of Arts and Sciences is such an organization. It adjusts disputes, redresses grievances, prevents trouble, smoothes the way for both actor and producer, sets proper standards for the industry, but makes no attempt to hamper, to restrict or to coerce, or to impose a closed shop. Its doors swing freely in both directions."[47]

With at least two factions struggling in Equity then — the Gillmore forces and the Nagel (AMPAS) group — the possibility of a third faction

Film Actors Organize

arose when the Gillmore supporters began to clash over tactics, at a meeting on July 5. Opting for a more aggressive approach was Clark Silverman who declared "an army going over the top isn't dignified," and added that he would "sock the first blow on the nose if it would bring this fight to a finish." Looking for a more moderate approach was a group that included Francis X. Bushman, George Jessel, and Charles Chase and they counseled for a "dignified" offensive. In response to Silverman's comments, Bushman replied, "I fear no man or body of men. I am not a catspaw for the producers or a groveling beggar for Equity." In other business at the meeting Gillmore refused to permit Gladys Grey to protest from the floor against her suspension from the ranks of Equity for having signed a studio contract in violation of the rules. Suspended that night, in addition to Grey, were Hedda Hopper, Cosmo Kyrle Bellew, Wheeler Oakman, Andre Beranger, Jules Cowles, Helen Millard, Mary Forbes, William Orlamond, and Holmes Herbert.[48]

In an effort to bring the producers and Equity together, Bushman spent much of the first week of July conferring with Cecil B. DeMille Louis B. Mayer, and Winifred R. Sheehan. DeMille told Bushman that in the two years he had been spokesman for the MPPDA no complaints from Equity had been presented to the studio members of the cartel. According to Bushman, when he queried Gillmore on that subject, the latter did not deny such was the case. On a return visit to DeMille by the actor, the former said producers were willing to make changes to the present studio contract and would even arbitrate the contract demanded by Equity, but the producers would not deal with Gillmore or anybody representing the union. Cecil added that the producers would have met with Equity if it had introduced itself in a "proper manner" but resented the methods the associations announcement of June 5 implied. Sheehan told Bushman anything DeMille said went for him and he saw no reason why the contract could not be arbitrated if the Equity connection was dropped. Mayer suggested to Bushman that the actors form another group to meet the producers.[49]

According to Equity, around July 9, members loyal to the union who had refused to sign a studio form contract had delayed the making and/or completing of over 50 percent of the films scheduled for that time. As well, the association reported a suspicion that the telephones at its west coast offices were tapped and that the contents of telegrams were known to pro-

5. Equity's Third Attempt, 1929

ducers "appears to have been confirmed," according to headquarters. Therefore, for the previous three weeks telegraphic communication had been carried out in code, while long-distance phone calls were no longer carried on with office phones. During the first two weeks of the Equity action, no such precautions had been in place.[50]

Also at this time, Equity claimed a gain of 1,000 new members from the film colony since it began its action. Gillmore's request that Equity members working in films contribute 10 percent of their weekly salary to the union relief fund was said to have met with little response. Most of the affected actors called the president's demand nervy and would not give any money. The more highly paid the player, it was reported, the firmer the refusal. A general feeling among the working actors was described as being against anything that seemed to be an enforced contribution.[51]

Film extras continued to be the forgotten players, at least as far as Equity was concerned. They were not then being invited to join Equity and no effort was being made to organize them, according to Gillmore. At the present time, he explained, the union did not have enough to offer the extras to warrant them spending the money necessary to become a union member and to pay the regular and recurring dues. Dave Allen, head of the Central Casting Bureau, explained the extras had been for some time receiving extra pay for overtime—thanks, though, to the California Labor Department mandate—on a more liberal basis than that which Equity was demanding in its contract.[52]

Producers were admitting, on July 9, that since the Equity action began five weeks earlier, about 200 people had refused to work unless given an Equity contract. The studios also conceded that about 30 extras had refused work from the Central Casting Bureau on the same basis. Mary Pickford stated that 13 members of Equity had successively turned down a small part in *The Taming of the Shrew* in the previous week until, finally, a non–Equity player was given the job. The rest of the cast had been engaged before June 5. With Equity members securing jobs as extras to spread the word for their association, all studios had increased their policing function with a watch being maintained for any of the so-called disturbers. "It is reported that at various studios where suspended members of Equity are working, or where players who took jobs that Equity felt belonged to its members are employed, there is still considerable breaking of light bulbs during the taking of talking scenes,' said a reporter.

Film Actors Organize

Cecil B. DeMille came forward to claim the producers had nothing to worry about and were getting enough players so that production was not being curtailed or halted.[53]

When Gillmore finally dealt publicly with the list of 164 names given out by the producers of reputed union members who had signed studio contracts since June 5, he said the list was misleading. Gillmore maintained that 114 names were unjustifiably placed on the list and that some of the other names were still being investigated by the union. Also, he declared that of a more recent list of 42 names supplied by the producers for the same reason, only three of the people listed were actually Equity members. It was also announced that starting July 8 "The Voice of Equity" would be a nightly radio broadcast aired on KMTR, Hollywood. Chester Conklin, heading the association's ways and means committee, reported that $4,892 had been received in donations from members for the relief fund.[54]

Reportedly, the producers held a secret meeting in the first week of July at which time a resolution to meet the union's demands was voted on and failed to pass by three votes. The reason for the supposed near change of mind by the studios was credited to the union's increasingly hardened stance, such as by placing a ban on loan outs and its order that all Equity members not under contract refrain from setting foot on any studio lot, and so forth. Meanwhile, more of the actors who had made public anti-union statements were having a change of heart. Monte Blue and Noah Beery were said to have made their peace with Equity. Francis X. Bushman and Jane Keckley were two of the 32 or so players who had signed Nagel's anti–Equity petition. Both now came forward, separately, to say their signing of that petition had been a mistake, a misunderstanding.[55]

With momentum of the union perhaps gaining in strength, a bombshell was dropped. On the evening of July 9, Frank Gillmore announced that a walkout of all Equity actors from the film studios had been ordered for Thursday, July 11. Producers declared that only a few actors would answer the union call and that the few that did would be minor players and easily replaced. Instructions for the strike had been sent to several hundred actors. At least that was what was reported in the *New York Times*. However, it was an erroneous report and no strike took place, or had been called.[56]

But, at an Equity meeting in Los Angeles on July 10 the hope was

5. Equity's Third Attempt, 1929

expressed the situation would be settled without resorting to a strike. It was announced at that meeting, with an estimated 3,000 in attendance, that a total of 63 chorus girls had walked out at Paramount, Warner Brothers, and First National studios. Upon invitation by Gillmore, 14 of the girls stood up and were introduced as the "shock troops of Equity." Gillmore remained silent as to the future action of the union. Previously suspended Equity members Gloria Grey and Jules Cowles were publicly announced as reinstated while the following players were suspended; Tully Marshall, Raymond Hatton, Louise Dresser, Anders Randolph, Anton Vaverka, and Henry Otto. All of them allegedly signed studio form contracts.[57]

In the wake of the above listed suspensions an editor with the *New York Times* pointed out the producers were confident Equity would not be able to execute its threats and even if some union members refused to sign studio contracts the producers could turn to a large supply of newcomers to draw upon. He concluded that "the producers are extremely sure of themselves, yielding not an inch. Their surrender will not be brought about until Equity officials are able, by slow educational methods as well as through spectacular suspensions, to bring home to the 'new talent' the high worth of its services."[58]

At the meeting on July 10 an open letter from the Central Labor Council of Seattle to Clara Bow was read out. It was signed by C. W. Doyle, that group's secretary. The letter dealt with the negative comments attributed to Bow in print with respect to Equity's activities. It asked Bow if she had made those remarks and pointed out that regardless of her success in motion pictures her place was with her fellow wage earners and not with the producers. She was given a "reasonable" amount of time to reply to the letter and if no reply was issued or if she admitted making the statements "action" would be taken by that labor body to bring about pressure to affect the patronage of Bow movies by friends of labor throughout the United States. Beginning that week the Equity news sheet distributed since the Equity action began was to be increased in size from four pages to 16. Distribution of the organ was to be made from house to house free of charge, so the general public could be better informed of the Equity story. A federal government mediator entered the situation on July 13, with a view to bringing the two sides together. He was Ernest Marsh, representative of the United States Department of Labor for the Los Angeles area. Marsh had been instructed from Washington to investigate the dispute

Film Actors Organize

immediately. Those instructions had come one day after Paul Dullzell had a conference with AFL president William Green, who got in touch with the office of the Secretary of Labor in Washington. As a result Marsh was quickly delegated to the task. Gillmore's earlier order that no Equity member not under a pre–June 5 contract was to set foot on any lot, and so on, was revealed to have come from a worry over the possibility that producers might make silent movies and add sound later after the dispute was resolved. That June 5 action taken by the union initially applied only to players and talking pictures, no mention was made of silent movies with the union thinking they were finished. However to cover all possibilities Gillmore, sometime after June 5, extended the union action to apply a ban on appearing in silent films as well, unless an Equity contract was involved.[59]

Odd jobs such as fruit picking, gardening, dishwashing, waiting on tables, and so on, were reportedly being taken by Equity members in the middle of July, by actors who were not accepting contracts for film work at the studios. Members of the union secured such jobs through the newly established Equity employment agency. Employment scouts went around the area lining up jobs it would list for its actor members, keeping up to 150 players employed daily through the job bureau. With 15 cars at the bureau's disposal it was able to provide transportation to and from work for players who got jobs in the San Fernando Valley. Most of the players given such work were small-part actors, bit players, and extras.[60]

As the action reached the end of six weeks plans were said to be in the works by Equity to file a damage suit against radio station KMTR as a result of being denied the use of that station. Meanwhile, Equity signed for four hours a week of air time over KMIC (Inglewood) and began broadcasting on July 10. Equity claimed it had signed with KMTR for six nights a week of airtime, from 7:00 to 7:15 P.M. at a rate of $25 a night and had given the outlet a check for $150 in advance for one week. When Gillmore went to the station to do the first broadcast he was refused use of the microphone and was told that KMTR would not be available to the union. According to union officials, the reason given was that the *Los Angeles Evening Herald* (a newspaper owned by Hearst), which controlled the radio station, had ordered the Equity time to be cancelled.[61]

During its first three broadcasts over station KMIC, Equity used the time to broadcast the principles of its struggle. On July 10 actors Helen

5. Equity's Third Attempt, 1929

Ware, Nance O'Neill, Alfred Hickman, Adele Rowland, and Irving Fisher all took to the microphones. Emma Dunn, Robert Keith, Jetta Goudal, and Reginald Denny all took to the air during the second session on July 11, while on July 13, Frank Gillmore was the main speaker.[62]

At an Equity mass meeting attended by some 3,000 people on July 15 the crowd heard denunciations of AMPAS and the CCB. As well, the suspensions of Eugenie Besserer and Phyllis Crane were announced. Women were estimated to outnumber men in the audience at that gathering by a ratio of five to one. Gillmore attacked Fred Datig, the casting director representing the producers, and his list of the 206 names of reputed union members who had signed studio contracts. According to the union chief 97 of those people were not members of the union. Of the balance, a union investigation found that 66 of the players had signed contracts that were not in violation of union rules (such as having negotiations commencing prior to June 5). Fifteen of those left had been suspended by Equity, 16 were still being investigated, nine had no address, and three were duplicated names. Thus, all 206 names were accounted for. Member Henry Otto had his earlier suspension lifted and was reinstated into the association.[63]

As the Hollywood dispute became more heated it attracted more national media attention. Somerset Logan wrote a long piece for the July 17 issue of *The Nation* in which he declared the situation in the film capital was getting closer to a strike situation, noting the studios had doggedly refused to negotiate with the actors or to recognize the union in any way. According to Logan, more than 70 percent of the players in the talkies were members of the association. He said the producers were receiving the powerful assistance of "entrenched privilege," including the local commercial organizations and the newspapers while behind the actors were the Los Angeles Central Labor Council and the American Federation of Labor. Logan said there was much abuse in Hollywood and that the maltreatment and abuses that the film players — especially the small-part actors — had suffered could scarcely be overstated. Actors were sometimes forced to accept contracts offering a lump sum for their part in a movie. In such agreements there was no stipulation as to the length of the working day, or the length of the entire engagement. An actor, upon engagement, had to take the casting director's word. As well, players were quite frequently paid nothing for rehearsals. Instances existed of actors being required to work up to 80 hours a week. The entire working schedule was hopelessly vague and inequitable to the actor. The proposed new Equity contract would correct such flagrant abuses, asserted Logan. Stars made out fine on their own but the small-part player and character actor were frequently victimized. "If they speak their mind, they are seldom re-employed at the same studio," explained Logan. "With the recent amalgamation of so many of the picture companies, and the antagonism of the producers' association, this is no slight matter."[64]

Logan went on to argue the producers were deliberately harassing the actors and had been doing so since June 5. As soon as Equity commenced its action "one player after another was called to a studio — where he had never worked before — and was offered a tempting non–Equity contract." Casting directors were looking over the files of players that had not been touched in years. He mentioned that the local newspapers had refused to print any pro-Equity statements yet often published "reputed interviews" with prominent actors in which the activities of Equity were condemned. He quoted a Gillmore statement from a recent meeting. "This uprising of the motion-picture actors is no passionate gesture of the moment. It is the result of eight years of striving to get the producers to meet us in a friendly conference and because of their indifference to our efforts this move was the only possible thing to do, if we intend to remedy the flagrant injustices which are now so common," said the union president. "We must win because our cause is just, and because in the offing there lies the sympathy and the association, if we need it, of the great American Federation of Labor." In conclusion Logan declared, "Equity is bound to prevail in Hollywood."[65]

As July moved along Equity began to face greater financial difficulties, although it would never directly admit the fact. Several "prosperous" film actors had received a call from the union to donate 10 percent of their income to aid the union in its fight. Emphasized was that the request was not mandatory but it was worded in such a way for the recipient to plainly understand that such a donation would be welcomed. Several Hollywood businesses also reported that they had been advised that the thing for them to do was to sell cheaper to Equity members than to their other patrons.[66]

On July 20 Equity filed a suit against character actor Tully Marshall and Warner Brothers studio. The union was suing for $1 million in damages and a court order restraining the defendants from executing a con-

5. Equity's Third Attempt, 1929

tract, signed July 1, alleged to be in violation of Marshall's agreement with Equity. In its suit Equity charged Warner had "induced and coerced" Marshall into breaking his agreement with the union by signing a studio contract and threatened "to continue to coerce and induce other members of Equity to break their agreements with Equity." Similar situations were suggested by the association with respect to the following players; Hedda Hopper and Holmes Herbert (MGM), Andre Beranger (Universal), Raymond Hatton (Paramount), and Phyllis Crane (First National). All of those named players had been suspended from membership by Equity. Also alleged in the complaint was that Marshall's newspaper interview that publicly denounced the union had actually been obtained by Warner, and it was Warner that was responsible for having the interview printed. It was part of a conspiracy, maintained the group, to "undermine the morale of Equity and cause it to cease operations" and "that as a result of said conspiracy and of the breach of the agreement between Marshall and Equity, plaintiff has suffered damages in the sum of one million dollars." When interrogated on the purpose of filing the suit local union attorney I. B. Kornblum said Equity was turning the tables on capital, which had always been in the habit of enjoining unions from inducing their employees to break contracts. If it won its lawsuit, Kornblum argued the union could then call out all Equity members who had signed with producers since June 5. The clause the attorney cited that beheld actors was a paragraph in the application for Equity membership that said, "I hereby affirm that if elected [to membership] I promise to obey and abide by the rules, regulations and mandates of the Actors' Equity Association and its properly elected officers under the constitution." With respect to resignation from the association, section 4, article 5 of the union's bylaws read; "Resignation of a member shall be effective only upon its acceptance by the council and such acceptance shall be at its discretion and be upon such terms and conditions as it may prescribe. Under no circumstances shall the council be obliged to accept any resignation while the good faith or loyalty of any member is under investigation or unless all his indebtedness to the association is paid."[67]

Equity used three more radio time slots for general broadcasts during the week ending July 23, in addition to continuing its brief hourly announcements over station KGFG. Station KTM (Los Angeles) was used on July 16 and July 17 while KELW (Burbank) was used on July 18. In all

Film Actors Organize

three of those hourly broadcasts Equity actors spread the gospel of the union with speeches interspersed with musical numbers, monologs and gags, all built around the fight with producers. Helen Ware was emcee on all three broadcasts. As well, an appeal for funds was made over the air by the actors. One of them, Creighton Hale, told listeners the unfairness of all the Los Angeles area daily newspapers forced Equity to resort to radio broadcasts. Claude Gillingham discussed the public's attitude toward actors, deprecating propaganda that led fans to think all screen actors were overpaid and spent their time riding around in Rolls-Royces, declaring that for every actor that rode in a Rolls, 150 could not afford the price of a Ford. After its radio broadcast on July 18, Equity announced it had temporarily abandoned radio broadcasting with cost said to be the chief reason. It was paying almost $375 for its hourly broadcasts over three small stations and for hourly announcements over KGFG. Those brief announcements over KGFG were to continue until the expiration of a one-month contract.[68]

At the same time Equity was then maintaining four or five offices in Los Angeles and Hollywood for the fight. One was described as a secret headquarters that was occupied only by Gillmore and his immediate staff. Other offices were occupied by various committees that had been set up since the action was started, and their clerks. By this time Equity had some 30 different committees. For example, Helen Ware headed the radio committee. One estimate that declared 360 union members were working in Los Angeles in the fight was claimed to be too low, with the real number closer to 1,500. Many were volunteers working for no compensation but expenses still mounted. Members who had lost employment prospects because they had obeyed Equity and refused to sign studio contracts were being financially taken care of by the union. However, officially Equity would provide no details, neither as to how many people were being helped, nor how much money they were receiving. Whenever questioned as to the financial cost of the action, union officials simply said, repeatedly, there were no problems.[69]

As the seventh week of Equity's action came to an end around July 24 the chief activities of the previous seven days included the launching of an initiative by the Los Angeles Central Labor Council asking for a nationwide union boycott of films made by producers Equity deemed unfair, an increase in the number of chorus players who had walked out,

5. Equity's Third Attempt, 1929

and expansion of the union's campaign organization to encompass eight separate offices in the area with approximately 2,000 members working one way or another in the fight, and an announcement by the producers that 72 more players had signed studio contracts. While the studios presented all 72 as being union members, Equity had not yet had a chance to investigate them. One estimate had it that Equity was then spending about $4,500 a week in the conduct of its campaign, including relief "loans." For campaign purposes alone, irrespective of relief demands, Equity was estimated to be then spending about $600 a week, or $2,400 a month. That total did not include the operating expenses of the union's regular office, whose expenses had increased only slightly in the current fight. Equity had then seven other separate offices in Hollywood, all but one were rented at a total cost of close to $900 per month. As well, the association had 17 extra business phones, at $5 each per month and a gasoline bill of $400 to $500 a month. Adding in the cost of its tabloid news sheet brought the total expenses to around $2,400 to $2,500 a month. Chester Conklin, head of the ways and means (relief) committee said $600 to $700 was issued in relief loans every day, six days a week, but donations to that relief fund averaged about $5,000 a week.[70]

That labor boycott idea had originated a few days earlier at a meeting of the Los Angeles Central Trades Council when a resolution was passed calling on all labor unions in the U.S. to take notice of "unfair practices and tactics on the part of motion picture producers and agents" in the present controversy. J. W. Buzzell, secretary of the Council, asked all members and friends of organized labor to write the players whose published statements in Los Angeles papers had been against Equity and tell them what they thought of such statements. Contained in the resolution were the names of the targeted players; Clara Bow, Lionel Barrymore, Marie Dressler, Conrad Nagel, Noah Beery, and Louise Dresser. To help in sending those people the non-laudatory fan mail the resolution listed the actors' addresses as well. Chorus Equity said that 22 of its members had walked out of four studios to that date; First National, Warner, RKO, and Paramount. Those were people who were working on movies without contracts and those who had completed one-film contracts and refused offers of further contracts for other picture work. Of 47 chorus boys called by Paramount to fill 24 jobs, 44 walked out when told that no Equity members would be engaged, according to Chorus Equity claims.[71]

Film Actors Organize

At an Equity meeting on July 22 held with an estimated 4,500 people in attendance, actor Lewis Stone, who had been earlier quoted in the newspaper with anti–Equity statements, spoke to a standing ovation after issuing a denial of the newspaper statements, saying he had never made them. With respect to a story in the *Los Angeles Herald* Stone said he never spoke to a reporter from the publication with regard to Equity one way or the other.[72]

When a journalist analyzed studio production at the end of July he found that for the month of July there was an average of 52 film units at work per week, as against 67 for July 1928, and 56 for June 1929. A comparison of production for the first seven months of 1929 against the same period in 1928 showed a monthly decrease of seven units. However, it was noted the decrease was not necessarily due to the union dispute but could have been a reflection of something else, such as a trend to fewer but more elaborate pictures being made.[73]

Because it was a Cecil B. DeMille picture and Conrad Nagel was in it, the night *Dynamite* opened (July 25) at the Carthay Circle in Los Angeles, the cinema had a trailer ready to throw upon the screen at the first sign of a disturbance due to the Equity situation. That was in the wake of the Los Angeles Labor Council resolution. At the first sign of a demonstration, went the plan, the feature film was to be cut off and the trailer screened. If the disturbance continued when the feature resumed showing the film was to be stopped a second time, the house lights were to come up and the police were to walk down the aisles "strongly" urging the disturbers to leave the building. Fifteen police officers were stationed in the cinema, in wait. However, no interruption took place. As well, it was reported that during the day on July 25 a police detective called upon Gillmore and warned him to do his utmost to prevent any sort of interruption during the screening. In order to counter the resolution of the Labor Council the trailer was devised from an idea by Harold B. Franklin, head of Fox's west coast theater division; the trailer was thought to have been sent to all houses in the chain as a precautionary measure. The trailer read, "Anger begins with folly and ends with repentance — and we apologize to you for this thoughtless outburst by a few misguided enthusiasts who bring discomfort to you and discredit to themselves — their opinion is their own — some of you may share it, but the great majority are indifferent and their peace and comfort must be our first consideration."[74]

5. Equity's Third Attempt, 1929

After eight weeks of action, at the end of July, the situation between the two sides remained unchanged. E. P. Marsh, the federal government mediator was still involved but admitted he could find no grounds for his direct intervention. He added that it was his belief that there was no hope for conciliation at that time and he doubted that any effective means would be found to bring the studios and Equity together within the next week or 10 days. The almost weekly list generated by the producers giving the names of purported union members who had signed studio contracts, contained 102 names in the latest release. But most of those names were said to be of chorus people. Meanwhile, it was reported, the studios were calling actors for parts. If they did not show up the first time they were called again. If there was still no appearance after the second call then all studios dropped their names as present or future prospects.[75]

Somerset Logan returned in print in the national media with a piece in the August 7 issue of *The New Republic*, observing the MPPDA producers maintained their "intransigent attitude" as they ignored Equity's demands. Logan them remarked the Los Angeles daily papers, the *Times*, the *Examiner*, and the *Herald* "consecrate valuable space to vilify organized actors." And "the newspapers, with few exceptions, print only stupidly biased comment — statements of individual stars and theatrical producers opposed to Equity: inadequate or false reports of meetings or no report at all: lists of actors opposing Equity's stand, many of which are blatantly false." In conclusion, said Logan, "Unquestionable a victory for Equity would mean the complete unionization of the film industry — a consummation devoutly to be wished. A more equitable distribution of the enormous spoils accruing from the production of motion pictures is inevitable. The star, the director, the producer and the stockholder have been consistently kind to themselves. Now the supporting casts and others connected with the industry are demanding what is no more than their due."[76]

On the evening of August 1 the MPPDA agreed that its representatives should meet with Equity, after a group of six prominent screen players sent a communication to the cartel in Los Angeles with a plea the two sides meet in an effort to settle their differences. A letter from the six addressed to J. Warner and the producer group proposed that its request for a meeting be favorably considered "in the interest of all actors and of the motion picture industry." Those six actors were Conrad Nagel, Lois

Film Actors Organize

Wilson, Edmund Lowe, Noah Beery, Louise Dresser, and Ralph Forbes. That committee of actors declared "we do not agree with all the particulars of the demands made upon you by the Actors' Equity Association through its president Frank Gillmore" but "we have ascertained that this conference will be entirely agreeable to the president of the Actors' Equity Association." When the meeting was held on August 2 no comment was released about it except that the two sides would meet again on Monday, August 5.[77]

On August 3, before that second meeting, the Boston Central Labor Union held that Clara Bow, Lionel Barrymore and four other prominent actors were "unfair" because of their attitude toward Equity. That group's resolution called upon "good union men and women to walk out of the theaters when these men and women appear on the screen." Marie Dressler, Conrad Nagel, Noah Beery, and Louise Dresser were the other players named. Boston took action pursuant to a request from the Los Angeles Central Labor Union, which declared that organized labor could assist in a fight between Equity and the studios.[78]

The second meeting between the two sides, on August 5, also remained shrouded in secrecy. In the face of that meeting the producers announced that another 58 supposedly union-member actors had signed studio form contracts. Thus, if the studios were to be believed a total of 515 such contracts had been signed since the union had banned the signing of those documents on June 5. Since that time Equity had suspended a reported 15 players from membership for signing such contracts.[79]

With no official information released about the meetings underway speculation abounded. One rumor had it that if any agreement was reached between the two sides it would contain a stipulation from Equity that it would not interfere with the non-union shop policies of the studios for a period of five, 10, or 15 years. Catalyst for the meetings being held in the first place was said to be Ethel Barrymore, described as an "ardent" Equity supporter. She was said to have opened negotiations for a mutual conference shortly after she arrived in Los Angeles from New York. The meeting on Friday, August 2, was a three-hour session at the home of Joseph M. Schenck and included Barrymore, Gillmore, Paul Turner (Equity attorney), Winifred Sheehan, Jack Warner, Irving Thalberg, Mike Levee, Ben Schulberg, and Schenck (the last six named represented the producers). All participants pledged to secrecy. When Barrymore arrived on the west

5. Equity's Third Attempt, 1929

coast, she said, she found Equity members divided by the attempted invasion of the studios by Gillmore, instead of being solidly together against the producers and behind Gillmore. That was the situation she said she found when she arrived in Los Angeles to appear for four weeks in a play, *The Love Duel*. Ethel then conferred separately with Gillmore and the producers. From her talks emerged the plan to have some of the Equity members present a petition for the producers to meet with Equity — those six actors named above were the prominent players who signed the petition/letter addressed to Jack Warner. By this time Equity's weekly cost of operation in Los Angeles had passed $10,000, having more than doubled in the previous 10 days. It continued to steadily grow. Demands for relief loan funds had reached $1,500 per day, although the union insisted donations, at about $1,800 per day, remained above disbursements. Equity claimed it then had 5,000 members on the west coast who were film players, having added 2,200 members since action began on June 5, to the starting total of 2,800.[80]

A different account claimed one impetus for the meetings had been the pressure brought to bear by central labor bodies such as the Boston group in declaring certain actors unfair and threatening a boycott. Studios were said to be greatly worried such a move could dramatically hurt the box-office. Paul Turner claimed the output of practically all of the studios had been reduced by as much as one-third. Reportedly, about 15 central labor union bodies in various parts of America had threatened the cinema box-office with unfair resolutions and declarations.[81]

In the wake of the second secret meeting an editor with the *Los Angeles Times* stepped forward again to attack the union. Sneering at Equity's claim the situation had reached a deadlock, the editor exclaimed, "It is an old and favorite piece of union strategy to proclaim at the psychological moment in an acute unionization campaign, that a deadlock exists. Then a cry is set up for arbitration. Such an appeal looks fair enough to the public, especially if it has been cunningly led to believe that one of the parties is the underdog." And "in such a case arbitration merely forces an employer to deal with, which means to recognize, the union. For an employer or employee fighting for the principle of free labor and free conduct of one's own business to be forced into such negotiations means that the union gets its toehold in the industry. And when a union gets a toehold in an industry it is relatively easy to force eventual submission to unionism."

Then he complained that the Equity "spellbinders" with years of experience on the stage were addressing clubs and other meetings wherein they presented only Equity's side of the situation. An especially ironic criticism since the Los Angeles papers presented only the producers' side. Meanwhile, the editor maintained, the producers held firm to their customary attitude that if the players wished to have a union it was their privilege to do so, but the producers insisted on their right to employ non-union as well as union members and to enter into individual contracts with players outside of Equity rules.[82]

Open and very public dissension appeared in Equity on August 11 as Ethel Barrymore (a vice president of the association) hurled charges at Frank Gillmore, following the recent attempts at reconciliation between the actors and the producers. She was on the committee with Gillmore when it met with MPPDA representatives in four secret conferences. Ethel charged that Gillmore had induced Equity at its closed meeting on August 10 to endorse by acclamation a settlement plan that had already been rejected by the heads of the studios, at those secret meetings. At the August 10 gathering, union members voted to endorse a plan of compromise on the basis of demanding an 80/20 union shop (80 percent of the players in a film would have to be Equity members, the other 20 percent could be non-union) instead of the 100 percent union shop. Ethel made her allegations as she prepared to depart Los Angeles for San Francisco, as her play moved on. About 3,000 members at the August 10 meeting endorsed Gillmore's plan for a settlement after he had revealed in detail what had taken place in the meetings with producers.[83]

Ethel also said she had begged Gillmore to call a meeting of the association when she could be present, on a Sunday or a midnight meeting, for example, which he had refused to do. Barrymore could not attend the evening meeting on Saturday, August 10, because she was on stage performing. On the night of August 12 Gillmore responded to Ethel's two main points: 1) Gillmore got members to endorse the 80/20 union shop when he knew it was futile; 2) the implication that the union president had called the meeting at an hour when her stage appearance precluded her from attendance. He explained that at the meeting he never presented a solution but simply wished to receive an endorsement of his action in proposing an 80/20 shop. As well, he apologized that the meeting was not convenient to the stage star and acknowledged she had asked for an after-

5. Equity's Third Attempt, 1929

noon gathering but Gillmore argued that many of the contract players were busy during the day. "It is also regrettable that Miss Barrymore, an Equity member-officer, should make any statement during the heat of the conflict after a discussion with persons on the opposite side and without any discussion with the executives representing her own people."[84]

With no results from the secret meetings at the start of August, the two sides remained firmly deadlocked as the dispute finished its 10th week. And after Ethel had virtually washed her hands of the Gillmore campaign in a public announcement the possibility of a new organization of screen actors being formed had begun to take root. Two petitions were then being circulated among the actors in Hollywood. One asked for the signatures of those who believed Equity had no place in the film field; the second sought the names of those who wanted Equity but only under its own local governing board and without Frank Gillmore. Names on the second petition included Ethel Barrymore, Ramon Novarro, Ronald Colman, Basil Rathbone, William Powell, Ralph Forbes, Montagu Love, and Phillip Strange. When Gillmore presented, and had passed on August 10, the 80/20 union shop proposal it was an item that had been rejected in those secret meetings with the producers. At those meetings the producers indicated a willingness to arbitrate but only upon the basis of a full non-union shop, although they were agreeable to having a film branch of Equity headed by Gillmore with an executive board under him of representative screen players. When Gillmore got the 80–20 union shop proposal passed he was seeking a mandate from the membership since the old mandate was understood to be for a 100 percent union shop. Thus Gillmore sought more flexibility for negotiations. That producers had already rejected such a plan meant nothing since in any union negotiations the two sides traditionally took extreme positions in negotiations and often moved suddenly and quickly. If the MPPDA adamantly refused the 80/20 shop on a Monday it did not follow they would do so a day, or a week, later.[85]

Late on the night of Saturday, August 10, after the Equity meeting was over, there was a gathering at a film star's home, ostensibly to honor Ethel, who attended after her downtown performance. That group consisted of about 40 prominent players and it was there that the idea for the two petitions was said to have originated. A general feeling from that group was that it was unlikely that even 25 percent of the contract players would walk out if called out on strike, and practically none of the high salaried actors, unless Equity could indemnify them against financial loss by the equivalent of their salaries. Movement for a new actors' union was said to be spreading strongly by word of mouth among the rank and file players who were disgruntled at the length of time the dispute had lasted "plus the influence of Miss Barrymore's statement and the original attitude of the moderate to high salaried contract actor who has not changed since the June inception." Under a rumored emergency plan, the producers had in mind to pool all of their contract players into one stock company numbering about 300, with MPPDA studios to then draw players from the combined pool according to their requirements. Few options seemed to remain to Gillmore, with one possibility being to get other labor unions to support the actors in case of a strike. J. W. Buzzell, executive secretary of the Los Angeles Central Labor Council had delivered many "morale" talks during the previous two months but acknowledged the labor council would not consider a sympathy strike at that time, describing such a move as "suicidal." Many Equity members did come out in defense of the union president, and many of them condemned Ethel. For example, Chester Conklin exclaimed, "It was a pretty poor thing for Miss Barrymore to do. Right now we're trying to get recognition for Equity and we should all work together to that end regardless of personal feelings. After we've gained that we can fight among ourselves all we want to."[86]

Reportedly, a couple of telegrams sent out from the Los Angeles Equity branch to the stage hands' union in New York and to the musicians' union in New York, asking for a position statement toward Equity in case of a strike call had not been favorably answered. Also, Gillmore had personally wired William Green, president of the AFL, at different times during the dispute. Green also lent a sympathetic ear but it was clear that support from the federation would be limited to moral support, there would be no sympathy strike from any of its affiliates if the actors struck. One unnamed labor leader said, in reference to Ethel's remarks and her prominence in the field that it was "a very bad condition in unionism."[87]

At that meeting of August 10, it was reported, there was an undercurrent of majority support at the start of the gathering for a 100 percent union shop or a strike. However, in the end Gillmore's 80/20 proposal was passed. It was to work, specifically, as follows; principal roles were to be 80 percent union members, small parts and bit roles were to be 80 percent Equity, chorus people 80 percent, and professional extras were to be

5. Equity's Third Attempt, 1929

80 percent union members. Definitions were: principal roles received a salary of $200 per week or more, small parts and bit players were paid from $125 to $199 weekly and $25 to $40 daily, extras received less than $125 weekly and/or below $25 daily.[88]

On Monday, August 12, Ethel Barrymore opened in San Francisco in the play *The Kingdom of God*. In a statement she released that day, in response to Gillmore, she said, "I spoke the truth in my statement. I wish no controversy and I shall not say another word. I feel sure it is unnecessary for me to state that I am 100% Equity and that every member of Equity knows this.... I am for the actor all the time. I have no ax to grind and I never have had. These are my people and they always will be."[89]

Around the same time, Roland Young and Ralph Forbes, both prominent actors and important Equity members, but aligned against the Gillmore faction, accepted studio contracts; acceptances that directly followed the disruptive August 10 meeting, which brought about the protest by Barrymore.[90]

Then, suddenly, Gillmore brought to a close Equity's "lost campaign" to organize the Hollywood studios. It came at about 8:47 P.M. Saturday, August 17, 1929, when the union chief issued the following terse statement: "The resolution of the council which forbade your accepting contracts of employment other than on an Equity form is hereby suspended." According to a reporter, that which preceded the announcement of that decision "was irrelevant" while that which followed "developed into a bitter harangue of Ethel Barrymore upon whose shoulders the entire blame for the failure of the campaign was placed by the speakers.... After 11½ weeks [actually 10½] it was no laughing matter for feminine bit players and chorus girls. These, with some of the men, bore the brunt of the long fight." A crowd estimated at 1,000 attended that final Equity meeting with the movement for a new organization to represent the actors said to be unformed at that time, but apparently gaining in strength. Ever since one week earlier when Gillmore sent his 80/20 ultimatum to the producers, to which the studio heads made no reply, it was believed that Saturday's meeting on the 17th would be the showdown with everything hinging on whether or not Gillmore had been successful in obtaining promises of physical support from other labor unions. Meanwhile, Ethel's statement to the press had strongly affected all except the hard-core Gillmore faction. "There is no doubt that 90% of the contract actors, whether veterans or newly arrived from the east, are lined up behind Miss Barrymore," according to a journalist, to be nominated to run against Gillmore for the Equity presidency at the next election. Speakers at the meeting on the 17th emphasized the decision to suspend was only a temporary withdrawal during further negotiations with other unions with an announced expectation that Equity would resume the struggle in less than a month. Clarke Silvernail, in his speech, declared he was not afraid of the entire Barrymore family and dedicated himself to "working for Miss Barrymore's suspension from Equity." Irving O'Hay became so vitriolic in referring to Ethel and her brothers that he had to be pencil-tapped to order by Gillmore, chair of the meeting. Equity was estimated to have disbursed about $50,000 of the approximately $55,000 it had received during the course of the campaign. Of the latter amount, $15,000 came from the union's New York headquarters, and $16,000 from Los Angeles fundraisers. Biggest labor donation was $1,000 received from Los Angeles musicians while large individual donations came from Mae Murray ($2,500), Marion Davies ($1,000), and $500 each from Walter Huston, Jean Hersholt, and Nance O'Neil. Another $17,500 or so came as donations from actors and labor groups. During that final week of the campaign the daily withdrawals from the union's relief fund had grown to $1,800 per day.[91]

With respect to the suspension of the campaign, a reporter with *Billboard* said it was "Largely as a result of the impaired morale of its membership brought about by the unfavorable statement given by Ethel Barrymore to the newspapers a week ago." Said Gillmore on the 17th, "Everyone responsible for organization policies shudders when he thinks of the borers from within, those inside the ranks who spread evil reports, who are defeatists. Equity had people such as these in this campaign. These borers from within showed themselves in members who lent their names to public statements denying there were any injustices to contend with and lauding the producers to the skies, in other words, denying their association. It is strange that none of these critics came to Equity officials for proof of unfavorable conditions, which are plenty." As well, he said, there was another group of members who had every right to their thoughts but when the battle started should have put those personal opinions aside and kept their mouths shut until the fight was over and then arraigned their leaders. Still another group contained those who broke the ruling of their Council and deliberately went to work while their fellow members

5. Equity's Third Attempt, 1929

remained out. Gillmore felt Equity could have handled all of those groups because their harmfulness was limited but "unfortunately, we had recently another kind, one whose big name caused her to be listened to by actors and public alike. This was perhaps the most cruel blow struck at Equity, which changed the advantageous position of a week ago into one that is difficult." He said it was hard for him to attack Ethel Barrymore, whom he admired, but said her position as first vice president was an honorary one and during the 10 years she had held that office she attended just one Council meeting, and that one only because it affected her personally. She was permitted to remain in Equity, he explained, because big names were often useful in the work of organization even though the real work was done by the little known. At the last of the four secret meetings held with the producers in early August, he added, Ethel had left early (she had a matinee performance that day) and all the business was done after she departed: "In my opinion no matter what Miss Barrymore may have felt, she should have remained silent. She should not have taken the risk of condemning her people, as she called you, to possible defeats." Gillmore declared the decision to suspend the organizing campaign came from Paul Dullzell in New York (but Frank was his superior). On the afternoon of the 17th Dullzell sent Gillmore a telegram outlining the results of a conference Dullzell had a day earlier with William Canavan, president of IATSE, who suggested a conference be held in New York with a view to devising some plan for carrying the fight to a victory. Frank left Los Angeles very quickly after his suspension order on the 17th and, allowing for a long, slow train ride, was back in New York on August 25.[92]

In an editorial in the *New York Times* on August 20, it was declared that in abandoning Hollywood, Equity and Gillmore had given the producers there cause for rejoicing. Those producers had little or nothing to say during the fight and in the days immediately following its end: "If there is dancing and singing and clapping of hands it is done in private. The war is off, at least temporarily, and they have the advantage." Comparing the union's stage strike victory in 1919 and its film defeat in 1929 the editor noted the ease and speed of the victory in the first case, and the physical support of other unions then, something notably absent in Los Angeles. In conclusion, said the editorial, "Equity has had a serious rebuff, but it is difficult to believe that it is permanently defeated."[93]

On August 20, Cecil B. DeMille, for the producers, issued a statement expressing "appreciation" to those who defied Equity during the campaign and told those who stood by Equity, "the controversy is ended." According to DeMille, Equity came to Hollywood with demands that meant "virtual control" of the motion picture business: "This control was predicated upon conditions unwise, impractical and unfair. The Equity movement did not have the approval or sympathy of a majority of the working actors and actresses in the motion picture studios." He added that it was a striking commentary upon the whole situation to reflect that during the more than ten weeks since the campaign began "and the consequent endeavor to prevent production; not a single picture was disbanded, postponed or canceled. During the same period, also, production in Hollywood was at its highest peak."[94]

When *The Nation* published a piece on the Equity defeat it noted that Gillmore laid the "chief blame" for the failure of the campaign on Ethel Barrymore. And while the producers offered no specific objections to any of the terms in the Equity standard contract, they "simply refused to give up their privilege of hiring actors under whatever terms they can make the latter accept." Pessimistic about the unionization of the Hollywood studios, the reporter commented, "The motion-picture industry is almost completely dominated by a few powerful organizations. It has almost unlimited resources, and the supply of minor actors is so much greater than the demand that unionization is extremely difficult." Still, he argued, "Equity will certainly win some day, but it is impossible to predict when." Real hopes for victory and unionization rested, he argued, with the loyalty of the more successful big stars because the producers could not get along without them, "and if they will unite to demand for their humbler fellows the fair play which they can get without difficulty for themselves, then they can speedily obtain it." However, he worried such solidarity would never emerge because the gulf between the floating extra and the pampered big star was so wide.[95]

Back in New York, Gillmore declared on August 27 that Hollywood producers used threats to make members break their agreements with the union: "It was $3,000,000,000 in capital against approximately 3,000 actors, most of whom live hand to mouth." Nor was it fair, he added, after the union had forbidden its members to break their agreements that the producers "should have used every argument, even threats, to make our people break their agreements with us as contained in their solemn affirma-

5. Equity's Third Attempt, 1929

tion of obedience to the regulations of their association when applying for membership in Equity." The union head said the case of Ethel Barrymore's "interference" would be put before the Equity Council. He stated the union had been on the verge of success when an "untoward accident" occurred that caused the association to feel that it was better to retire temporarily, but only temporarily. "That we shall ultimately succeed cannot possibly be doubted," he said. "The struggle is only postponed for a short time, for the spirit of the actors in Hollywood, which I learned to know so well, will never submit to their being the only important group in the studios not represented by an organization."[96]

At a meeting of the Equity Council on August 23, Ethel's alleged interference with the Equity campaign was discussed. Although no official statement was made at the end of that meeting it was reported that any action concerning Barrymore had been deferred to an unspecified later date.[97]

With business back to normal in Hollywood, the producers issued another statement, near the end of August, which said, "Striking members of the motion picture industry who refused to work during the recent battle between Equity and the producers will be accepted back into the fold; there will be no discrimination in casting and the producers will hold malice to no one." Rumors were then circulating that many of the things Equity had demanded in its campaign would appear in the new AMPAS contract, expected to make its appearance in a short time. However, both the Academy and the producers officially denied all, including even the existence of any new and forthcoming contract.[98]

For the 17,541 extras registered with the Central Casting Bureau there was an average of 621 jobs handed out each day during the first 10 months of 1929. Also that year there were about 3,000 freelance feature players who worked from studio to studio on a picture to picture contract and who were paid from $150 a week to $2,500, when they were employed. The average number of daily placements from that group was 555. Before talking pictures arrived that latter group had contained about 6,000 people, but many did not make the transition. As for the extras, sound movies created a demand for voices, dancers, and musicians, and so on, with the result the registration totals for extras increased from 12,000 to 17,541.[99]

After the defeat of Equity in its 1929 campaign, Cecil B. DeMille commented, "The motion picture industry has brought contentment and prosperity to thousands employed therein. The conditions of employment are fundamentally sound.... We believe that many of Mr. Gillmore's supporters were recruited in part from the ranks of those who unfortunately were out of employment and in part from those who have never been able to obtain employment."[100]

Also after the Equity defeat, a reporter writing in *The Outlook and Independent* said he did not accept the Ethel Barrymore situation as the reason for the sudden Equity withdrawal from Hollywood. Rather, he said, "More likely Equity found the enemy too strong to vanquish by a single push." As well, he felt Equity would have to recruit the assistance of the craft unions if it hoped to be successful in organizing the players.[101]

6
Organizing Founders; Salary Cuts, Again, 1930–1933

The complaint department of AMPAS handled 27 complaints filed by people engaged in film production in 1929, and in 17 of the cases secured satisfaction for the complainer. Its official title was the Conciliation Committee, composed of one actor, one writer, one director, one producer, and one technician. Only five of the 27 cases considered by AMPAS in 1929 got as far as the Conciliation Committee. Thirteen of the grievances went no farther than to the desk of AMPAS secretary Frank Woods for disposal; that was the first step. Most of those settled there were actors' claims for pay. If Woods could not settle a complaint the case moved on to the executive committee of that branch of the Academy (five branches in total) to which the complainer belonged, or would have if he had been a member of the Academy. For example, a complaint by an actor went to the actors' branch of AMPAS. If no settlement was reached there at that stage it moved on to the third and final step — the Conciliation Committee. Of the 27 complaints in total, 19 came from actors; three were still pending. Complaints were handled for all those in the industry, whether or not the individual was a member of the Academy.[1]

During the last two weeks of January 1930 a committee of actors and producers held a total of seven meetings, and came to a partial agreement on the basic conditions and hours of employment for actors. Studios expressed a willingness to establish 54 hours of work as a weekly maxi-

Film Actors Organize

mum. Many more details were to be worked out and it was declared that meetings of the two committees would be held twice a week until an agreement was reached that could be submitted to the players in the industry for ratification. Then, it was felt, an organization of picture players would be perfected that would be independent of Equity. Irving Thalberg and Mike Levee represented the producers on the committee with the actors' representatives being Conrad Nagel, Sam Hardy, Wallace Beery, Jean Hersholt, and Lawrence Grant. William DeMille, president of AMPAS, attended the meetings as a "neutral." The AFL was said to "view with alarm" those negotiations because they felt they would result in the formation of a company union [beyond the AMPAS group, widely seen and branded as a company union] outside of AMPAS and leaving Equity outside the pale. Reportedly, the Federation had approached several of the film industry craft unions with a view to affecting a strategy that would prevent Equity from being completely frozen out of the film field. Various actors, numbering about 10, had attended several of those seven meetings. Of those who did some six or so of them had been active on the Equity side during the 1929 campaign.[2]

As February began, reports surfaced from New York that Equity might again attempt to organize the film colony, but an agreement had just been reached in Los Angeles between the producers and a committee of film players. Revisions in the standard contract used by the MPPDA studios intended to remedy alleged objectionable working conditions were to go into effect immediately, as a result of that series of meetings, with those sessions having been inaugurated by the actors' branch of AMPAS. That actors' committee ratified a previous agreement of the Hollywood players to refuse "to support or countenance a strike or any radical action by any group of actors that might be injurious to the motion picture industry so long as the letter and spirit of this agreement is observed." Included in the newly revised AMPAS contract was a provision guaranteeing a player a 12-hour rest period between calls; producers were to give reasonable notice of dismissal (although there was no definition included of the term "reasonable"); when an actor started work on a film he was to remain on salary until the film was completed; if an actor was called back for retakes within six months after completion of production he had to be paid at the salary he received during the original filming. It was agreed by the producers that actors employed by the day, to which the standard contract did not apply,

6. Organizing Founders: Salary Cut, Again, 1930–1933

were to have an eight-hour day with one-eighth of the day's salary for each hour of overtime worked.[3]

In the end that contract, which replaced the AMPAS document of two years earlier, did not have a clause for a maximum number of working hours for players engaged by the week or by the picture, or those under long-term contract to the studio. Biggest gain in the document for the players, and morale booster, was said to be the provision for a minimum of 12 hours rest between calls to the studio. In the past it had been common for players to be compelled to work 16 to 18 hours on a film and then to be told to report back for the next day's shooting within six hours of completing the previous day's work. Reportedly, some 250 of the foremost players in the freelance and term contract groups approved the revisions to the contract, through their committee of about 10 actors. Although Equity's campaign had been a failure it was felt by many observers that some of the concessions contained in the revisions came about because of the Equity demands of 1929.[4]

In the wake of that revised studio contract, Equity officials moved to state that members of the association who were declared "traitors" to the cause of the association in the 1929 campaign were no longer held under suspension, according to the New York headquarters. Through its Los Angeles representative, Equity approached prominent members in Hollywood who agreed to let bygones be bygones and start afresh. At a meeting of the Council it was announced that a general amnesty was declared for all those who broke the rulings of the association and that within 60 days all members having placed themselves in good standing would have their suspensions lifted. That is, they were to pay any and all dues in arrears, including for the period suspended. Those failing to take advantage of the lifting of the suspension within the time designated were to be dropped from the membership rolls. More than 150 members were suspended as a result of the 1929 campaign in Hollywood. Many of those were said to be desirous of appearing on the legitimate stage from time to time but could not do so because their suspension barred them from the legitimate stage.[5]

In April 1930 Equity's nominating committee announced its official slate of candidates that would run in the next election, slated for May that year. All of the old guard were re-named to run, such as Frank Gillmore for president, with the one exception that Ethel Barrymore was dropped as the candidate for first vice president, a position she had held since the election following the stage strike of 1919. Gillmore acknowledged the nominating committee had probably taken into consideration Ethel's actions and attitudes in the 1929 campaign. When the union's move to discipline Barrymore was suddenly dropped in the fall of 1929 it was rumored at the time Ethel would no longer be an officer of the association after her term expired.[6]

Out of 746 voting member attending Equity's 17th annual meeting in New York on May 26, 1930, only 22 declared themselves discontented with the regular slate provided by the nominating committee, and thus that slate took office. After the vote the meeting was turned over to a general discussion. In his report, Frank Gillmore stated the Equity question would be put to a test in Hollywood in the near future, but there was no further discussion of the Hollywood situation. According to the treasurer's report at that meeting, the total cost of the 1929 Hollywood campaign was $53,477.89, with total contributions toward the campaign amounting to $41,608.91. Total assets of Equity were listed as $446,392.29.[7]

By the summer of 1930 it was reported that Equity, three times beaten on the film lots, was sitting back waiting until a sufficient number of film producers had begun to put on a number of Broadway plays. For a short time, in the period around 1929–1930, there was a pervasive idea that film studios would expand into stage play production. While, of course, it did not happen it seemed then to be a logical adjunct to the talking film production. If the Hollywood studios invaded Broadway then Equity planned to take industrial action against the film industry's stage plays unless Hollywood recognized the union in the film field. Several of the studios announced fairly elaborate plans for the forthcoming Broadway season, and in the previous season several shows had been backed financially by Warner and Paramount. But the idea that Hollywood studios would invade Broadway never materialized.[8]

Biggest event that took place between the end of Equity's 1929 campaign and the summer of 1930 was the economic Depression that set in late in 1929. That became a catalyst for the Hollywood studios to once again launch moves for efficiency and to try and implement cost cutting measures. Another such economy drive had started a few weeks earlier and producers were said to be cutting expenses everywhere at the source. Producers brought up the old idea that movies could be both cheaper and better. All the MPPDA studios were involved in the cost cutting. At MGM

6. Organizing Founders: Salary Cut, Again, 1930–1933

every department head was asked to save money; to use fewer employees wherever possible, several departments had been eliminated and some were merged. All this reportedly came in response to a box office slump. MGM's goal was to cut expenses 25 percent on all productions. Adding to the slump was a large drop in foreign revenue after the arrival of sound films. However, that drop was short lived as subtitling and dubbing technologies soon were in place and solved the initial problems.[3]

Trying to get work as a film extra was always a very tough job but within the previous few months it had gotten even harder as the type of films made with sound differed from the silent era. Casts became more limited and mob scenes became less frequent as film settings moved from outdoor to indoor locales. A little over a year earlier the Central Casting Bureau closed the registration books to prospective extras yet hopefuls continued to pour into Hollywood. The CCB's books were closed with a registration of 17,541, of which 3,000 were considered regulars. For the previous year the daily average of extras used was less than 500. Many hopefuls continued hanging on and trying because of fan magazines, and so on, that told of how stars such as Janet Gaynor, Charles Farrell, and so on, were once extras. "Less than a dozen of any note today in pictures got there from the mob. Hays office has tried to hammer this point home before but one fan blurb spoils it all," declared a reporter. "Chances against new extras used to be 1,000 to 1. Today the odds have been quadrupled."[10]

By the end of 1930 the studio economy wave that had affected writers and other studio employees in the previous few months had been extended to take in the players. As option renewals came up players had been told an economy drive was on and if they wanted to re-sign at a lower figure than was stipulated in the option the studio would not object. Otherwise, the contract would not be renewed. According to this report the number of featured players who were getting less than $500 a week was greater than it ever was in the past 10 years. However, the account did remark, "Biggest evil in the salary jumping has always been one studio bidding against the other."[11]

At a meeting of the Academy in January 1931 the 115 actors present were unanimous for the continuance of the revised AMPAS contract, with the 12-hour rest period provision. Its trial year was coming to an end the following month and the basic agreement to use that contract for four more years then had the signature of 17 producers and 424 players.[12]

Film Actors Organize

In the spring of 1931 it was reported that high star salaries and competitive bidding for the services of established box office names had been cited in the newest edict to the producers from eastern bankers whose money was then financing the film industry. This supposed bankers' ultimatum resulted in a secret meeting or two, which resulted in still another gentlemen's agreement to leave one another's stars alone. If that practice of poaching were eliminated it was believed the actors would not be so independent when new salary discussions came around. Supposedly, there was then underway the dropping of players by the studios whose salaries were creeping upwards as each and every option period arrived. Within a two week period one studio had dropped five players who had reached "dizzy salary altitudes" and, said a journalist, "With but a few outstanding exceptions the name players are not getting anywhere near the pay checks of the favored ones of two and three years back."[13]

Film studios were then going in for what was called a new type of contract. It was an arrangement whereby the producer paid the salary and dictated what the player should or should not do with his spare time. Warner was taking the lead in that department and one of its contract people could not do any outside work without Warner Brothers' consent. Then, if the outside work was a radio appearance and the time was commercial, the air appearance was considered the same as when the studio loaned out the star to another studio for a picture. Many of the studios had financial interests in such things as vaudeville, radio, and so forth. Underlying it all was the idea that it was an unsound idea for a player to hold down three or four jobs at one time. That is, a poor performance on the radio or on the legitimate stage could be just as damaging to an actor and his future box office potential, as a poor performance in a film. "Its purpose from filmdom's perspective is that a screen actor is chiefly a screen actor and that whatever he does aside from that must come under dictates which will govern his commercial employment," declared a journalist.[14]

More moves to cut overhead and production costs came from all the majors in the spring of 1931. Paramount announced it wanted an annual cut of from $2 million to $3 million while Universal was said to be imposing salary reductions of up to 25 percent on all who were paid salaries of over $100 per week.[15]

Paramount's reductions affected all but long-term contract people. It scaled reductions from five percent to 25 percent (an average of 11 percent)

6. Organizing Founders: Salary Cut, Again, 1930–1933

to represent a supposed saving of $100,000 weekly. Wage cuts were five percent for all receiving up to $50 per week; 7.5 percent for those with salaries from $50 to $99; 15 percent on salaries from $100 to $249; 20 percent on salaries of $250 to $500; and a reduction of 25 percent on all those with salaries of over $500 per week. Efforts were to be made to arbitrate reductions with contract talent, since those term contracts precluded the studio from unilaterally imposing salary cuts. It would be up to the stars and directors to give their consent to cuts. At any event, it was officially declared that players who insisted upon their contracts being observed to the letter would have something to think about at renewal time. Universal was said to be the first studio to introduce salary cuts. People there who earned $30 a week and under received no salary cuts; from $30 to $50 the reduction was 10 percent; from $50 to $100 the cut was 15 percent; from $100 to $150, 20 percent; and those paid over $150 weekly received a salary cut of 25 percent. Similar cuts were expected from the other major studios.[16]

According to a September 1931 report the acting talent for movies was costing the industry $3 million less per year than the talent used two years earlier. Going back to 1926, the last all-silent year, the drop in salaries was closer to $5 million. While there was some reduction in the pay of directors and writers it was not on such a heavy scale as that imposed on actors. However, it was acknowledged that a few superstars had been able to resist cuts, including Norma Shearer, Greta Garbo, Richard Barthelmess, Richard Dix, Gloria Swanson, Ronald Colman, and Joan Crawford. Players then drawing $500 to $700 a week compared in many cases with the stars of a few years earlier who were drawing anywhere from $2,000 to $10,000 a week. One way of reducing player salaries was at option time when a studio refused to pick up the player's option unless the actor agreed to sign at the studio's lower offer.[17]

Another one of the reports that Equity planned a new effort to organize Hollywood surfaced in the fall of 1931 when it was reported that "it feels certain of bringing the screen contingent into the fold next time and is lining up to force its self-drawn contract upon the studios." Frank Gillmore was then in Los Angeles and expected to stay in Hollywood for one to two months. In New York Equity again claimed AMPAS was a producer set-up: "Putting through the contract with the Academy as the credit medium was just a political move and will be appreciated as such by pic-

Film Actors Organize

ture people when disputes arise." As well, Equity maintained the current AMPAS actor contract was "literally a facsimile of its own" document that was used for stage actors. As it pondered whether or not to make another attempt at organizing the film field, Equity strived to make membership in its Hollywood branch as easy as possible. They then claimed 3,000 members on the west coast with the influx of stage actors from the east having swelled the stage faction in films by 50 percent in the previous two years. Expulsion had virtually been dropped by the association. There was not then a member, according to Equity's New York headquarters, who was classed as expelled in Hollywood. Reasons for placing a member on suspension had been minimized with only the failure of a member to obey union instructions under a call to arms being a reason for placing a member on suspension. As Equity saw it, film studio crafts on the west coast were then 90 percent unionized, but the association admitted slightly less than 25 percent of the film players were members of Equity.[18]

In its effort to assess the situation Equity was described as marking time, awaiting an expected upswing in actor discontent as salary cuts were imposed. So tentative was the association that Gillmore, in his first couple of weeks in Hollywood refrained from calling a meeting of the Los Angeles Equity branch while he was on the west coast. There was a fear that the producers would have such a meeting monitored and that actors attending such a gathering might be subject to reprisals or blacklisting. At least that was the reason given by the union president for not assembling the members.[19]

Studio heads met in Hollywood during the last part of November 1931 in several secret sessions, in the hope of reaching an agreement on an economy plan — namely the control of actors' salaries. Attending one or more of those meeting were Joseph Schenck, Nicholas Schenck, Louis B. Mayer, Adolph Zucker, Carl Laemmle, Harry Warner, Jack Warner, and Winifred Sheehan, among others. At the last of the series of meetings one of the attendees was Will Hays. However, rumor had it that little or no unity had been reached. Cuts of various percentages went into effect late in November in the studios. First the cuts were imposed at Fox, and then at Warner cuts ranging from 10 percent to 25 percent were implemented for all employees, including contract players with no renewals at option time for "most" players who refused the cuts. Although the studio meetings maintained the utmost secrecy it was said that an effort was being

6. Organizing Founders: Salary Cut, Again, 1930–1933

made to bring all the studios into an ironclad understanding to hold all high-salaried contract players to their present salaries, refusing to exercise any options that called for an increased rate of pay on the extension. "This calls for a second angle, whereby all studios will refrain from doing business with those who refuse to accept renewal at the figures they are now receiving and who leave, in the hope of bettering their salaries at other studios," said an account. It was believed a star would renew at his current rate if he realized other offers from other studios would not be forthcoming.[20]

At the end of 1931 one estimate had it those Hollywood pay envelopes for actors in 1932 would be about $5 million lower than they had been in 1931. And that was said to be a conservative estimate. Total studio payroll for talent, office employees, department heads, the chief executive officer, and so forth, was said to have been $24 million in 1931, going down to around $20 million in 1932. Also, another approximately $1 million was expected in reductions imposed on the craft people "although to date these have not been severe because of union agreements." Virtually nobody in the Hollywood film industry was said to be getting a raise.[21]

Over the year 1931 film extras were paid a total of $1,766,479, down about $700,000 from the previous year. On average there was work for 606 extras per day with the average pay check being $9.32. Jobs for extra were the scarcest they had been for six years; two out of every three placements were for male extras. Of the roughly 17,500 registered at the CCB, 619 averaged one days' work a week; 218 extras averaged two days per week. Even the average pay was down, 42 cents from the previous year. Besides those registered at the CCB many others, unregistered and out-of-work, competed for the jobs. For example, many studios handed extra jobs to their own ex-employees. Despite the fact the producers were supposed to hire extras only through the CCB, studios often ignored the rule and hired from outside. Those 218 extras that averaged two day's work a week consisted of 144 men and 74 women; only 63 averaged more than two days per week.[22]

When the actors' branch of the Academy met on March 30, 1932, the players condemned the recent activities of the producers as the latter attempted to bring in a draconian method of actor control and salary suppression as the MPPDA cartel flirted with the idea, again, of imposing the waiver system as it was then employed in baseball — when a player signed with a team he was their property for life, or until the team waived him. Actors declared they would not take the matter lying down. At the meeting Edwin Loeb, representing the producers, said an observer, "was the target of accusations that the studio heads were attempting to make chattels of the players similar to the situation in organized baseball." Players were angry they had not been consulted by the producers as to what they planned to do, as they had been consulted on the freelance contract and the day-worker agreement. Admitting that their own competitive bidding system and inside dealings were chiefly responsible for inflated actor incomes, the major studios — with the exception of one cartel member, Columbia — were trying to establish what a spokesman for them described as a medium to protect themselves against themselves. Legal authorities were said to have studied the waiver system set-up that was to be applied to film players and, according to the MPPDA, had pronounced it outside the bounds of coercion or restraint of trade. Producers could band together and set prices and be within the law according to lawyers in the industry familiar with the plan and it intentions. The producer committee named to set it up was headed by Edwin Loeb, a Los Angeles lawyer who had been described as the Hollywood sheriff designated to break up star raids and to stop poaching.[23]

One of the things that committee studied was the work of Judge Keneshaw Mountain Landis, the czar of baseball, who supplied the model and format used when Will Hays was appointed czar of filmdom. His appointment to that position copied that of baseball, which had adopted a czar-type leader position when the sport was plagued by inflated player salaries and by moral problems — the fixing of the 1919 World Series, for example. Baseball's waiver system method of dealing with its players was again, in the spring of 1932, being closely studied by film lawyers who admitted its adoption by producers in relation to their term contract people would be more beneficial to the studios than was the current option system of dealing with talent. Instead of taking up or dropping an actor's services at option time, on the baseball premise the studios could retain the performer under contract until they chose to exercise the waiver. Then if the star were sold to another company the first studio could keep all the profit in such a transaction. Organized baseball's contract system entitled the club to a player's services for as long as it wished to hold him. That despite the making of periodic contracts. Those were solely for salary val-

6. Organizing Founders: Salary Cut, Again, 1930–1933

uation purposes and usually ran from one to three seasons. When the contract expired the player continued to be the club's exclusive property and remained so until the latter wished to dispose of him. When the time arrived for the making of a new contract and if the player and club failed to agree on salary, the club was empowered to either bar him from organized baseball or trade him to any other club. Under the waiver system overtures by baseball club managers or officials to players on opposing teams were barred among the clubs. Thus, competitive bidding and the consequent salary boosting arising from that method were said to be "practically unknown in baseball." From the no tampering clause in organized baseball, film producers obtained their inspiration for "no star raiding" among themselves.[24]

Despite the resolve to slash salaries, and so on, little happened until early in March 1933 in the wake of the continuation of the Depression and the financial storm of the "bank holiday" (the Emergency Banking Act mandated a 4-day bank closure, or holiday, at this time to allow banks to be inspected for solvency and then, hopefully, to be reopened). On March 8 it was reported that salary reductions of from 25 percent to 50 percent for eight weeks had been accepted by employees at three major studios while a forth studio was on a four-week "pay holiday." Two other studios were expected to fall into line shortly and yet another studio was considering such cuts. The studios at which pay cuts were accepted at mass meetings were Columbia, Paramount, and MGM, with the salary reduction proposal having originated from AMPAS. Reportedly, savings of $5.2 million from the normal payroll would be achieved during the eight weeks, including the $800,000 from the Fox studio where the 1,900 employees agreed to forego salaries for four weeks — they all worked normal hours in that period. At the same time 15,000 unionized studio craft people were called to meetings of their own unions over the next day or two to consider the pay cuts. Salary reductions could not be imposed on the craft people because they were unionized; reductions could be imposed on actors, writers, and directors as none of them were organized. At Warner Brothers studio writers and directors nearly all signed the pay cut agreements; actors took the matter under advisement. All term contract people at Paramount, including players, directors, writers, and executives, agreed to the reduction. Under the AMPAS initiative salaries of $50 a week and more were slashed 50 percent, with a minimum, after the cut was imposed, being fixed at $37.50. Salaries below $50 a week were cut 25 percent, with the minimum salary set at $15. The pay cuts were decreed by a committee of executives on March 7, following a secret meeting in New York with Will Hays. The reduced pay scale was retroactive to March 4 and was promulgated as an emergency measure to prevent a general shutdown of the industry due to the banking holiday and the consequent decline in theater receipts. Extras were not affected by the pay cuts. Included on the committee that mapped out the cuts were Sidney R. Kent (president of Fox), Nicholas M. Schenck (president of MGM), and Samuel Goldwyn (independent producer, affiliated with United Artists).[25]

On March 9 film producers announced that 97 percent of the contract film players had agreed to accept the stipulated pay cuts for eight weeks. That announcement came from a group headed by Louis B. Mayer (MGM). However, those producers were still waiting to hear from their 15,000 unionized employees. When the pay reduction was initially advanced at AMPAS, assent to it was withheld by the actors' branch of the Academy and by the directors' branch. Directors in the Academy adopted, instead, a resolution offering to donate their salaries for four weeks rather than modify their existing contracts. The writers' branch of AMPAS approved the action of the Academy in creating a fact-finding committee, but reserved formal approval of the general wage cut.[26]

At the AMPAS actors' branch meeting on March 10 to consider and discuss the wage cuts a storm of protest erupted with the session described by a reporter "as strictly anti-everything, and especially the recommendations of the Academy board of directors and the actors' executive committee." And "an incipient revolution to turn the meeting into a new actors' protective body was started by [Lawrence] Grant, but was railroaded in order to continue the business called for," which was, of course, the rubber-stamping of the producers' proposals for wage cuts.[27]

For the first time in memory not one foot of film was shot in Hollywood studios, on March 13, 1933, when the producers ordered a halt in filming for the day as a step in the industry's efforts to cope with what it self-described as a financial emergency. During the previous week the producers had held mass meetings in almost all of the studios and obtained almost unanimous agreement from their unorganized employees, including clerks, stenographers, publicity staffs, maintenance workers, directors, writers, and most of the actors. However, on March 11 the unionized

6. Organizing Founders: Salary Cut, Again, 1930–1933

employees delivered their answer to the salary reduction plan — no. Thus, studios threw open their doors on March 13 for the sole purpose of holding more mass meetings at which the producers planned to request the unorganized employees to agree to work three more weeks — on top of the original eight — either without salary or on half salary, and consent to the studios continuing to pay the unionized employees full wages. Those three weeks were also to be used to try and come to a better resolution of the situation with the unionized people.[28]

That crisis came to a sudden and peaceful end when a solution was reached on the evening of March 13 that allowed film production to resume normally on the 14th. Under that settlement union labor and unorganized employees earning $50 a week or less were all unaffected; those receiving salaries of $50 to $74 a week had a 25 percent reduction imposed (with a $50 minimum after the cut was imposed); those between $75 and $99 were slashed 35 percent ($65 minimum); and those earning $100 and more per week received a 50 percent reduction. Said a reporter; "Thus, the vast majority of the employees are either not touched or reduced only a small amount, the brunt of the revision being carried by the high-priced executives and stars."[29]

Announcing that no studio would have to close down because of the "salary emergency," AMPAS said on March 22 that the number of employees voluntarily taking salary reduction at all studios averaged 93.9 percent. Major studios and their percentage of employees accepting the cuts were as follows: Columbia, 97 percent; Warner Brothers, 97 percent; RKO, 96 percent; Fox, 95 percent; Paramount, 93 percent; Universal, 91 percent; and MGM, 90 percent.[30]

Towards the end of March 1933, it was reported that several agent members of the Artist Managers' Association were behind a move to organize all screen players, with a view to affiliating with Equity, so they might be accorded full support by the AFL. Working under cover a number of agents were lining up stars and other contract players for the purpose of holding a meeting within the coming few weeks to launch the organization. Agents claimed they were trying to unionize players as a means of forestalling any possibility of a general studio readjustment of salaries of their clients after the expiration of the current reduction. A general worry was the studios would not restore the salaries to 100 percent but would ask for a permanent cut of, say, 20 percent. "Back of the effort to organize is said to be an agency feeling that the actors' branch of the Academy did not properly protect the talent in the recent situation," explained a reporter. "They also indicate they will ask members of the Academy to resign individually or collectively to join the proposed union."[31]

Yet, in the middle of April six of the major studios announced the restoration of full salaries to all whose pay had been reduced, retroactive to the time of imposition; two other majors followed suit almost immediately. In other words, it was almost as if there had never been any pay cuts at all; it was a result of tremendous pressure brought to bear from all sides, including the very vocal protest from the AMPAS actors' branch. Conrad Nagel resigned as president of AMPAS on April 21 after a stormy meeting of the Academy's board of directors. His resignation was precipitated by criticism of Nagel's handling of negotiations with Will Hays, head of the MPPDA. The intensive struggle of the previous few weeks in the industry had resulted in many questions of Academy policy with which Nagel felt he could not agree, according to a statement from the board of directors. A spokesman for the anti–Nagel directors said the resignation had been accepted after Nagel had conferred with Hays about Warner Brothers in extending the recent salary reduction from April 10 to April 17, whereas the Academy ruled the employees should have been returned to full pay on April 10. According to a statement from Nagel, he had appealed to Hays to persuade Warner Brothers not to extend the period of salary reductions and that he resigned when the Academy directors criticized his action in making that plea to Hays. AMPAS had vigorously fought the economy measures sponsored by Hays and the MPPDA studios during the previous week. It was an action that caused a journalist to observe, "Created originally by the film executives to protect themselves from Actors Equity and the American Federation of Labor, it has risen to the defense of the actor and now finds itself in the ironical position of opposing the producers who have given it their financial support." One of the economy measures worked out by the producers the previous week was to form a central artists' bureau through which the studios would exchange artists, sets, properties, stories, and so forth. That plan, which the membership of the Academy strongly opposed, was said to promise a substantial savings to the studios, at the expense of the medium-salaried actors, writers, and technicians, who would be hired exclusively through the proposed bureau.[32]

6. Organizing Founders: Salary Cut, Again, 1930–1933

Another reporter who wrote about the new artists' bureau observed that four of the five Academy branches — actors, writers, directors, and technicians — had all passed resolutions against the proposed bureau. And that this had created a split between AMPAS and the major studios. "With the break out in the open now, it is believed that the producers will withdraw financial support from the Academy which they set up four years ago to head off unionization of Hollywood by Equity and the AF of L. Ironically enough, the organization the producers originally put up as a dummy has become strong enough to defy them."[33]

One estimate published in May 1933 said that Hollywood could only give employment during the year in major films to one out of every 10 actors in Hollywood. Based on actor employment figures for the previous 12 months [all statistics are exclusive of the 17,000 or so registered extras and their work in films], of the 9,830 players, principals, and bits, only 1,102 got jobs during the year at the major studios. An additional 441 worked for independent producers. Of the 1,102 who were employed, 232 were under term contracts at the various studios and used repeatedly. There were also 200 favored freelancers who were almost constantly busy, leaving the rest of the huge talent pool to divide up the remaining jobs, which for the most part occupied only a few days. Those 1,102 different people were employed in 404 movies made by the majors while the 441, with some duplication, were in the casts of 47 independent films. Screen credit on those major films went to only 497 players while the bit parts were divided among 605 people.[34]

Also that month, the enrolment of 28 stars and featured players in AMPAS had brought total membership in the Academy to almost 1,000, with the actors' branch being the largest of the five. Membership was as follows; 200 stars, 100 freelance players, 100 directors, 55 assistant directors, 129 screenwriters, 140 production executives, 40 art directors, 80 sound technicians, 50 first cinematographers, 15 film editors, 30 technical executives, and 25 special members. However, events of the previous few years had more and more revealed to the actors that AMPAS was no more than a company union. Anger and disillusionment spread among the players to the extent that even the somewhat exclusive and favored actors' branch of the Academy — presumably loaded with the players thought to be the most loyal to the cartel — was beginning to snap at the master. The stage was being set for a revitalized effort to unionize the Hollywood players.[35]

7

The Coming of SAG, 1933–1936

Another example of the weakness of the unorganized was brought home to the film players late in 1933 with the introduction that year by the federal government of the National Industrial Recovery Act (NIRA, and under it the National Recovery Administration — NRA). It was a far-reaching plan under President Franklin D. Roosevelt to bring the U.S. out of the Depression. Part of the NRA involved setting a code for hours of work and wages for virtually all occupations and industries in America with some of the underlying ideas being to establish minimum wages for all occupations and to set maximum weekly hours so employment could be better shared. Under the NRA each industry was responsible for establishing its own industrial code, after consultation with all relevant groups. Once a code had been agreed to it went on for inspection and final approval by the NRA. However, in the middle of 1935 the program was struck down by the United States Supreme Court on the ground the federal government did not have the power to regulate wages and hours of work. Representatives of unionized workers were involved in all their respective industries in drawing up the individual codes, over the life of the NRA. Many of those codes were in place and in use when the Supreme Court rendered its decision and, by mutual consent, continued to be used after the decision. In the acting field Equity was involved in the conferences that eventually produced the theatrical code. But film players and vaudeville actors had no unions and no obvious representatives. A group set up suddenly, the Actors' Betterment Association, led by its president Eddie

7. The Coming of SAG, 1933–1936

Dowling, was trying to win some sort of recognition for the actors outside of the legitimate stage world. Hollywood film players were being represented by AMPAS but it then had little credibility among the screen players and even its long-term loyalists, such as Nagel, were disaffected and disillusioned.[1]

And a new union for film players was formed in July 1933, Screen Actors' Guild (SAG), which was then reported to be staging a heavy campaign for members, promising an eventual union shop condition in the film field and to provide an employee body that would be as strong in pictures as Equity was in the legitimate stage field. It proposed to ally itself with the equally new Screen Writers' Guild (SWG) in an anti–Academy body. Some of those involved who were actively involved in canvassing for the new organization were Academy members, dissatisfied with the condition of the actors' branch in that organization while others were former stage players and Equity members. Some 50 actors attended the first SAG meeting with many of those said to have signed up on the spot for membership. Temporary officers of the new group included the following: Ralph Morgan (president), Alan Mowbray (vice president), Kenneth Thomson (secretary), and Lucille Gleason (treasurer). They were to resign when sufficient members had enlisted in SAG to warrant the union holding elections. According to one report, SAG was born on a May evening in 1933 when six actors — Ralph Morgan, Grant Mitchell, Kenneth Thomson, Berton Churchill, George Miller, and Alden Gay Thomson — met to determine what, if anything could be done to prevent the blanket 50 percent salary reduction that had just been announced by the studios. When the meeting broke up that night the Screen Actors' Guild had been tentatively formed. Two months later it was incorporated.[2]

When the NRA had made it clear that it would demand codes for every branch of show business — it essentially recognized actors as "labor" as opposed to giving them the "professional" designation, which would have rendered them exempt from an NRA code — there was a flurry of activity in unionization in Hollywood as seen, for example, with the new groups for actors and writers. If a group subject to an NRA code was officially unionized then representatives of that union would be represented at all code hearings. The Actors' Betterment Association, then some five months old, had a reported 2,000 plus members. Originally organized by actors for social/fraternal reasons it tried to step into more of a union-type

Film Actors Organize

role due to the NRA hearings. An even younger organization was the Burlesque Artists' Association, which then claimed 500 burlesque members. Yet, SAG would founder for a few months and be more or less dormant for some three months before its name was taken over, with its consent, by a somewhat different group that was prepared to energize SAG.[3]

Meanwhile a lame duck AMPAS actors' branch was preparing its proposal in August 1933 to be presented for NRA conferences. Said an account, "It is expected that provision will be made for two types of contract: one for Academy members and the other for non-members. This is necessitated by the recent acceptance of the new constitution which bars non-members from Academy benefits."[4]

Equity could not entirely forget the film field. In meetings for an NRA code between producers and the AMPAS actors' representatives protest was made by both sides to a statement credited to Equity's president Frank Gillmore in which it was claimed that in NRA matters he represented all actors, both legitimate and screen players. Actors went on record to the effect that they did not consider that Gillmore had a right to speak for Hollywood players, especially those holding Academy memberships.[5]

Early in September 1933 charges of trickery, misrepresentation, and so on, were tossed around as a result of a group of agents reported to be headed by the firm Joyce-Selznick, and circulating petitions that would set up an actor code-representing body independent of the Academy. Petitions circulated contained the names of the following as the originators of the document: William K. Howard, Russell Mack, John M. Stahl, Norman Taurog, William Wellman, Miriam Hopkins, George Bancroft, Eddie Cantor, Richard Dix, Clark Gable, James Gleason, Edmund Lowe, Groucho Marx, and George Raft, and were meant to be seen as a committee to represent the petitioners in Washington at NRA conferences. However, in the immediate aftermath of their names being made public several of them — Hopkins, Stahl, and Taurog — claimed their names were used without authority and obtained by misrepresentation. AMPAS considered the matter to be one of treason since most of those named to be on the proposed committee were members of the Academy and thus had been disloyal and treasonous. As a result, AMPAS threatened to expel from its ranks anyone whose name was on that committee list and who could not satisfactorily explain its presence. At an actors' branch AMPAS meeting on September 8 Adolphe Menjou declared that not only the members of

7. The Coming of SAG, 1933–1936

this committee whose names were not gotten by misrepresentation, but all Academy members signing the petition, should immediately resign. It was plainly indicated at that AMPAS meeting that those who went into opposition to the Academy knowingly would be held answerable and expelled if they did not resign in the meantime. Telegrams from Hopkins, Stahl, and Taurog, claiming trickery in getting their names, were sent to Academy representatives at the code sessions, to be used in an effort to discredit the fledgling group. Joyce-Selznick reported about 1,000 actors had signed the petition, with Frank Joyce of that agency then on his way to Washington to argue for the signers and, incidentally, to fight the inclusion of the AMPAS agency code in the film industry pact.[6]

Later that month a report by the Academy's investigating committee declared it had found evidence of sweat shop methods in the treatment of bit and extra players. One result of that was the presence in Washington of Dave Allen, head of the Central Casting Bureau, who went east with the Hays delegation following the presentation of the report to the Academy board of governors and the branch executive committees. There was a worry in Hollywood that the film extra situation would be injected into the NRA hearings — hence the presence of Allen in the nation's capital. That report stated there seemed to be a policy to keep wages down to the lowest level and to take advantage of the distress of unemployed players. Pay of extras had been radically cut in the previous few years and that those then getting between $7.50 and $15 a day had seen their pay reduced on average by 20 percent. Also, that while two years earlier $2 and $1.50-a-day extras were unheard of, such low salaries were found to have been paid during 1933. During the previous year many former well known names in the acting world were working as extras for $3 a day and that while the average paid per call in 1930 was $9, it had been reduced to $7.48 during 1932. Only 69 people averaged as much as two days' work in the first half of 1933 as extras and no one had averaged three days or more. Charges of graft, said the report, had been heard but none were substantiated "although there was plenty of evidence that favoritism and discrimination at Central Casting office was in existence, with relatives and close friends being given the breaks."[7]

Still in September, the fight of Equity for recognition of its jurisdiction over film actors continued and moved from Hollywood to Washington, D.C., when Frank Gillmore spoke at the public hearings on the motion

Film Actors Organize

picture code, and accused AMPAS of being a company union. He claimed for Equity the right to represent actors in all hearings and conferences of the code. William Green, AFL president, also attacked the Academy as being dominated by the producers and not truly representative of the actors. "In the opinion of observers here, the Academy will have hard sailing after the settlement of the code question, due to the attitude of labor leaders and the bringing out into the light the question of its domination by producers." Gillmore strongly objected to the constant references to actors in the code, submitted by the producers, tying them up with the Academy. Equity, he said, was not consulted in the drawing up of the code, although Equity had jurisdiction over the motion picture field according to the charter it held under the AFL (through the 4As) and more than half of the players in Hollywood were members of Equity. Of the 2,583 players given screen credit, he said, 1,418 (54 percent) of them in a 1933 analysis were Equity members. Among the character and bit players, he added, around 80 percent belonged to his union. On the other hand, Gillmore continued, the Academy had only 296 actors as members out of all the actors in Hollywood. He filed a brief of Equity's suggestions for code provisions for actors. J. T. Reed, president of the Academy, admitted his group had only 296 actor members but went on to argue they were the "important" players, which caused a reporter to declare Reed's remarks were "tacitly indicating that bit players need not have either labor representation at the hearings or recognition under the code." Later in the hearings film executive Sidney Kent unintentionally intensified the effect made by Gillmore's speech by offering his own defense of the Academy in which he said AMPAS was a "much-needed forum for the settlement of production disputes."[8] As a result of continued and growing dissatisfaction with the way actors' concerns were dealt with by AMPAS, 26 film players met on Sunday night, October 1, 1933, at the home of Frank Morgan and those who were members of AMPAS resigned from the Academy by wire to form a new actors' organization "for the protection of all Hollywood players." A wire was also sent to the NRA code Deputy Administrator Sol A. Rosenblatt informing him of the action. The following telegram was sent to the Academy: "The undersigned hereby resign from the Academy of Motion Picture Arts and Sciences in all capacities, this resignation to take effect at once. We have no feeling of resentment in resigning but feel that an organization for actors can only produce better results for the members of

7. The Coming of SAG, 1933–1936

our profession." It was signed by the following: Adolphe Menjou, Frederic March, Robert Montgomery, Chester Morris, George Bancroft, James Cagney, George Raft, Gary Cooper, Ralph Bellamy, Boris Karloff, Warren William, Frank Morgan, and Kenneth Thomson. The wire to Rosenblatt scored the producers' film code as being in direct violation of the "principals of the NRA" and said that "all the undersigned who are members of the Academy of Motion Picture Arts and Sciences have this night resigned and are forming an actors organization open to all motion picture actors." That wire was signed by the 13 players listed above and by Ann Harding, Paul Muni, Otto Kruger, Eddie Cantor, Charles Butterworth, Ralph Morgan, Lee Tracy, Spencer Tracy, Miriam Hopkins, Zeppo Marx, Chico Marx, Harpo Marx, and Groucho Marx.[9]

When the *New York Times* published its account of the action of the 26 actors listed above it identified the same 26 players but listed Paul Muni in the first category — Academy members — instead of as a non–Academy member, as had *Variety*.[10]

Late on the evening of October 8 in Hollywood the players, severing all connection with the New York stage and film actors' group, but with the old Screen Actors' Guild (the organization initially begun the previous July) had, said a newsman "what is perhaps the strongest group of thespians in the country." At the conclusion of a mass meeting 501 leading actors signed up for membership in SAG, "heretofore only a small organization." The new members were obtained after speakers declared the players faced a crisis in the proposed salary control regulation the producers were trying to place in the NRA code then under consideration. A protest against the inclusion of anti-raiding clauses and maximum salary provisions produced for the code by the MPPDA cartel was announced by SAG.[11]

Two days later Eddie Cantor, president of SAG, explained the union was mainly for the protection of the "little fellow." The actors had no fight then, he insisted, and no immediate grievance; they wanted to be together in a common cause in the same manner that their employers were, with an authoritative voice in the NRA conferences and other conventions that affected the entire industry. Actors long ago should have had their own organization, he added, but somehow never got around to it. The suggestion by producers at the NRA hearings in Washington, that a salary board be established — a suggestion not immediately quashed — "was the spark that set off the firecracker. It gave the actors further cause to believe that the Academy of Motion Picture Arts and Sciences, which was representing them, is producer-controlled. Maybe the Academy is not controlled by the men we actors work for, but nevertheless it never could be above suspicion." Further, Cantor said, "If the actor group of the Academy had a meeting no one could speak his mind as freely as he'd like — because the minutes would be available to the producers. Naturally the Academy could not represent the actor in the same way that his own organization could." Cantor reiterated the newly formed guild was for the little fellow and that players such as himself and, say, Ann Harding and William Powell, did not need a guild "nor any of the others who are fully protected by iron-clad contracts. But to make the organization mean anything, to give it power and worth, it must have the important as well as the less important people in it." The SAG that had formed in July, and apparently remained dormant effectively disappeared on October 8 with little of the old group left except its name and a shell with most of those early members presumably staying on. That handover, though, was done with the consent of the originals, as a new and different leadership moved SAG from dormant to active.[12]

Just days before SAG's October meeting *Variety*, once again, observed that the aim of the major Hollywood studios was to have a completely open shop: "Intention of the majors is to fight all other groups who are organized for collective bargaining, and to discourage any new organization that might spring up later." For example the majors had recently had a battle with IATSE, one of the craft unions, which resulted in a brief strike. Rumor had it that the majors would continue to fight IATSE and perhaps even take on the then very powerful American Federation of Musicians. As well, the studios were said to be ready to attack the fledgling Screen Writers' Guild and its own creation, AMPAS: "There is a good chance that the major companies will also go after the Academy at a later date. Company heads ... are burned plenty over the organization's stand on the producers' code, and the antagonism generated toward certain clauses and conditions." And "the Academy has gotten out of control, and has expressed too militant sentiments toward the majors during the past 18 months.... But the greatest blow to the major companies was dished out by the Academy last March when the 50% cuts were forced on employees, and the Academy, by smart maneuvering, took the entire matter out

7. The Coming of SAG, 1933–1936

of the hands of the companies and dictated when each firm was to restore full salaries."[13]

When *Billboard* discussed the newly formed SAG it said the actors finally wised up to AMPAS, wherein "some of the officers were producers, and the actors' contracts could not be enforced," and 26 of the players (13 resigning from AMPAS) went on to form SAG. In this account it said a few days elapsed before the group took over the charter of the original SAG group. Practically all of the group of 26 (25 in this account), it was reported, were members in good standing of Equity; "Some actors are a bit worried about their employers' attitudes, which are not as friendly as they were when everybody belonged to the good old frat, the Academy, and the rumor is sifting through from up top that producers would wreak vengeance upon the wayward stepchildren if they had a chance. Reportedly, Sol Rosenblatt then stood in good stead with the film folk because he had tossed the Academy out of the code hearings (that is, no longer giving it a voice as the actors' union representative) after he heard what Frank Gillmore and a couple of others from labor bodies thought of a company union. "Gillmore's heated denunciation of the Academy in Washington, in fact, may have had something to do with why the group of leading film actors broke loose," speculated the reporter. SAG's new set of officers were: Eddie Cantor, president; Adolphe Menjou, vice president; Frederic March, vice president; Ann Harding, vice president; Kenneth Thomson, secretary; Morgan Wallace, assistant secretary; Groucho Marx, treasurer; Lucille Gleason, assistant treasurer. The board of directors included all the above and Ralph Bellamy, Boris Karloff, Claude King, Robert Montgomery, Frank Morgan, Ralph Morgan, Chester Morris, Ivan Simpson, and Spencer Tracy.[14]

In its coverage of SAG's formation *Variety* called the development the most serious blow leveled at AMPAS since the latter's inception. At that mass meeting on Sunday night, October 8, 1933, at the El Capitan Theater in Hollywood, of more than 800 attending, 503 actors flocked to the stage to sign membership blanks in the new SAG. Writers, in forming the Screen Writers' Guild, were the first to make the leap from the Academy roster, but with smaller numbers. That actors' meeting strengthened the stand and overall movement of the breakaway faction from AMPAS. Lawrence Grant and Jean Hersholt were among the Academy members signing up with SAG on October 8. Cantor emphasized the new associa-

Film Actors Organize

tion was against no individual or group and had but one mission — actor protection. He indicated "he had heard that threats had been made against actors attending the mass meeting" and that "some Academy members say we are going screwy forming a Guild organization. But we are not screwy. We just want to be 100% represented in an organization not subsidized by any one." Robert Montgomery, speaking in defense of the 14 Academy members who had originally walked out, said SAG had no animosity against the Academy but was of the opinion that only a 100 percent actors' organization could work effectively for the players' benefit.[15]

On October 16, 1933, it was reported that in the hope of obtaining a voice in the film field, actors had filed application in Sacramento for a charter for the Hollywood Picture Players' Association, which would also embrace the extra ranks. Sponsors of that new group felt their interests were in conflict with existing groups and it was imperative that the supporting players and extras have no "entangling alliances" with any other producer or actor group, or any so-called labor union. Sponsors of the new group were J. Buckley Russell, Robert P. Chapman, Col. Starrett Ford, R. C. Huestin, Richard Kipling, W. R. Deming, Harry Strathy, Frank Pharr, Edward Reinach, and Herta Reinach. It was not heard from again.[16]

On October 15 a joint meeting of SAG and SWG was held, attended by 1,200 people, wherein it was declared that unless the proposed NRA code was changed to meet with the agreement of the creative talent in Los Angeles there would be a general walkout of actors and writers. Frederic March indicated that the money paid to talent was, proportionally, of little importance in film making — stating that of every dollar going into a box office in America, only 11 cents came back to Hollywood, of which 40 percent to 50 percent went to labor. Eddie Cantor panned the producers for their waste, inefficiency, and undercover tactics and referred to Hollywood as a "sink of corruption." He added, "But we have a weapon and we can use it. That is, not to work, and to let them make their own pictures." A total of 183 new members for SAG were signed up following the October 15 meeting.[17]

At the same time, as SAG gained strength, *Billboard* observed the group had moved to a commanding position in the industry with the status of the Academy "correspondingly weaker and its ultimate death now figured as only a matter of time." Equity when contacted in New York and Los Angeles was noncommittal, watching it all with interest. Eddie Can-

7. The Coming of SAG, 1933–1936

tor, president of SAG, was a member of Equity's Council, and so was Frank Morgan, one of the SAG directors. In Washington, Deputy NRA Administrator Sol Rosenblatt had left AMPAS entirely out of the industry's governing body in his first draft of the code. Rumors then circulated that some of the film directors, from the directors' branch of AMPAS, were holding secret meetings with a view to forming their own organization, along the lines of SAG and SWG, which they later did.[18]

SAG announced on October 26, 1933, that extras and bit players would be taken into the union in its fight against "salary control" features of the proposed code. "For the first time in motion picture history," said Kenneth Thomson, secretary of the guild, "there are no class distinctions and no castes among the players. The star and extra will work together to solve their mutual problems."[19]

An editorial in *Billboard* at the start of November 1933 declared, "With the best of intentions, Eddie Cantor is recruiting a stupendous army of film actors in Hollywood to resist, and even when necessary to wage an offensive campaign against, producers.... In the case of the Screen Actors' Guild, however, the gun is not yet loaded." The editor believed that a large membership did not make a victorious army; it was equipment and leadership that were crucial. Further, he argued, SAG was then unequipped. It could not enforce contracts because it had no affiliation with the AFL and if it came to a showdown there would be deserters who would not agree to cut off their own earning power by striking, unless such an order had the backing of the AFL: "This is only the obvious conclusion from many attempts in past years. They have always failed. However, with the support of the AFL and all its branches, the SAG could be effective." As to the question of leadership, the editor worried that it was obvious that sooner or later Cantor would return to Broadway and the legitimate stage and where would SAG be then? In conclusion, the editor declared that "Actors' Equity has nearly everything important that an organization should have, including an enforceable contract, and generalship that has endured for years, and it is possible that the SAG may deem it wise to call upon Equity sooner or later."[20]

In response to the above editorial, SAG issued a reply a week or so later in which it denied it would affiliate with the AFL. Membership in the group was said to then exceed 2,000 players.[21]

Some 10 days later, still in November, SAG continued to downplay

Film Actors Organize

the idea it was seeking to affiliate with the AFL or that it would merge with Equity. American Federation of Labor officials in Washington pointed out the obvious; the only way SAG could come under its jurisdiction was through an affiliation with Equity. At that time, Equity claimed a membership of 1,000 in the Hollywood film colony, with most of them delinquent in their dues. On the other hand, SAG was said, in this account, to have a membership of 1,550, nearly all paid up in their dues. Leaders in the SAG movement in Los Angeles claimed there never was any intention of an affiliation either with the AFL or with Equity and that its pledge to members during the formative period of the guild was that the organization would also be a Hollywood organization, controlled in Hollywood and with headquarters in Hollywood, and free of control by any outside body. And that pledge clearly had Equity in mind, said those leaders.[22]

Contrary to the boast that Kenneth Thomson had made in October with respect to extras being taken into SAG and a classless union of actors existing, the class factor was soon in place. After its formation SAG quickly developed senior and junior branches with the division based on how much the individual actor earned in the film world. All below a certain amount — all extras and bit players — were consigned to the junior branch. Only members of the senior branch got to vote on SAG business and proposals, such as proposed contract items, or changes in the constitution, and so on. Those "little people" that Cantor spoke of SAG helping would, to a large extent, not have a say in proposals adopted, or rejected, by SAG that affected them.[23]

In a May 1934 speech to SAG members outlining future plans, Eddie Cantor slammed AMPAS, stating the Academy in the previous year "sold the actor down the river to the producer" and had it not been for SAG the producers would now be able to regulate salaries "and pretty nearly control the destinies of players." According to a journalist at the meeting, when Cantor condemned the Academy the audience "nearly tore the roof off, which indicates the high regard the players have for the nearly defunct Academy, which is a producer set-up."[24]

By the fall of 1934 it became more and more the conventional wisdom that it was only a matter of time before AFL affiliation by SAG would be necessary. But for SAG to get independent jurisdiction (a charter of affiliation with the AFL) under the 4As it would be first necessary for Equity to renounce its own jurisdiction over film actors and then for the

7. The Coming of SAG, 1933–1936

4As to grant that jurisdiction to the Guild. Equity continued to insist SAG had only to join Equity in order to achieve AFL affiliation. "Observers in the film field, however, see small chance of such procedure being followed," said a reporter. "The majority of Guild members, according to reports from the coast, feel that the screen actors' organization should be run entirely by and for people in the picture field and, in addition, the producers with whom the Guild is presently negotiating for a closed shop are reported unalterably opposed to Equity because of the organization's demands during the strike several years ago."[25]

SAG's first negotiations with the producers, in its efforts to establish a union shop, took place in September 1934 but went nowhere. Irving Thalberg, for the producers, met with a SAG committee.[26]

Denials by SAG that it would affiliate with Equity began to fade away and on October 19, 1934, Kenneth Thomson, Arthur Byron and Robert Montgomery (all for SAG) met with Frank Gillmore and I. B. Kornblum (Equity attorney) at Montgomery's home in Los Angeles to discuss the preparation of a "working agreement" between them. It was understood that SAG officers would maintain control of SAG, when and if it affiliated with Equity, and that SAG would remain in Hollywood.[27]

Observing SAG's move to negotiate with Equity for affiliation under a separate AFL agreement, film producers were said to have interpreted that action as the first move toward a strike. That SAG move came in the wake of the SAG representatives involved in the ongoing conferences to establish an NRA code for the industry pulling out of the conferences on the ground the producers had informed the players the producers were unalterably opposed to the various clauses demanded in the code by the actors. In the evening of the day after the actors' pullout from the NRA code proceedings SAG directors met in a secret session with Gillmore and passed a resolution to ask Equity to share its federation affiliation with the guild so that the film union could go into the AFL as an autonomous body. A proposal to that effect was sent to the Equity Council. Still smarting from 1929, the producers continued to insist "we will stand where we have always stood. We shall not recognize Equity or any other organization affiliated with it." Among the demands made by the actors in the NRA conferences (all five actors representing film players were members of SAG) and rejected completely by the producers were: a new standard form of contract for freelance players; a new standard form of contract for day players; a basic day of eight hours, with 15 hours set as the minimum period of rest between calls to the set.[28]

With the producers and SAG at an impasse in the middle of October, Eddie Cantor declared the producers would not meet the actors halfway and the only recourse left to his group was to join the AFL. That SAG would join the Federation, if at all possible, was assured by Cantor himself.[29]

That move toward the AFL caused an editor with the *Los Angeles Times* to declare, "From the standpoint of their own personal interests, members of the Screen Actors' Guild will make a serious mistake if they affiliate with the American Federation of Labor through the Actors' Equity Association, or in any other manner." His reasoning for that conclusion was the same as found in so many similar editorials in the past. That is, the motion picture industry was built up to its present position on the open shop system and its future welfare, as well as that of everyone in the industry, depended on the maintenance of that system; "The past activities of the A.F.L. in the motion-picture field have never been in the constructive interest of the industry, but always disruptive and destructive."[30]

By the end of October an agreement between Equity and SAG looked to be close to reality. Under the proposed pact SAG would actually be part of Equity but would have the power to act on its own — local autonomy, and so on. Equity, however, would not relinquish its jurisdiction in the film field to SAG. Thus, if SAG disappeared in the future the agreement terminated and the jurisdiction over film actors remained with Equity. Fees to the AFL would be payable to Equity, which would send the money on to the Federation (unions affiliated with the AFL paid the federation 18 cents per year for each of its own members). Such an affiliation was said to work to strengthen both bodies. If SAG took action against the studios, the producers could not send to New York for more actors as Equity would not allow it. Using this plan SAG would not receive a separate AFL charter but would operate as an affiliate of Equity and come under its AFL charter. When it came time for the memberships of the two unions to vote on the proposed agreement only class A members of SAG (and Equity) would have a vote. There was also a class B membership of around 200 players and about 1,750 extras, all members of the junior division, out of a total SAG membership of about 2,500.[31]

With the proposed affiliation between SAG and Equity still in the

7. The Coming of SAG, 1933–1936

works Eddie Cantor remarked, "I do not believe that the producers in Hollywood are meeting the Screen Actors' Guild halfway. They are interested in doing away with the Guild. The only other agency in Hollywood is the Academy of Motion Picture Arts and Sciences, but that is producer-controlled and amounts to a company union." He added that "many producers are stubborn, pig-headed and feel like czars. They aren't, though. They live in Hollywood all the time and they don't know that there are other parts of the country. If we join the AFL the producers will have brought it upon themselves." According to observers, producers were standing pat, but were becoming more worried. They were trying to discredit SAG's latest move by claiming it was incendiary and amounted to preparation for an unwarranted strike. The actors, on the other hand, noted the fact the producers had turned down all their attempts to have arbitration or a fair hearing, holding to their present position to maintain conditions precisely as they were.[32]

During November 1934 the majors made a few moves of their own. For one thing they put an end to the Producers Arbitration Agreement, originally drawn up and signed in 1931 to prevent talent raiding, before a player's contract had expired. Most of the major studios had signed on to the pact. When drawn up in 1931 it was expected to correct raiding, following the lifting of Ruth Chatterton, Kay Francis, and William Powell, from Paramount by Warner Brothers, in a well publicized poaching incident. The agreement was signed secretly by the majors — Columbia had not signed — and when its existence was disclosed a year later, the Academy complained loudly with an allegation of double-cross and "it resulted in considerable toning down of the document and bringing its operation out into the open." Such agreements by the majors, whether formal and in writing or informal and verbal, never worked very well or accomplished much. One or another of the majors was always ready to ignore such a pact. Nevertheless, the producers had still another reason to dislike the Academy as, once again, its own creation proved to be something of a Frankenstein monster.[33]

Also in November, rumors of a desperation move by producers circulated. Several important studio heads were said to be willing to withdraw from AMPAS in order to make the organization more attractive to talent expatriates by removing the "producer-controlled" or "company union" stigma. While the Academy denied such a move was afoot a reporter remarked it was nonetheless known that such a scheme had been widely discussed. Some producers went so far as to admit that if the key members of the two Guilds, actors and writers, would return to the Academy then the producers would be willing to exit in the interests of harmony. "They even would agree to a collective bargaining setup, something they have been adamant in refusing to Equity or the Guilds," said the reporter. It was an example of consideration being given by the cartel to a desperate plan to try and negate or ward off SAG and SWG. Somewhat earlier the same idea had been waved as an olive branch by Academy officers to certain actors and writers then prominent in the Guilds that previously had deserted the Academy.[34]

In something of a surprise move in the middle of November 1934, Equity's Council decided by a vote of 13 to 8 that SAG would become a union on its own, and not an affiliate of Equity. The general membership of Equity and the class A membership of SAG still had to approve the plan; SAG's directors had already given their approval. That meant SAG would receive its AFL affiliation charter from the 4As. Equity's position switch came after SAG secretary Kenneth Thomson and the union's attorney, Lawrence Bielenson, journeyed from Los Angeles to New York to appear before the Council to make a pitch for becoming an independent union. It was understood that the SAG representatives frankly told Equity that its name meant little in the film field since it failed to organize the film players during any of its several earlier efforts. Equity people admitted its union was standing still as far as membership on the west coast was concerned and therefore was not in a position to refuse SAG a charter any longer. Given the impasse with producers in Hollywood at the time, SAG felt that unless it could show strength within the coming few months it might not survive, and therefore it felt the backing of the AFL was important. An affiliation such as recently proposed would likely come to nothing, SAG reasoned, because Equity was on the outside looking in as far as the studios were concerned. As a separate and independent union, SAG would pay its per capita tax directly to the AFL, as well as a smaller one to the 4As. Under the arrangement of being an independent union, Equity delegated its jurisdiction over motion pictures to SAG, which would have complete autonomy. The grant of jurisdiction, however, was recallable upon four months notice, a condition Equity insisted on having in the agreement.[35]

7. The Coming of SAG, 1933-1936

Negotiations between the actors and producers, for an NRA code, continued off and on late in 1934 and into early 1935, but with little in the way of results. When the five actors representing SAG filed a lengthy brief with the NRA in Washington at the start of 1935 it was to ask for a hearing on the actors' proposal for working conditions, which had been turned down by the producer representatives. In that brief the frustrated actors declared "history shows that no agreement with producers is worth the paper it is written on." Further, it stated that actors had been tricked, hamstrung and lied to 'and that every dishonest practice known to an industry, the code of ethics of which is the lowest of all industries, has been resorted to by the producers against the actors." The five actors on the committee were; Robert Montgomery, Claude King, Ralph Morgan, Kenneth Thomson, and Richard Tucker. In that brief the actors cited data compiled by the NRA's Sol Rosenblatt. For the year 1933 1,563 actors were employed, excluding extras. Of those players who worked, 432 (28 percent) earned less than $1,000 that year; 382 (21 percent) made between $1,000 and $2,000; 158 (10 percent) earned from $2,000 to $3,000; 108 (seven percent) were in the $3,000 to $4,000 bracket; 82 (five percent) made between $4,000 and $5,000; 64 were in the $5,000 to $6,000 bracket; 42 made between $6,000 and $7,000; 38 earned from $7,000 to $8,000; 23 were in the $8,000 to $9,000 bracket; 25 came in the $9,000 to $10,000 bracket, 196 earned from $10,000 to $50,000; and 63 earned over $50,000. Thus, over 25 percent of the actors who worked in 1933 made less than $1,600; about half the actors who worked that year made less than $2,000. And that was gross income. Out of that came an agent's fee of 10 percent, for most of them, and the cost of a wardrobe. With respect to the proportion of a film's budget that went to actors was data that showed that in the boom years of the industry, 1927-1929, the motion picture industry spent around $150 million each year on production while worldwide box office revenue amounted to some $2 billion a year, meaning that product cost around 7.5 percent of gross receipts. Even during the worst years of the Depression when production costs dropped to $100,000,000 per year and receipts were $1 billion, the ratio was still only 10 percent. According to figures obtained from United Artists around the same time, only 18 percent of the cost of production went into actors' salaries. So, in the worst year of the Depression, with the grosses at their lowest point, actors received only 1.8 cents of each dollar that came into the box office. More Rosenblatt data from a different source, for 1933, showed the cost of production amounted to eight percent of the box office receipts. And of that eight percent, one-fifth went into actors' salaries. That meant actors during 1933 received 1.6 cents of each dollar that came into the box office.[36]

The alliance between Equity and SAG, which had been under consideration in one form or another since the latter formed, took its final form on January 16, 1935, when a charter was granted to SAG by the Associated Actors and Artistes of America (4As). That latter group had the AFL charter for the amusement field; its officers were; Frank Gillmore (international president) and Paul Dullzell (executive secretary) who were also, of course, the president and secretary, respectively, of Equity. As officials of the 4As they signed the charter, as did Montgomery and Thomson, vice president and secretary, respectively, of SAG. Gillmore said in a statement that "the Screen Actors Guild of Los Angeles is now a component of the American Federation of Labor. It is wholly autonomous. I want it clearly understood that Equity is not a dictator in this situation. The Screen Actors Guild has been given complete authority, with a few restrictions which have been noted in the agreement already exchanged with them. This means that they have the right to conduct their own business independently of Equity."[37]

At a SAG membership meeting on January 16, emboldened by its new AFL affiliation, the union was preparing itself for a fight with the producers to force acceptance of the working conditions it proposed to the NRA for the film code, even if that federal body denied its request for a hearing. From the speakers' platform that night, Robert Montgomery declared that whether or not the government granted it a hearing on the code as requested, SAG would continue to fight until all the actors' demands were accepted. A telegram from Gillmore that welcomed the Hollywood players as fellow members of the AFL was read to a cheering audience. SAG leaders said the organization would attempt to halt any producer move to renew the AMPAS agreement under which the current "no strike" contracts were in effect. Those contracts were based on the Academy agreement that expired in March 1935 and had provisions for arbitration under Academy jurisdiction. SAG's intentions, it was understood, were to demand recognition of itself as soon as the AMPAS agreement expired and to force into future contracts between SAG members

7. The Coming of SAG, 1933–1936

and studios a clause establishing player allegiance to SAG, even ahead of contract provisions. Further, union leaders said they would refuse to agree to any Academy arbitration after the March expiration date, and if unable to get arbitration under Guild machinery, would take every contract violation into the courts.[38]

Producers, though, made a countermove at the start of February that caused the threat of a player strike to dwindle. They offered a new, five-year contract (through AMPAS) that carried concessions that were said to even exceed those demanded by the players through the NRA. That contract for freelance actors, and a new one for day players was formulated by a committee of AMPAS producers and AMPAS actors and was then in the hands of the members of those two branches of the Academy for ratification — just a formality. Behind the producers' move for a new contract, as a renewal on March 1 of the current pact, was thought to be a gambit on the part of the studios to eliminate any strike talk by removing the cause. "Virtually only thing left for the Screen Actors' Guild to demand is producer recognition of the Guild and, with it, the American Federation of Labor," said a journalist. Demands made by actors and turned down flat by producers in the NRA code negotiations were said to be found in the proposed new contract, some in an even more beneficial format for the actors. Still, SAG was leery of the offer, questioning the intent of the producers in offering such concessions at that time. However, on the surface SAG admitted that "it would then seem as if the producers willingly granted all the demands [made by SAG in its brief to the NRA] and went the Guild a few points better." That proposed new AMPAS pact offered a 12-hour minimum rest period between calls; paid retakes; holiday pay; a work week based on six days, and overtime (one-sixth of a week's pay) if work was required on the seventh day of a week. The day player contract then in place allowed a four-hour (maximum) lay-off in the day. For example, an actor could be called to the studio and worked for four hours, then be "laid-off" for four hours, and then worked another four hours. It meant an actor could be at the studio for 12 hours but paid for only eight hours; under the new pact that practice was eliminated. One point SAG did not like was that under the new AMPAS agreement arbitration, not binding, was to be done at the Academy; SAG wanted disinterested, and binding, arbitration.[39]

After considering the matter for a few days SAG declared it would reject the new AMPAS agreement and continue to fight for its own contract and for recognition of its own organization. "This is not an Academy achievement. The concessions are the result of pressure from the Guild and will continue just so long as pressure is applied," said SAG officials. "The new contract offered to free-lance players by the Academy of Motion Picture Arts and Sciences reminds us of the story of the man who gave a bad check. When faced with the fact that the check was bad he agreed to write another bad one." A reporter with *Billboard* declared, "It is agreed among insiders that producers are on the run and that the Guild will get all of its demands. Producers felt that by offering concessions they could get players to return to the Academy and thus cripple the Guild. This is not working out. Players are strong for their organization. And signs of weakening among producers is cementing Guild members more closely than ever."[40]

A week later a reporter with the same publication observed that the producers had the idea that their new contract would wean many SAG members to the "scarecrow" Academy but many observers believed it would have just the opposite effect. SAG contended the new pact had no means of enforcement (no effective and binding arbitration) while the producers insisted the Academy would take care of that aspect. "The Guild points out that the Academy is a producer union and that it would enforce only what the producers please, which is probably the case.... The players want a new contract and recognition and nothing short of this will be considered," according to the reporter.[41]

If producers thought their new contract proposals would bring back the actors in droves to the Academy they were disappointed. At the end of February 1936 there were said to be less than 100 players in the Academy, while SAG claimed 4,000 members.[42]

One month later a different publication stated there were less than 30 actors who were members of the Academy while SAG claimed a paid-up membership of 2,300 actors. It also observed that AMPAS had not profited by new members, despite the new AMPAS agreement.[43]

Late in May 1935, Robert Montgomery replaced Eddie Cantor as SAG president. Serving with Montgomery were: James Cagney (first vice president); Ann Harding (second vice president), Chester Morris (third vice president), Kenneth Thomson (secretary), Boris Karloff (assistant secretary), Warren William (treasurer), and Noel Madison (assistant treasurer).[44]

7. The Coming of SAG, 1933–1936

Toward the end of May 1935 a reporter declared that a comparison of the proposals by SAG with certain features of the AMPAS contract showed why SAG had such a strong growth in membership in the previous months "and why it is fast becoming an important figure in Hollywood studio circles and is destined soon to control the actor-producer relationships with an iron hand." Main differences pointed out were that the only arbitration of contract disputes offered by the Academy was through the Academy and that the producers refused to bind themselves to a contract with a representative actor body. "The Academy has adopted some of the Guild proposals but avoided the most vital one, which made the producer responsible for keeping his promises," concluded the newsman.[45]

As of the summer of 1935 there was reportedly not much chance in Hollywood for actors seeking work. Records showed there were then in Hollywood around 11,000 people listed as players (excluding extras) yet only about 25 percent could be assured of any work at all during the year. Actual figures showed the ratio of players to jobs was around 19 to one. Over the previous year about 75 percent of the total number did not work a single day. And new faces showed up daily in Hollywood, arriving from the legitimate stage, radio, and other sources. Only 318 players were then assured of a weekly pay check — those were the players under term contracts. Added to that, was the fact that only an average of 253 supporting players from the freelance list were used each day. That number, however, was made up almost wholly of repeaters, due to the popularity system whereby casting directors confined their calls for support players to actors who had been in recent pictures.[46]

At a SAG meeting in August 1935, the union's attorney Laurence W. Bielenson told the membership of the benefits to be derived from the Wagner Labor Bill (some of the provisions of the now defunct NRA had been incorporated into the Wagner bill — enacted shortly after the NRA was struck down by the Supreme Court. It was formally the National Labor Relations Act. Among other provisions it made it easier for workers to organize and made it more difficult for management to refuse to bargain with unions that legitimately represented the majority of the workers). He said there would no doubt be attacks on it by big business as to the constitutionality of the bill but that the production of motion pictures was interstate commerce and therefore fell under the scope of the Wagner bill.

Film Actors Organize

Bielenson said it was his firm belief that the producers would be forced to recognize the two guilds (SAG and SWG) and deal with them under the collective bargaining clauses of the Wagner act.[47]

Out of around 2,500 established feature film actors dependent more or less upon motion pictures for a livelihood, only 974 participated in one or more film acting roles that included screen credit in 1935, according to an AMPAS survey. Results showed that out of 439 feature length movies shown in Los Angeles during 1935 only 974 actors were cast in 2,189 principal roles. That meant an average of 2.5 roles per actor, including those under term contracts and freelance players. Further analysis showed that of the group of 974 working, featured players, 59 performed 400 roles, 237 had 903 parts, and 678 appeared in 881 roles.[48]

Extras had an 11 percent increase in the number of placements they received in 1935, from the Central Casting Bureau. There were 278,486 jobs for extras that were paid a total of $2,571,293.64, for an average pay of $9.23 per day. Of the total expended, approximately 60 percent went to male extras ($1,521,017.60 for 182,650 placements). Women earned a total of $724,154.60 from 86,001 jobs. As there were always new applicants for registration on the CCB list, the number of interviews given at the bureau office to hopefuls averaged 87 per day in 1935, as compared to 64 the year before. Weather, and other causes, meant there was a daily average in 1935 of 48 calls for extras being cancelled, as against just 17 job cancellations per day, on average, in 1934.[49]

Laws prohibiting the United States Army and Navy from turning equipment, military bases, and personnel, over to Hollywood studios for feature films were in the offing early in 1936 as a result of strenuous protests to the United States Congress about the cooperation of military and naval services with the film industry. Apparently the 1927 directive from the U.S. War Department banning such use of the military had not gone into effect, or perhaps had been ignored. Stirred up by SAG, the Los Angeles Central Labor Council and the AFL submitted complaints to Secretaries Woodring of the War Department and Swanson of the Navy Department, complaining that soldiers and sailors working free in Hollywood productions had deprived civilian talent of months of employment in recent years. Efforts were said to be in the works to have the Congress write into appropriation bills amendments stipulating that such practices should stop. According to the complaints, 100,000 man-days of employment — involv-

7. The Coming of SAG, 1933–1936

ing upwards of $1 million in wages — had been lost to film extras and studio civilians in the previous five years because of the general aid given Hollywood by the Army and Navy. Emphasized in the complaints was that the studios saved tremendous amounts of money by getting the federal government to foot the bills, not only for talent, but also for gasoline, sets, costumes, and equipment.[50]

Listing 17 films made with Army and Navy personnel in which civilian actors could have been used, unionists focused attention on Army cooperation with Warner Brothers in making *Captured*, pointing out to Congressmen the "scandalous" arrangement by which United States noncommissioned officers and enlisted men were dressed in German uniforms while American Army planes were repainted to resemble German ships. Arguments were reinforced with a list of 80 semi-military and semi-naval films made in the same period with civilian actors taking all the parts of officers and enlisted personnel. "If some pictures can be produced without calling on the Government, virtually all can be made with civilian talent," argued the unionists. Critics pointed out that the Navy especially had spent thousands of dollars of taxpayers' money maneuvering ships for film purposes adding that huge sums were frittered away every time an anchor was weighed. Movies named by the complainers as having used military personnel and equipment to save the Hollywood studios money included *The Leathernecks Have Landed* (Republic), *Here Comes the Navy* (Warner Brothers), *The Fleet's In* (Paramount), *Rendezvous* (MGM), *All Quiet on the Western Front* (Universal), and *Cavalcade* (Fox).[51]

During the year ending March 1, 1936, a total of 4,000 freelance player contracts were issued by AMPAS, from the major studios that were signatory to the Academy codes. Some 2,500 of those contracts went to featured players and small-role actors, guaranteeing players from one to 10 weeks of work at $90 or more per week. The other 1,500 contracts were issued to bit players, dancers, singers, and so on, at weekly stipends of from $66 to $90. Studios who were members of the Academy also made in excess of 13,000 day-player engagements. Approximately 20 percent of the 2,500 engagement of featured players were secured by players without agents. A total of 93 agencies figured in the balance of the deals with 12 of those firms (13 percent) having been responsible for about 51 percent of the agent-arranged contracts.[52]

Late in August 1936, SAG leveled charges at the majors of cheating

Film Actors Organize

the extras. It came in the wake of a report from the CCB that showed of the 15,275 persons given work, 13,463 earned less than $200 each for the first six months of 1936. SAG filed some suits and was contemplating others, charging the studios were paying extras $7.50 a day for speaking parts in defiance of the producers' agreement to pay $25 a day for such work. Included in the CCB's report was the warning to "Stay out of Hollywood" as the Bureau still tried to discourage hopefuls from making the trek to the film capital. The report also showed that 1,277 earned between $200 and $500 during those six months and just 533 people earned in excess of $500 for the half year. Meanwhile, SAG was reported to have been gathering data and had a wealth of affidavits and other material to substantiate its allegations of cheating by the majors. It was SAG's contention that when the producers agreed to continue the provisions of the NRA after the death of that agency their resolution was, in effect, a labor contract and that they specified that people speaking lines germane to the plot would be paid $25 a day. But the studios had demanded the extras do that bit work for the usual $7.50 a day check and the players, worried about the possibility of being blacklisted, complied. It was pointed out by SAG that the savings to the studios by such practices were tiny, running perhaps to $100 on a $150,000 production.[53]

On the heels of SAG's threatened barrage of salary lawsuits against the majors for cheating extras and bit players, the MPPDA decided to get tough against any of its member studios and their executives who cheated in violation of the producer agreement to abide by the labor regulations of the former NRA code. Due to that it was expected SAG would drop all of its lawsuits. SAG had gone thought something of a lull of a year or more in its efforts to gain recognition and to collectively bargain for its first contract with the Hollywood producers. There had been some confusion and uncertainty when the NRA had disappeared and still more uncertainty over what the Wagner act meant and whether it would stand up in court. But as summer ended in 1936 the time seemed ripe for the union to make its first independent foray against the violently anti-union Hollywood film cartel. It was time for SAG to try and do what Equity had failed to accomplish on several occasions.[54]

8

SAG Negotiations and First Contract, 1936–1937

A news account dated September 22, 1936, speculated that SAG would soon serve an ultimatum on the MPPDA for recognition and for a union shop in the Hollywood studios. Plans for such action had been underway for a year or so and a week earlier Kenneth Thomson, SAG executive secretary, was elected one of the California State Federation of Labor's vice presidents. As well, at that convention a resolution was adopted declaring for a closed shop in the studios. Thus, SAG believed it had solidified itself properly with the AFL and was in an appropriate position to call a strike, if it was deemed necessary. Further, Gillmore had served notice on 24 important actors, members of Equity, to join SAG. All those actions strengthened the belief of observers that actors were set to try very soon for recognition and the closed shop. Equity's desire to see SAG strengthened was said to be apparent on Gillmore's last trip to the west coast when he announced that Equity would close its Hollywood office. In line with that, Gillmore announced the list of 24 Equity members told to join SAG. They were to be expelled from Equity in four weeks if they did not join SAG — all had been film players for some time. Included in the 24 were Lionel Atwill, John Barrymore, Lionel Barrymore, Alice Brady, Lloyd Nolan, Jack Oakie, and Rosalind Russell. Frank Gillmore explained those named had refused to abide by an agreement between the two unions calling for membership in both groups, if the player worked on stage and screen. Most of those named were freelance actors. For some time the majors had been moving to protect themselves against such moves as those

149

made by SAG and Equity by putting important players under term contracts. Producers, it was said, felt that no walkout could occur under those term contracts (they specifically banned the signer from walking out or going on strike) as the producers had been legally advised that those people would have to comply with the provisions of their contracts or be subject to litigation that might prove costly. MPPDA executives began to pay more attention to the labor situation when word reached Hollywood that the California State Federation of Labor had adopted a resolution calling for a full union shop in filmdom, covering all crafts, actors, writers, and directors. As a further move the state labor body adopted a resolution to modify the current personal employment act to reduce the length of option contracts from seven years down to three years [it was under that provision that studios signed players to contracts that ran for a period of up to seven years], thereby eliminating a bill passed by the state legislature several years earlier that had been enacted at the instigation of the producers and had increased the length of such contracts to a maximum of seven years from five years. SAG then had an estimated membership of about 3,000 of whom more than 1,000 were in the Class A or senior Guild, with the remaining 2,000 in the junior Guild.[1]

When journalist Douglas Churchill mentioned the expected SAG initiative, he declared that "the impending fight will not be limited to the studios, it is indicated, for Los Angeles is notoriously an open-shop town, and leading industrialists are attempting to inspire producers with the courage to resist the organization trend. The cry of 'Red' has always been an effective weapon in California in combating labor troubles, and this has been used in discussions of the actors' demands." Churchill felt the biggest weapon the actors had was their ability to draw on AFL support. Specifically they could get the unionized projectionists in theaters across America to refuse to handle Hollywood product — if the players struck — and in so doing close every cinema in the United States and thus instantly financially cripple the studios.[2]

Kenneth Thomson told the SAG board of directors on September 28, 1936, that no definite move would be made to force the studios' acceptance of a 100 percent closed shop until the annual meeting, in April 1937, of producers and craft union heads, signatory to the present studio basic agreement between the studios and most of the craft unions, which bargained as one with the studios. That basic agreement, which could be

8. SAG Negotiations and First Contract, 1936–1937

opened once a year on narrowly focused items, such as wage rates, ran for a number of years, and expired in April 1937. Major studios were then staffed by technicians and craft people that were 90 percent unionized. Thus, Thomson let it be understood that a full demand for a closed shop, of both technical and creative talent, would be made in April 1937.[3]

Late in March 1937, Kenneth Thomson was in Washington, D.C., to meet with William Green, president of the AFL, to enlist his support to put pressure on George E. Browne of IATSE for the inclusion of SAG in the studio basic agreement with the craft and technical unions. It was said to be understood that in the event Thomson could not get the support of Browne the only alternative for SAG would be to go over to the AFL's rival, the CIO (the Congress of Industrial Organizations, 1935–1955, sprang up as a rival to the AFL but the two bodies finally came together into the organization that exists today, the AFL-CIO). Browne was reportedly not kindly disposed to SAG due to its hands-off policy during the last, brief IATSE strike. Officially, though, Thomson denied all the rumors, declaring he had no differences with Browne and laughing off any talk of going over to the CIO.[4]

As April began SAG, with a membership then said to be over 5,000 strong, was poised to make another attempt to win union recognition from the producers. It met on April 4 with representatives of some of the craft unions and the studios in an effort to acquire a contract, a basic agreement, an arbitration clause, and other concessions. According to SAG, it had been promised the support of five other unions in the industry. Thomson was to represent SAG. Joining him were representatives from the painters' and laborers' unions that, like SAG, had not been recognized by the producers. A year earlier at a similar meeting the players had made a similar request, but it was not considered. SAG would be backed by some 17,000 other unionized workers in Hollywood, according to Thomson. Attending that April 4th conference were Daniel J. Tobin, general president of the International Brotherhood of Teamsters and Chauffeurs; George Browne, president of the International Alliance of Theatrical Stage Employees and Motion Picture Operators (IATSE), Dan W. Tracy, president of the International Brotherhood of Electrical Workers, Joseph N. Weber, president of the American Federation of Musicians, and William L. Hutcheson, representing the United Brotherhood of Carpenters and Joiners of America. According to Thomson the film extras, freelance actors,

151

Film Actors Organize

and bit players would be the ones most affected by union recognition. SAG wanted to see the extras and small bit players benefit from improved working conditions and also wanted the right to supervise the contracts as Equity did for the stage players.[5]

A day later it was reported that SAG would not shrink from calling a strike if its demand for recognition and collective bargaining was not met by the studios. In this account SAG's membership was said to be 5,600 people, of whom 3,500 were extras.[6]

As a result of the meetings between the producers and the various craft unions, on April 5 the producers announced a pay increase of 10 percent had been granted to the craft unions (not SAG) named above, except for the musicians who had not asked for an increase and whose pay remained unchanged. However, the Brotherhood of Painters, Decorators, and Paperhangers, represented by its president L. P. Lindelof, refused to participate in the agreement because the studios would not recognize the union's jurisdiction over hairdressers, makeup artists, scenic artists, and art directors. That pay raise affected an estimated 20,000 workers in the film industry. Both SAG and the Painters, though, remained outside of that basic agreement between the studios and the craft unions. Producers' representatives who attended the meetings on April 4th and 5th were as follows; Nicholas Schenck (MGM), Sidney Kent (Fox), Robert Cochrane (Universal), Albert Warner (Warner Brothers), Leo Spits (RKO), Harry Buckley (United Artists), Barney Balaban (Paramount), and Charles Schwartz (Columbia).[7]

Thus, after those two days of meetings, as expected, the producers' labor committee, headed by Pat Casey, reached an agreement providing for a 10 percent pay increase to four unions under a five-year basic agreement and stood willing then or at any later date to take back the Brotherhood of Painters into the agreement, with the pay increase, if and when it gave up its claim to jurisdiction over the other job categories. Musicians remained within the newly extended basic agreement but at the same rate of pay. The fact SAG was trying to join the basic agreement and its threat to cause trouble was not taken too seriously by the film cartel. As well, the discussion to include the laborers' union under the basic agreement was not resolved. SAG requests to join the basic agreement had fallen on deaf ears as, said a reporter, "the producers are reported refusing to believe that the SAG will strike, or if it does, that the organization can cause much

8. SAG Negotiations and First Contract, 1936–1937

trouble." Producers were refusing to talk to SAG but not, it was explained, because actors wanted a closed shop. Among other things it was pointed out that SAG, or any other group seeking recognition, first had to obtain approval from the producers' Labor Group, from where recommendations were made to the producers' committee. The latter could not discuss inclusion of any union organization until the Labor Group had passed on its application. Thus, since that had not happened with respect to the players' union, SAG was still out in the cold, so far as direct negotiations with the producers were concerned. That also applied to hairdressers, makeup artists and the others who were trying to ally themselves with the Painters. Because of the fact the producers could not see what connection or relations those groups had with the Painters, the latter were also out in the cold. The Brotherhood of Painters had been a signatory to the basic agreement of 1932 (the one that had expired in April 1937) but had withdrawn from it because of the refusal of the producers to let the union take on the other job categories. In this account, abut 15,000 employees were covered by the pay increase, which totaled about $3 million a year. Over 3,000 laborers then worked at the studios. Of that number, less than 50 percent were organized as members of the Utility Workers' Union. Trade unions in various fields were then fighting for jurisdiction over film laborers, complicating the situation for the studios. It was the jurisdictional fighting that kept the laborers from being recognized as a union by the producers, and being included in the five-year basic agreement.[8]

As April progressed there was growing general labor unrest among film workers. When the United States Supreme Court held the Wagner bill legal and constitutional it caused considerable anxiety among the producers due to the fact there were several labor organizations outside the recently signed basic agreement, including SAG. Those producers were worried because it appeared the Wagner bill compelled the film producers' cartel to collectively bargain with them. When the Supreme Court validated the Wagner bill most observers agreed that, under its provisions, the producers had to bargain not only with SAG but with any other unions outside of the basic agreement, provided each union represented the majority of workers in that occupation. Although the issue of pay had been resolved with all the unions within the basic agreement — the increased pay came into effect on April 26 — the producers continued to negotiate with them on working conditions and other minor points. Rumors circu-

Film Actors Organize

lated that the MPPDA might still refuse to deal with SAG, Wagner notwithstanding, and stall for a longer period by taking the matter to court as a test case. Meanwhile, as a result of a meeting a few days earlier it was revealed that SAG was discussing plans with the Painters for the formation of a federated group of all those outside the basic agreement, to compel collective recognition by the producers of that group as a whole. Those who would go into the federated group were actors, makeup artists, painters, plasterers, laborers, scenic artists, culinary workers, machinists, office workers, script girls, animators, writers, cutters, assistant directors, and unit managers. Recognition of the Studio Utility Employees Union in the producer/craft union basic agreement came that week with a truce in the union jurisdictional disputes and a line drawn between the duties of the Utility workers and the IATSE grips. Even then the Brotherhood of Painters was threatening a strike while the CIO had opened a drive to organize the film industry with a vertical union (the CIO favored industrial organization, one union for a plant or industry, while the AFL favored craft unionism with multiple unions, by craft, within a plant or industry) and to supplant the AFL. Various crafts that previously opted to go with the Painters were then looking for a different union home. The CIO planned a special drive into the ranks of SAG believing members would be in a receptive mood since their application for inclusion in the studio basic agreement had been turned down by the producers.[9]

At a meeting on April 24, the demand for immediate action or a walkout was voiced by 700 members of the Brotherhood of Painters. The fight by film labor bodies, led by the Painters and SAG, led to the formation a few days earlier of the Federated Motion Picture Crafts (FMPC). As well, there were the filing of protests and discussion of strike votes if negotiations failed. Sixteen, or so, organizations outside of the producer/labor basic agreement were aligned in the new FMPC, including actors, painters, makeup artists, scenic artists, costumers, and so on. Each member of the FMPC planned to negotiate a separate agreement with the producers but asked for collective bargaining with the federation. Kenneth Thomson, for SAG, met with the producers' labor representative Pat Casey for several hours on April 27 to present SAG's demands. For the actors Thomson wanted recognition of SAG; increased wages for extras and bit players; notification a full day in advance if a player was to be needed on a specific day; and the curbing of the powers of assistant directors, who

8. SAG Negotiations and First Contract, 1936–1937

were alleged to widely engage in nepotism and favoritism when it came to casting. Thomson emphasized SAG had no grievances with respect to the higher-salaried players, but that his organization was more interested in the day worker, the bit player, and the extra, and improving conditions for those categories. All of the labor unrest then found in Hollywood had reportedly slowed production in the studios with the result that production schedules were running far behind schedule.[10]

On the night of April 30, 1937, some 3,000 technical film workers went out on strike with picketing of the major motion picture studios in Los Angeles underway on the morning of May 1. It was called by the FMPC, an AFL affiliate composed of 14 craft unions and SAG. However, only four unions were affected by the original strike call; scenic artists, hairdressers, painters, and draftsmen. Other craft unions joined the strike on May 1 as each group held a meeting of its members, explained the situation, and took a strike vote. As a result, hanging over the head of Hollywood was the threat of a strike by 10,000 people. SAG, with a reported 3,000 members had a mass meeting slated for the evening of May 2. The other 14 bodies in the FMPC had a total of 7,000 members. A strike call had been issued on the 30th by Charles Lessing, head of the FMPC, after he had walked out of a conference with film executives that day when they rejected a demand for a closed shop. Studios had, however, agreed to recognize the federation as the bargaining agent for the group it represented. Also included in the federation were; plumbers, engineers, molders, boiler makers, machinists, blacksmiths, carpenters and linoleum workers, sheet metal workers, culinary workers, and costumers. Whether the five major unions in the film industry (the ones within the basic agreement, the musicians and the other four who received the pay raise) would strike in sympathy with the FMPC was then unknown.[11]

With respect to SAG's position on the strike, before its own mass meeting was held, the SAG board declared, "It is up to the individual players at this time whether they want to pass through the picket lines. The executive board of the Guild cannot advise them. Likewise it is up to the individual stars and lesser players whether, with the make-up artists on strike, they want to make themselves up." Among the early arrivals at the MGM studio on May 1 were Clark Gable, William Powell, Jean Harlow, Jeanette MacDonald, and Greta Garbo. Their only discomfort was the inability to get breakfast on the lot because the commissary chefs had

Film Actors Organize

walked out. At their studio only four of the regularly employed makeup artists and hairdressers failed to appear for work. Pickets at Paramount studio made no effort to stop Jack Benny, Bing Crosby, Bob Burns, Martha Raye, Irene Dunne, Jean Arthur, or Randolph Scott from entering the lot. Those players worked as usual throughout the day. When Gable first arrived for work he sat in his car and observed the pickets. When asked by a reporter if he was a strikebreaker he replied, "No. I'm just here to see the fun. Of course, I'll work if the company does." It did and so did Gable. Marlene Dietrich applied her own makeup at her studio and James Cagney, considered to be one of the most ardent proponents of unionism among the stars, was reported to be "out on his boat." In his statement Lessing said, "Nothing much is going to happen today. Saturday is a quiet day at the studios. We feel certain that the other unions of the federation, including the Screen Actors Guild, will join us in the strike after they hold important meetings tomorrow." Pat Casey, for the MPPDA, claimed that not more than 1,500 of the more than 40,000 studio workers were involved in the strike and that production had not been hampered at all. For SAG to call a strike a vote of 75 percent in favor by the senior members — those who earned $250 a week or more — would be necessary.[12]

Picketing of all major studios ceased on May 2, for one day, as 40 representatives of the FMPC gathered in a closed meeting to discuss strategy. According to this account four unions having 2,500 members were then on strike.[13]

An editorial in the May 4 edition of the *Washington Post* explained the FMPC consisted of 18 AFL unions with an estimated membership of 16,000 while SAG numbered 1,600. They were part of an industry that in 1936 took from the public about $1 billion in the form of gross receipts paid in at cinema box offices. In 1936, moreover, about 500 feature films had been produced at an estimated cost of $135 million, illustrating the important place the industry held in the United States economy. Although the strike underway had been called primarily to secure bargaining rights for the FMPC, the editor thought it would undoubtedly direct attention to the great disparities in wage and salary scales prevailing in the film capital. "If members of the actors' guild earning $250 per week and more should decide to align themselves with the craft unions in the present contest it would be a strong vindication of the principle of industrial unionism," said the editor. "Yet any dispassionate observer would be inclined

8. SAG Negotiations and First Contract, 1936–1937

to conclude that the motion picture studios are not naturally good experimental laboratories for organization of the C.I.O. type."[14]

Although the strike had spread by May 4, movie-making continued. The number of pickets at nine major studios increased to an average of about 1,000 in total on duty at any one time as the strike spread to encompass 11 unions of the FMPC. It was said there were then about 6,000 workers on strike. Actors continued to pass through the picket lines into the studios as they awaited a final decision from SAG as to whether the 3,600 actor members of the union would join the strike, either by a formal walkout or by declining to cross the picket lines. No decision was reached at the May 2 mass meeting, with the matter deferred for one week to Sunday, May 9. Some 2,000 members attended the May 2 gathering. SAG directors planned to confer with producers on May 5 to discuss Guild demands. Robert Montgomery, SAG president, conducted the May 2 meeting and declared the senior members of SAG "will stand directly behind" the junior members — those receiving less than $250 a week, and who had no voice in the vote that, when called, would determine whether or not SAG joined the walkout. By this account SAG had 1,200 senior members and 4,400 junior members. Urging active support of the FMPC actor Lionel Stander told the meeting, "With the eyes of the whole world on this meeting, will it not give the guild a black eye if its members continue to cross the picket lines?"[5]

Widely-circulated reports that non-union workers were being hired by studios was confirmed on May 4 by Pat Casey, the man who dealt with labor issues for the MPPDA. He said that about 150 people had been hired to replace striking employees. Meanwhile, the strikers announced that downtown Los Angeles and Hollywood cinemas would be picketed and placarded beginning on the evening of May 4 in a move to boycott distribution outlets of the studios and put more pressure on the producers. Lessing said that placards were then being prepared that read "Studios on Strike — Do Not Attend Theaters." Placards were to be attached to automobiles that would be parked in front of cinemas showing films made at the MPPDA studios where the FMPC-affiliated workers were on strike. As well, added Lessing, an appeal was being sent to labor organizations throughout the United States and Canada to establish similar boycotts against cinemas until the producers granted union recognition to groups affiliated with the FMPC. Reports of a revolt by several stars against the

157

Film Actors Organize

"hands off" attitude maintained toward the strike to that point by SAG were met with complete denials by union officials. Those reports, said to have originated at the union's strike headquarters, said Richard Dix and Elissa Landi refused to cross picket lines out of sympathy for the strikers. However, when a journalist finally reached Dix the actor told him he was "accepting" the Guild's policy. Although the FMPC claimed that a number of minor actors turned back at the picket lines, reporter Alan McElwain observed that "the stars swept by on foot or in limousines or swanky sports roadsters with hardly a glance at the men with the strike armbands. Greta Garbo, Clark Gable, Marlene Dietrich, and Gary Cooper were among them. Others were Constance Bennett, Jean Harlow, Mary Astor, Jeanette MacDonald, Gypsy Rose Lee, and Douglas Fairbanks, Jr." Pickets tried to at least embarrass scab actors by taking their photos. Striker William Cullen explained, "We are building up a rogue's gallery for use as a strike weapon. It will be sent to the American Federation of Labor."[16]

Aubrey Blair, secretary of SAG, announced on May 8 that top-flight actors in Hollywood had voted to strike on May 10 unless producers granted the demands of the lower-salaried players. Blair explained that the star actors in the senior section of the Guild had been voting secretly in the homes of actors and more than the necessary 75 percent majority had been obtained, which was a mandate to call a strike. He said that many of the highest paid and most glamorous stars on the screen would join the picket lines on that Monday and "only immediate and unqualified action by the producers can forestall a strike." That balloting was done over several days at the homes of James Cagney, Frederic March, and Chester Morris, and replaced the original idea to hold the voting as part of the SAG mass meeting slated for Sunday, May 9. Among other items, SAG was seeking higher wages for the low-salaried players, and recognition as the sole bargaining agent for actors. Also, it wanted to outlaw the $3.20 daily wage that was paid to some extras and win a guarantee of $25 a day minimum for bit players — those who spoke from one to 100 lines per picture. "Stars with a quarter of a million-dollar contract are laying them on the line for the sake of the $5-a-day actor," exclaimed Blair. "We are determined to better the lot of the poorer paid actors." Among the senior SAG members — earning at least $250 a week — who had been most active in the SAG strike movement were Robert Montgomery, Eddie Cantor, Joan Crawford, Franchot Tone, Jean Muir, James Cagney, Frederic March, and

8. SAG Negotiations and First Contract, 1936–1937

Chester Morris. The Los Angeles Central Labor Council demanded the AFL place nine major studios — Columbia, MGM, Paramount, RKO, Fox, United Artists, Universal, Warner Brothers, and Hal Roach — on the "unfair to labor" list. The boycott of cinemas in the Los Angeles area had spread to include three in Santa Monica. It was still hoped to extend the theater boycott nationwide.[17]

In his recap of the FMPC strike situation on May 9, reporter Douglas Churchill noted its steady disintegration. SAG, after much brave talk, decided that the situation did not merit hasty action, while six of the 14 unions involved in the strike withdrew from the FMPC and negotiated settlements of their own. The International Alliance of Theatre Stage Employees (IATSE) provided strikebreakers in those areas where FMPC people remained formally out on strike. Meanwhile, the CIO sent words of encouragement to the strikers but was popularly believed to have done little except to contribute to the general confusion. The Screen Playwrights, the industry-favored organization (another company union) had supplanted the SWG at this time, and remained discreetly silent. With respect to studio tactics, Churchill observed that for years the studios had used the simple expedient of seeing that two union factions were kept alive. When one made trouble, the industry allied itself with the other. It was a method used in 1921 when IATSE struck. Ten years later the Federated Crafts, which had enjoyed the support of the industry in the earlier fight, decided a strike was necessary. But before events were well underway IATSE was aligned against them. That strengthened IATSE to such an extent that in 1933 it believed it would be successful in its effort to organize the industry, but a six-week strike was defeated, not by the producers but by another union faction. Summarizing the past 16 or so years of labor disputes in Hollywood, Churchill concluded the unions involved had been without effective leadership and at times without purpose: "There has been a notable absence of skill in handling their campaigns. Whether ignorance, lack of valid issues or deficiencies in various qualities on the part of their leaders are responsible for the unbroken series of defeats can only be surmised."[18]

A different recap of the strike at the same time also pointed out that squabbling among rival unions continued to block efforts by union chiefs to win their demands. The striking unions, in some cases, said the report, "found that their places were being taken in the studios by members of their own union carrying cards of a rival organization"—IATSE. In explaining the situation the reporter remarked, "To understand a walkout which apparently is being defeated by its own strikers acting as strike breakers, it is necessary to consider several elements. Los Angeles is the self-styled open shop capital of America, and venerable methods of disrupting union action have not been weakened by time, Wagner act or no Wagner act. Backed by a militant non-union city, the studios, while appearing to embrace organization, have yielded little and have kept the unions in hand." By this account the current difficulties went back to 1926 when the producers signed a basic agreement with all the recognized unions of the time, the Painters among them. To increase their membership the Painters took in unrelated crafts and when their demands for recognition for these new trades were denied in 1932 they withdrew from the pact with the understanding they could be readmitted (without jurisdiction over the extra crafts) whenever they chose. In January 1937 they renewed the demand (as part of negotiations for a new five-year basic agreement) to include those other crafts. When the demand was again denied it led to a strike. The FMPC was opposed in its current struggle by IATSE; the latter did have friendly relations with SAG, though. For IATSE the strike was a chance to strengthen its own position and to that end it had been issuing union cards to members of the rival union, the FMPC. Such a card allowed a striking FMPC worker to turn around, renter the studio, and work as an IATSE member at the very job he had walked away from. As well, several of the crafts that the producers refused to recognize as part of the Painters' union had petitioned Pat Casey for recognition which he indicated he would grant. By around May 8 some 800 workers, at most, were out on strike. Reportedly, the strike had little effect on production and the MPPDA had adopted an official policy of silence on the whole strike issue.[19]

A working agreement between the studios and SAG was arrived at on May 9, diminishing the likelihood the Guild would back the craft strike. Six of the nine major studios granted the primary demands of the Guild for a union shop, improved working conditions, and better pay for film extras. Heads of those six studios — RKO, Paramount, MGM, Universal, Columbia, and 20th-Century-Fox — also promised to bring the three others — Warner Brothers, United Artists, and Hal Roach — into line. Samuel Goldwyn (an independent producer affiliated with United Artists)

8. SAG Negotiations and First Contract, 1936–1937

issued a statement in which he said, "I am shocked to find that my name is not included in the list. I have never and will never be an enemy of the fair demands of labor." At a meeting of 4,000 SAG members who accepted the union's proposal to continue negotiations, Robert Montgomery said, "We have an agreement with the producers, but it has not yet been committed to a full contract." The FMPC's 11 unions still off the job continued their picketing and strike. As well, Montgomery told the meeting the producers had abolished the old $3.20 a day minimum for extras and agreed to pay a $5.50 minimum per day for extras doing "mob stuff."[20]

Actors celebrated the fact that SAG had won a closed, union shop. It came about due to increased pressure on the studios during the last few days. On May 6 the producers agreed to practically all of SAG's demands and even went so far as to offer an 80/20 union shop. Their argument against the full closed shop was that something like 25 of the more famous Hollywood stars did not belong to the Guild. Immediately SAG went after those stars — Greta Garbo, Marlene Dietrich, Jean Harlow — and a score of others who kept aloof from SAG from the beginning were signed up. A federal mediator became involved in the strike on May 7. One day later the Los Angeles Central Labor Council voted support of the FMPC, condemned IATSE as a strike breaker, and put the nine strike-bound studios on the unfair list. Aubrey Blair, business agent for the actors, threatened the producers with a strike unless the closed shop was granted and before the actors' meeting on the evening of May 9. On Sunday, May 9, there were pickets in front of all Los Angeles cinemas; IATSE suddenly confronted the producers and demanded the closed shop for the actors. Otherwise no projectionist (they were members of IATSE) in the United States would screen a film in any theater in the country. Later on May 9 the producers reached an agreement with SAG that included the union shop, or so it was reported.[21]

And so, on the morning of Monday, May 10 the actors went back to their studio where it was work as usual, despite the fact the FMFC, or what remained of it was still on strike. A bitter Lessing exclaimed, "It is a dirty double-cross. The actors sold us out," as he commented on the agreement reached by SAG and the studios. Picket lines remained up around the major studios and the larger theaters in downtown Los Angeles. In Hollywood, though, players such as Clark Gable, Eleanor Powell, Greta Garbo, Gary Cooper, and Marlene Dietrich, among others, passed without incident. In reply to Lessing, Aubrey Blair of SAG said, "We have given the Federated Crafts as much support as possible. The crafts called their strike prematurely. We were to have met with them at 6 P.M. on April 30 to discuss the strike. But at 3 P.M. of that day, Lessing called us and said the strike was on."[22]

The Pacific Coast convention of the International Longshoremen's Association (meeting in Seattle) protested on May 10 against the action of SAG in calling off a threatened film strike. The longshoremen unanimously approved a protest sent to Robert Montgomery, SAG president, declaring SAG's move represented "another attempt of your employers to split the program of unified union action." It went on to state the actors' duty was to "refrain from appearing on the job or in any way to help your employers to break the strike."[23]

Later on May 10 Charles Lessing, having cooled off somewhat, moved away from his earlier statements in which he accused SAG of a double-cross and of being in collusion with the producers. He said he would have liked to have had the actors' support but held no animosity toward them: "We can win without them, and we will win."[24]

With most contract points resolved it appeared, on May 10, that SAG had won a 100 percent union shop, a minimum of $50 a week salary for stock players, a $5.50 per day minimum wage for film extras, and an increase from $15 to $25 per day for bit players. All players had to belong to SAG if they wanted to appear in pictures. For its part, SAG had to accept as members any and all who applied. Thus, if a studio casting director wanted to case a relative of someone influential he could do so, provided the relative first joined SAG. The union was obliged to take him.[25]

The first official rift in the SAG-producer agreement came on May 11 with conflicting interpretations of the terms of the deal. Producers claimed the pact called for an 80/20 SAG shop while the Guild insisted the agreed ratio was 95/5, the five percent maximum of non-union players per film being allowed to take care of established players who "conscientiously" were opposed to joining any union. That is, a certain percentage of non–SAG members at the time of the contract signing were grandfathered into the pact.[26]

Meanwhile, the FMPC continued its strike and on May 14 it declared that every actor who crossed studio picket lines would be classified as a "strikebreaker." The executive committee of the strike charged that SAG

8. SAG Negotiations and First Contract, 1936–1937

had played into the hands of the producers by accepting a separate agreement that FMPC leaders contended did not guarantee the union shop that the Guild sought.²⁷

As of May 17 the strike continued but two more of the unions involved dropped out of the strike and returned to work that day. FMPC had called for a nationwide boycott of cinemas and while they did receive sporadic picketing in support in some cities, there was no real effect. At a mass meeting on May 16 SAG members ratified a 10-year contract with the film cartel. One condition in the pact had SAG pledged not to strike for 10 years. Chief feature of the contract was the guarantee of a union shop for every player in the industry, except that a maximum of 10 percent of the stars and featured players were being exempted during the first five years of the agreement's life. A producer of 40 or more films annually could use up to three non-union stars in only two of them; if the studio made less than 40 films annually, then a maximum of three non–SAG players could be used in only one of the pictures. SAG agreed to keep membership open to all comers and to impose no unreasonable dues and initiation fees. The contract expired on May 15, 1947. Thus, for stars and featured players the contract mandated a 90/10 union shop for the first five years and a 100 percent SAG shop for the last five years. For the entire life of the pact a 100 percent union shop was mandated for freelance and stock players, extras, stunt men, and day players.²⁸

In something of a desperation move the executive committee of the striking FMPC, on May 18, formally requested labor unions throughout America to boycott all films in which five well known stars appeared; Robert Montgomery (SAG president), Franchot Tone (SAG vice president), Frank Morgan, Humphrey Bogart, and Edward Arnold (all three were SAG directors). In telegrams to the AFL and to the CIO, the committee asked that the actors be put on the "unfair" list because they refused to recommend that Guild members decline to cross picket lines at studios.²⁹

One day later, however, that same executive committee of the FMPC voted to repudiate the appeal made a day earlier. It wired a retraction of its desire to boycott the films of the five actors to all concerned organizations it had wired in the first place. Charles Lessing explained that the boycott appeal had not been authorized, adding that he was opposed to "bringing personalities" into the strike. The FMPC strike slowly fizzled out.³⁰

Film Actors Organize

Once SAG had formally approved and signed the deal with the producers there was a flood of applications for membership. Near the end of May applications for membership and/or reinstatement in the Guild were reported to be coming in at the rate of about 450 per day. The SAG initiation fee for junior members was $10 with quarterly dues of $1.25. Senior members paid an initiation fee of $25 and dues on a sliding scale. Players earning up to $15,000 annually paid $30 in dues annually; those in the $15,000 to $50,000 bracket paid $60 in yearly dues, above that dues were $100 yearly.[31]

A month after SAG had reached its settlement reporter Hubbard Keavy declared he knew there would have been no actors' strike. He had been sure they would not. "The actors never expected to strike. They knew that if they did, public sympathy would be so against them that the movies would have to hire a new set of puppets." He argued the ringleaders — Robert Montgomery, Boris Karloff, Lionel Stander, James Cagney, and Frank Morgan — had put themselves out on a limb but they would not have called for militant action. Keavy said that 98 percent of the actors would have ignored a strike call, if one had been issued, because if an artist under contract refused to work, for any reason, he voided his agreement and immediately became liable for damages for denying to his employer anticipated profits. And, for the period of that contract he would not be allowed to work for anyone else at the only calling he knew. "An actors' strike would have been the world's greatest fizzle," he concluded. And, "I didn't expect to see stars doing strike duty. Imagine a corporation — which is just what an actor getting a half million a year amounts to — in a picket line. It doesn't make sense."[32]

By late in July 1937, SAG membership was an estimated 10,000 making it the most powerful labor organization in the motion picture industry. So busy was the SAG office in Hollywood that 25 full-time employees had been added to the staff. A little earlier the Screen Directors' Guild completed organization and thus the film world was fully unionized.[33]

A few weeks later a realignment of the entertainment field took place under a revitalized Associated Actors and Artistes of America (4As). In a move that further weakened it, Equity relinquished its radio jurisdiction and agreed to give it to the American Federation of Radio Artists (AFRA, later AFTRA, American Federation of Television and Radio Artists). Frank

8. SAG Negotiations and First Contract, 1936–1937

Gillmore, president of Equity, and the 4As, was given a five-year contract as executive director of the international body, the 4As.[34]

Late in 1937 it was reported that out of a potential field of about 65,000 professional performers, the different units of the 4As had organized to that date between 16,000 and 20,000 performers. Summing up the different "claimed" memberships of the leading units, the total of organized players reached about 24,000 but that figure was thought to be misleading since it probably included overlapping membership and perhaps members not in good standing. Before the formation of AFRA a leading 4As official put the 4A total at about 16,000. The latest figures were: SAG, 9,000; AFRA, 4,000; Equity, 4,000; American Federation of Actors (AFA — a vaudeville group that had taken over from the defunct White Rats), 6,000; Chorus Equity 700; American Guild of Musical Artists, 500. The powerful American Federation of Musicians was never any part of the 4As.[35]

SAG's union shop, as laid out in its contract, was in effect only within 300 miles of Los Angeles. Supposedly that was because there were few SAG members, outside of New York City, in places such as Denver and Seattle, for example. However, by the summer of 1937 SAG was fighting to extend its Guild shop jurisdiction beyond the 300-mile limit. In September SAG moved checkers into Sonora, Truckee, and Flagstaff, among other places, to wage extensive membership drives; a similar drive was also underway in the New York area. Protests had been filed with producers over the actions of the studios in hiring non-union people and serving notice that the Guild would pull members off productions unless SAG people and extras were given work when available, even outside the 300-mile limit. When 75 non-union cowboys were hired in Sonora for Universal's *Courage of the West* by the producer, Joe Lewis, the film's director, telephoned a protest to Los Angeles but was advised the Guild did not have jurisdiction beyond 300 miles from Los Angeles except that SAG members on such productions had to be paid the Guild scale. To that time, SAG had already organized Guild chapters at many location points outside the 300-mile zone, but membership was not then sufficient to enforce the 100 percent union shop.[36]

Later that September, SAG declared it had a 100 percent Guild shop in the east; that is, the New York area studios as the last of the holdouts had signed on to the SAG-producer agreement.[37]

Film Actors Organize

When journalist Morton Thompson looked back at SAG, in April 1938, and what it had accomplished he was extravagant in his praise for the actors' union. "The incredible has now become commonplace. The Screen Actors' Guild rules the roost. It is probably on its way to becoming the richest and most powerful labor union in America," he exclaimed. "The stars have stepped down into the ranks to fight for the extras, the bit players, the masses. Their victories have been crushing and complete. What the S.A.G. dictates, the producers do. The result has been a startling betterment of working conditions, somewhat increased pay."[38]

9

Conclusion

Actors in all branches of the amusement business were slow to organize into unions in America, relative to other occupational groups. Partly that had to do with the idea that actors were artists and somehow above that which was taken up by the ordinary workman and trades person. They were also perceived to be too independent to maintain the discipline and solidarity necessary for a union to function effectively. As well, some of the slowness had to do with the transient nature of the profession with actors on the road much of the time and working, when they did, in small work units the composition of which regularly changed. It was a far cry from a large group of relatively unchanging employees who all labored in one big plant. Variations in salary were very large in acting, much bigger than was found in most occupational groupings and that added to the organizing difficulties. However, despite the difficulties actors did manage to form unions effectively from time to time. Many of the attempts were brief and fleeting with a fledgling group announcing its presence only to disappear almost as quickly as it had appeared. Some of the associations that appeared and lasted for short, or longer, periods of time tried to disguise themselves and their purpose by posing as social or fraternal organizations and then trying to slowly take on more union-type activities. None lasted very long or were very effective. If one did have any staying power it was only because it backed away from any union-style role and stuck with being a fraternal grouping. (For details on the early period of actors — not film — attempting to organize, see Kerry Segrave, *Actors Organize: A History of Union Formation Efforts in America, 1880–1919*. Jefferson, N.C.: McFarland, 2008.)

Film Actors Organize

Prior to 1920 there were only two unions in the amusement field that emerged and lasted; two that were openly unions and functioned as such. Those that had pretended they were not really unions had done so because the capitalist class in the amusement field was as virulently and aggressively anti-union as the capitalist class in any industry in America. First successful union to emerge and to last, at least for a time, was the White Rats Actors Union of America. It organized the vaudeville players but when faced with a tremendous hostility from the vaudeville producers, biased reporting from the media that denied them access; and a smear campaign against the Rats' leadership, the Rats collapsed and effectively disappeared from the scene at the time of World War I. Contributing to their downfall was an erratic and shaky leadership and a seeming lack of a coherent strategy. The only other actors' union to emerge in the years before 1920 was the Actors' Equity Association, which organized players from the legitimate stage. It spent six years trying to be recognized by the theatrical producers and to negotiate but got nowhere. Finally, in 1919, Equity called, and won, a strike against the producers. It meant they would survive, although Equity spent much of the 1920s in battles to win a full union shop and in fighting a rearguard action against the stage capitalist class, many of whom despised the idea of accepting unionization in their industry. When the Rats had struck it had been disaster; when Equity struck it had been success. One difference was that in the latter case other unions of craftsmen, such as stage hands, went out in sympathy with the players, and that support was crucial. No such support was extended to the Rats, and that was a factor in their defeat. Those two unions reached their peak in strength at different times and each made a few efforts to cross-organize. That is, the Rats tried to recruit stage players and Equity tried to recruit vaudeville artists. No union had much success in cross-organizing, although there were some recruits. Those came, for the most part, from players who went back and forth between the vaudeville stage and the legitimate stage.

Film actors were the last of the acting community to be organized. In addition to having to overcome the difficulties listed above there was an extra hurdle to deal with. The state of California and the city of Los Angeles had the well-deserved reputation of being especially anti-union areas, more than most parts of America. It wasn't just the actors in Hollywood that were slow to organize but all of the creative talent such as screen-

9. Conclusion

writers and film directors were also late in organizing with each of the three occupations not successfully being organized into unions until the middle 1930s.

The first attempts to unionize film actors took place in the New York City area as that was the center of film production in the earliest years of the industry; production shifted to California over a period of five or so years in the 1910s. One of the earliest moves to form a union was an effort made in 1912, followed by a second attempt in the summer of 1913. Details of the first effort were not reported while the second attempt was suddenly ended by the actors when it became known to those behind the attempt that the producers had infiltrated their supposedly secret meetings and stood ready to blacklist any actor caught agitating for a union.

Throughout this period, and into the 1920s and 1930s, working conditions were often quite poor for film actors, although the public was fed a disproportionate diet about the huge wealth and extravagant lifestyles enjoyed by the players. Such stories were more or less true but they only applied to a tiny percentage of actors, the favored few on long-term contracts with Hollywood's major studios at rates of pay that were so high as to be almost incomprehensible to the public. For the vast majority of actors the work was erratic and did not pay particularly well. Players had the extra expense of agent fees and they had to supply all of the clothing the part they had signed for demanded — not, of course, for period pieces wherein the studios supplied the period dress. Players were worked long hours and often for seven days a week. A contract stipulated a weekly rate of pay and the studio was free to work the actor for 40 hours a week over five days or 100 hours over seven days, the pay remained the same. Meal breaks were irregular and given only when it suited the producer. After a player worked a long day finishing up at, say, 11:00 P.M., the producer might inform him five minutes before he left the lot that he had to report for work again at 7:00 A.M. the next morning. There was no minimum rest period between calls to the studio. For hourly workers pay did not start until the actor arrived at the location. First he traveled to the studio and then he was transported to the location (when it was an on-location shoot). He was not considered to be at work, and on the payroll, until he arrived on the set, not when he arrived at the studio. Film extras were paid so little that they often had difficulty in paying the carfare necessary to reach the studio. Many of them walked to the studios, usually situated in

Film Actors Organize

outlying areas, setting off very early in the morning. Since a film shoot might be delayed by weather or cancelled for various reasons, they could arrive at a studio only to find they were not needed that day. They received no pay for the day and were not even reimbursed for car fare. Or they could arrive at the studio and spend hours waiting around before finally being told they would not be needed at all. Again, they received no pay, even though they had been kept on the lot for hours, and no bus fare. Those in the ranks of the players put up with such conditions because each one feared he would be blacklisted out of the industry if he complained. And there were lots more actors and hopefuls ready to step in as replacements. Even then the dream of making it in Hollywood was pervasive. A reality for Hollywood's film actors all through the period covered by this book was that most of the time most of the actors were unemployed. And it was usually a vast majority that was unemployed at any given time.

A more substantial effort was made in 1916, still in New York, to organize the players with the catalyst being a continuation of poor working conditions, especially as they applied to film extras. Those involved in the effort had talks with the American Federation of Labor and soon were taken under the wing of the White Rats. However, pressure was brought to bear on them by the agents who supplied the producers with extras, taking a middleman's extortionate share. Along with that went a fear of having the blacklist applied against any actor who was involved in union activity. A final factor was an internal dispute in the fledgling organization and within a few months the Motion Picture Extra People's Association disappeared.

Equity was accepting film players as members as early as 1917 but not with open arms or much enthusiasm; in order to become a member of the stage union a film-actor applicant had to have at least two years' experience in acting on the stage in spoken drama. With the film industry then being mostly in the Los Angeles area many of the film players, including stars, featured performers and small-role players, had no stage experience at all, let alone two years. Around the same time all of those major studios in the Hollywood area reiterated their firm desire to remain a completely open shop industry, as they battled any and all attempts to unionize any portion of their industry, whether such attempts came from creative or craft personnel. All the major newspapers in Los Angeles joined in the crusade to repel all unionization efforts.

9. Conclusion

By 1920, or shortly before, efforts to unionize actors were all centered on Hollywood and would remain so. While a couple of new groups tried to emerge their efforts were unsuccessful. Actors' Equity Association became the organization that dominated the effort to organize the film players into a union and it would remain dominant and active in pursuit of that goal over the entire decade of the 1920s, with three major efforts undertaken. The first attempt took place in 1920–1921 and began when Equity executive Frank Gillmore spent a good deal of time in Hollywood recruiting members for his association. Even then there was internal dissension as some of the new film members wanted a fully independent union of their own, chartered directly by the American Federation of Labor, as opposed to being a part of Equity. Six months later Gillmore, having been back and forth from his New York City base, continued to push for members and implied the producers would have to grant the film actors a union shop once they had recognized Equity as their bargaining agent. Then in July 1921, there was a brief strike in the film industry when some of the craft unions walked out. Pleading the actors were not then ready to walk out in support of the technical employees and that the actors' position with respect to unions was too fragile, Gillmore got the striking labor unions to agree not to ask for support from the actors. Once that was granted Gillmore retreated and left immediately for New York. Such weakness on the part of Equity led to a collapse of the association's first effort to organize the film actors.

Big stars in Hollywood were the least in need of union protection but it was also true they were necessary as members of any union that hoped to be successful. That is, the stars would have to show a willingness to sacrifice that was thought to be opposite to the egotistical and temperamental nature of the superstars of the screen. In its first effort the vast majority of Hollywood's stars were notable by their absence from Equity's membership rolls. Not much happened over the next few years, with respect to unionization. Only sporadic noises were heard. Producers, perhaps emboldened by all the failures to organize took advantage of the situation to attempt to impose salary cuts on the players and to implement speed-up rules to work the players even longer hours than in the past. Some of the abuses imposed on the film players in this period were so egregious that the state labor department of California became involved and, after investigating working conditions, established state regulations with respect

Film Actors Organize

to the working conditions of the film extras. Conditions had reached such a low level that Hollywood's major studios felt compelled to establish the Central Casting Bureau as an industry initiative to regulate working conditions for extras in the industry. One of the reasons for taking that step was to forestall even more government regulations, a constant worry to Hollywood at the time. Attempts to control and limit salaries in the period up to 1927 were not successful, as Hollywood remained its own worst enemy. Studios continued to raid each other for talent and to poach stars from one another no matter how many gentlemen's agreements they had reached; and there were many, some of the formal kind, some of the informal variety. Movie studios were prone to blame greedy actors for escalating salaries, and overall high film production costs, rather than face the fact that they, themselves, were mostly to blame. Actors in the star and featured categories benefited enormously, of course, from such studio behavior.

The last seven or so months of 1927 saw Equity make its second major attempt to organize the actors. And that attempt came in the wake of yet another try by the majors to reduce salaries. First, though, Hollywood's major studios launched what they undoubtedly saw as a pre-emptive strike. They resorted to a method long used by the capitalist class when faced with unionization efforts on the part of its workers — they established a company union. That company union was the Academy of Motion Picture Arts and Sciences (AMPAS) and was, obviously, presented as something quite different. One of its functions was to act as a sort of public relations agency, a cheerleader for Hollywood as the film industry tried to create more and more buffers between itself and the government in the hopes such efforts would deflect the government from stepping in to impose any more regulations on the industry. Hollywood then faced two major types of problems from the government and the public. One pressure was somewhat technical and did not overly involve the public, at least at an emotional level. That was anti-trust and restraint of trade allegations that came from the federal government. First raised in the middle 1920s those allegations would lead to a dramatic breakup in the industry with the majors having to sell off their cinema holdings, among other things, but that did not happen until the end of the 1940s. A second pressure involved both the government and the public in growing moral protests over the Hollywood lifestyle both in the sense of film content on the screen,

9. Conclusion

and the lifestyle, salary levels, and general goings-on of high-profile actors off-screen. Due to that pressure a so-called czar, Will Hays, was hired to supposedly fix all the moral issues (he had been formerly a high-profile politician who far from being an independent individual who would clean up the industry was merely a highly-paid minion of Hollywood's ruling elite). From that came the infamous Hays production code, the direct ancestor of the current film rating system.

Because AMPAS was set up by the major Hollywood studios and because they funded it and were an equal part of it (there were five supposedly equal branches; producers, actors, writers, directors, and technicians) it had little credibility from the start. Designed to thwart unionization efforts by writers and directors, in addition to actors, it was successful in the sense that it delayed unionization in all those three areas of the film industry for a number of years. Trade publications, such as *Variety* and *Billboard* (neither of which could be called pro-union), recognized AMPAS for what it was and sneered at it for being a company union; other publications, such as the *Los Angeles Times*, also saw it for what it was — a way to block unionization — but heaped praise on it as the answer to all the actors' problems, which were few and far between anyway, if the *Times* was to be believed. Another point that gave AMPAS away was that membership was not open to any and all film players, but was open by invitation only. With such a hand-picked selection of actors, presumably the most loyal among its ranks, AMPAS succeeded for years in dividing the actors and sowing dissension.

One month or so after AMPAS had been established the majors got together to once again announce plans to implement salary cuts, to lower overall production costs, and so on. All that was enough to re-energize Equity and in June 1927 the association asked all the creative talent in the film capital to decline to sign the proposed salary cut agreement with the producers until it could study the situation. Surprisingly, the producers own creation, AMPAS, also rebelled against the proposed cuts. Although AMPAS succeeded in delaying unionization among the actors it never was the perfect lap-dog organization the producers must have envisioned. Pressure from the actors' branch of AMPAS and from Equity caused the studios to announce at first that the salary cuts had been deferred for a month. Actually, they were really dead but by announcing a deferral the studios saved a little face. One thing that resulted from the salary cut proposal

Film Actors Organize

was a large number of actors signed up with Equity. In July an emboldened Equity submitted its demand for a union shop in Hollywood, along with demands for various improvements in working conditions. Arrogant producers, though, ignored Equity and its demands, refusing even to meet with them. As far as the producers were concerned a meeting with Equity was tantamount to recognizing the association even if all the producers did at the meeting was to dismiss all their demands and then stomp out of the room. Studios continued to point to AMPAS as the place where actors should take their grievances. Near the end of July 1927, Gillmore shocked the actors at a mass meeting when he announced that Equity's attempt to win the union shop for the players, and other demands, was being suspended temporarily. At the meeting several actors came out in support of AMPAS. The Academy had announced it was meeting one of the key demands made by the players through Equity — a standard form contract. When AMPAS declared it would issue one in the near future it was enough to maintain the support of key actor-members of AMPAS, increase the division among players, and lead to a second bitter defeat for Equity. The players who were on the executive council of the Los Angeles Equity branch were also, in most cases, members of AMPAS. A bitter Gillmore felt he had been undermined by such people but, nevertheless, advised the members at the mass meeting to support their local executives — which also happened to be the AMPAS faction.

That standard form contract was issued and went into effect at the start of 1928 and did contain many of the demands Equity had been making a few months earlier. The association had been successful in beating down the attempted salary cuts and in winning many of its demands — indirectly through AMPAS — but it had not been recognized by the producers and had suffered a second humiliating defeat. While the players had won a standard form contract the AMPAS variety of that document was seriously flawed. Equity was after a dispute settlement mechanism for its contract in the form of disinterested, binding arbitration; the AMPAS version offered no binding arbitration at all and arbitration only through itself. Thus, the producers could dictate what was arbitrated and, anyway, it was not binding. As Equity, and others, would point out over the coming year a contract, no matter how many beneficial and generous clauses it contained, was functionally useless if it lacked an efficient dispute settlement mechanism.

9. Conclusion

Equity's fortunes had fallen so low in 1928 that there was occasional talk of the actors forming a new union of their own, although nothing came of it. Attacks on the contracts, for various other reasons besides dispute settlement, intensified in 1928 to the point that AMPAS had to take a second look at the document and reword it to clear up many of the vague and ambiguous clauses, although the arbitration clause remained the same. More noises were made by Equity with respect to a return to Hollywood to try yet again to organize the players. Nothing much happened although the association did mail out a questionnaire to its Hollywood members near the end of 1928 in an effort to gauge support. In its past efforts Equity had felt it had been called to the film capital, that it arrived and expended considerable time and energy in trying to organize the players only to be let down and disappointed by those same actors who all seemed to get cold feet and back away at the most crucial times. That questionnaire tried to ascertain whether the majority of players would really be behind the association if it showed up once more to fight for the players. In May 1929 Equity had a standard form contract of its own prepared and ready for actors' use; it was similar to the one used by the group's theatrical stage members. Early in June 1929 Gillmore returned to the west coast. It had been rumored that this marked the start of yet another assault by Equity, but so many similar rumors had made the rounds from time to time over the years that nobody paid much attention to that one.

Without any prior warning, Equity's Frank Gillmore announced on June 5, 1929, that henceforth actors in the association could not appear in sound films unless the casts of such films were 100 percent Equity and contracts signed after that date had to be on Equity's standard form film contract. Other demands were also made at that time as Gillmore kicked off Equity's third attempt to organize the film players and to win recognition and a first contract from Hollywood's film cartel. By far that attempt was the association's most intense and vigorous campaign. Although some observers referred to the action as a strike it was not since actors were never instructed to walk out en masse from the studios. Initially the producers adopted the strategy they had used in the past; they ignored the association and its demands completely. As well, the producers maintained a strict media silence, officially. Once again Gillmore was in Hollywood and once again he would be there for months. Los Angeles newspapers quickly adopted the position of refusing to give any space to Equity statements or press releases. While they allowed anti–Equity statements, often unfounded, to be made in their pages they never allowed the association to respond to, or rebut, those allegations. Many of Hollywood's biggest stars turned up one by one in the pages of those newspapers to denounce the union and to wonder why it had come to Hollywood in the first place. As before, Equity's support came mostly from the lower-paid players, stars remained hard to find among the association members. Time passed but very little happened. Equity had nothing to offer the extras, and was even slow in coming up with a standard form of contract for such players. As well, Gillmore seemed to have no real strategy in mind, despite the lessons of previous defeats, all led by Gillmore. Actor after actor defied Equity's demand that no player sign up on studio-form contracts and did that very thing. Producers delighted in seeing the names of such players were published in weekly lists in the trade press and they soon mounted, apparently, into the hundreds. After doing nothing at all about the situation Gillmore began to denounce the lists as containing names of players who were not Equity members. Yet many were, and Equity seemed to have no response. Mass meetings were held in Hollywood by Gillmore on a weekly basis, presumably to keep the players emotionally involved. But even among the faction loyal to the union chief to the end came questions as to what was the strategy Equity was going to use to win its demands. Gillmore never had any answer. A faction of players loyal to AMPAS continued to sow dissension. With little or no way to get its side of the story aired — due to a newspaper blackout — Equity was forced to buy radio air time in an attempt to tell its side of the story, besides issuing a small news sheet the union distributed. This dispute became heated enough that it attracted national media attention as some observers felt an actor walkout was almost inevitable.

More and more money was spent by the union as time passed and no progress was made. Behind the scenes Gillmore worked hard to try and line up a promise of physical support from film industry craft unions and from other federated labor bodies both locally and nationally. However, he could never get more than a promise of moral support from them, perhaps not surprising since Equity had never extended that type of support to any film industry craft union during any of their strikes. After eight weeks of action by Equity nothing had been gained by the union. Not only had the producers refused to recognize Equity or to negotiate with

9. Conclusion

the association but hundreds of Equity members had defied the association's injunction to refuse to sign any film contract that was not an Equity document.

At that point Ethel Barrymore entered and became the catalyst for a series of several secret meetings between Equity and the studios. It was a change of heart by the producers and reflected a worry on their part (unfounded as it turned out) that federated labor bodies in America might be able to order, and successfully bring off, a labor boycott that might hurt the box office take. Misunderstandings and misinterpretations between Barrymore (an icon of the stage, and screen to a lesser extent, she was still held in high regard by unionists because of her pro-Equity activities during the 1919 theatrical stage strike in New York City) and Gillmore led to the pair making public, personal attacks on each other. More internal dissension was the last thing Equity needed but it was what it received. In the face of that final straw, the lack of physical support from other unions, the apparent absence of a coherent strategy to press its demands, the lack of major stars behind Equity, and its continued fragile state, Equity's third attempt to organize the players suddenly collapsed not long after the Barrymore/Gillmore row became public. In a terse statement on August 17, Gillmore declared the order to Equity members not to sign contracts on anything but an Equity form was suspended. Despite that third humiliating defeat many observers felt the association would ultimately prevail; that it was only a matter of time. Even Equity executives seemed to share that view, even if they had no idea when or how that victory might occur. In the few years that followed there would be a report here or there that the union was preparing yet another assault on the film capital but it was all over for Equity. They would never be a factor or a force in Hollywood again. Another problem the union had never dealt with, or every apparently acknowledged, was the geographical factor. Although it made perfect sense for a union of stage players to be headquartered in New York City, it made much less sense for a union of film players, the bulk of whom lived and worked in the Los Angeles area, to be in a union that had all of its executives, and headquarters in New York City. As well, by this time Equity had achieved a pariah status among the studios. Its very name fired the anti-union film cartel into a frenzy. That same kind of pariah status had dogged the old vaudeville White Rats union to such an extent that for the last dozen or so years of its existence — only in a skeletal form

Film Actors Organize

then — it had to actually drop the name White Rats completely and adopt another. That geographical divide perhaps played a part in Gillmore and other Equity executives, all living in the New York area, misreading the mood on the west coast as to whether or not the Hollywood players were ready to organize and what they could be counted on to do. All too often they did little except to develop cold feet at the most inappropriate times. Of course, none of that explained Equity's seemingly complete lack of strategy once its executives were in Hollywood. A weakness in the players and a reluctance by them to display solidarity might have been overcome at least to some extent by a strong leadership with a well developed action plan in place. But a weak membership commanded by a befuddled leadership was a formula for disaster. Equity's role in Hollywood was effectively finished on that August night in 1929, except to drag its feet a bit when SAG sought to stand as an independent union, rather than being an affiliate, or part, of Equity.

Stepping into the Equity void, AMPAS in 1930 quickly issued a new standard studio form contract for actors, one that incorporated many of the demands made by Equity in 1929. Again, it was done to forestall any future efforts Equity might have had in mind. By that time, the Depression had taken firm hold of America and the producers used that as a reason to announce, again, that efficiencies were needed in the industry, and so on, if it was to survive. Always emboldened in the wake of a union's failed organizing efforts, the producers declared that one of those efficiencies would be a reduction in actors' salaries. Finally, in March 1933, a dramatic salary reduction of 25 percent to 50 percent to last for eight weeks and to be applied to all studio personnel was announced. However, once again a storm of protest arose and the cuts were not implemented. For one thing, cuts could not be unilaterally imposed on the industry's craft people because most of them were in unions and had contracts that could not be unilaterally tampered with. Cuts could be unilaterally imposed on actors, writers, and directors, however, because none of them were organized and those AMPAS contracts they labored under always meant whatever it was the producers wanted them to mean. It was one more object lesson for the actors to be exposed to; the unorganized were very weak and vulnerable if and when the capitalist class decided to impose draconian measures.

One more such example came to the players in the period 1933 to 1935 when the government's NRA was in existence, as part of President

9. Conclusion

Franklin Roosevelt's efforts to blunt the worst effects of the Depression. Every industry had to generate its own industrial code and every union that legitimately represented the majority of workers in its area got a seat at the table for its industry when all sides sat down to bargain and establish minimum wages, maximum hours of work, and so on. In the end the NRA was declared unconstitutional by the United States Supreme Court and faded away but the film players were once again confronted by their weakness because they were unorganized. Equity sat down at the table with the theatrical producers and participated fully in drafting the NRA industrial code for the theatrical stage industry. However, when the film producers negotiated the film code they sat down with no actors' representatives except ones from their own creation, the company union AMPAS. By that time AMPAS had no credibility among actors, except for a small number of hard-core loyalists. Later in the code process SAG representatives replaced the ousted AMPAS people but by then the NRA was almost finished. Once the NRA was gone many of its principles were installed in what came to be known as the Wagner Act and made it easier for workers to become unionized and harder for employers to refuse to negotiate for no reason. That is, the economic forces of the early 1930s, with no direct relationship to the film industry were making it easier for unorganized workers to organize and to negotiate with their employers. At the same time it was becoming increasingly difficult for the film cartel to arrogantly pretend a union wasn't there. As well, the regular attempts to cut salaries, though unsuccessful due to the producers' own greed and their unwillingness to trust each other, and the ease with which the film producers got what they wanted in the NRA code made the organization of actors more likely. Screenwriters and directors also formed their own film industry unions at roughly the same time as the actors, for many of the same reasons.

The Screen Actors' Guild was formed over the period of May to July 1933 but lay dormant until October of that year when a new leadership group stepped in to take over the name and the charter of the group and to give it a new energy. It was as if a new union had formed in October. Actors left AMPAS in large numbers to join SAG; many of the new members were the stars that were perceived as being necessary to any actors' union in Hollywood that hoped for success. As a first order of business SAG wanted to affiliate with the American Federation of Labor directly

Film Actors Organize

and stand as an independent union, as Equity did. The latter dragged its heels for a short time as it tried to get the new group to be a part of itself, to be an affiliate of Equity. However, with the track record that it had in the film capital it could not hold out for long and soon it relinquished any claim on the new group, ceding its jurisdiction over film actors to SAG, although it was a recallable grant of jurisdiction, on four months notice. At the end of summer in 1936 the Wagner Act was awaiting its constitutional challenge and would soon be declared legal. Actors had flocked out of AMPAS and into SAG, despite another new contract that had been put forward by AMPAS as the cartel used its old gambit in an effort to stave off unionization. It was just about time for the players to try again.

A delay took place that stalled SAG action until the spring of 1937 when a producer labor agreement with a number of their craft unions expired. Known as the basic agreement, it usually ran for five years but was reopened year by year, on demand of either party, to readjust wages, but not to alter the general basic agreement. One of the craft unions, the Painters, was out of the basic agreement as it attempted to extend its jurisdiction. Those outside occupations, such as makeup artists and hairdressers, the Painters, and SAG remained outside that basic agreement as the other craft unions reached a new agreement. At the end of April the Painters, SAG, and some 15 other crafts announced they had formed the Federated Motion Picture Crafts (FMPC) and were on strike against the studios. Initially, only a few of the craft unions went out on strike with the other groups, including SAG, having to wait until mass meetings were held, the situation explained to the membership and a strike vote taken. SAG members continued to work and to cross picket lines with their leadership taking the easy way out and announcing it was up to its members to determine individually if their conscience allowed them to cross the picket lines. That FMPC strike would slowly peter out over time as it was beset by internal dissension, not the least of which was another industry union — IATSE, who had signed the new pact with the other craft unions still in the basic agreement — acting as a strikebreaker.

While the striking FMPC unions expressed in public confidence SAG would join them in the strike it did not turn out that way. First of all, the SAG mass meeting to vote for or against going on strike was deferred for one week. That deferral had been made in order to hold negotiations with the producers, who finally realized the inevitable must happen. Just hours

9. Conclusion

before the deferred meeting was to be held it was announced that a working agreement had been reached between the studios and SAG, with only the language and some small details to be worked out. Among the more important points won by the actors in the 10-year agreement was the closed shop, actually a 90/10 shop for stars and featured players for the first five years of the pact and then a 100 percent union shop for that category in the second five years; a 100 percent closed shop prevailed for all other categories of players, at least on films shot within 300 miles of Los Angeles.

And so, in 1937, SAG had achieved union recognition from the producers as the sole bargaining agent of the players and it had achieved a first contract with the film cartel. It did, however, draw a certain amount of criticism for the lack of support it extended to the striking FMPC unions. Nevertheless, by 1937 the notoriously anti-union film industry, operating in the equally notorious anti-union city of Los Angeles, in the notoriously anti-union state of California, was finally fully unionized. With the screenwriters and the film directors having organized at roughly the same time as the film players, every occupational grouping in the film world had a union in place.

Notes

Chapter 1

1. "Photoplay actors fail to form new organization." *Variety*, July 25, 1913, p. 8.
2. *Ibid.*
3. "Extras forming union for mutual protection." *Variety*, August 25, 1916, p. 20.
4. *Ibid.*
5. "Supers call mass meeting and arrange for a charter." *Variety*, September 1, 1916, p. 13.
6. *Ibid.*
7. "Row in extras' association." *Variety*, November 3, 1916, p. 23.
8. "A.E.A. film membership." *Variety*, December 21, 1917, p 50.
9. "Unionists plan to shackle film workers flat failure." *Los Angeles Times*, August 20, 1916, sec 2, p. 1.
10. "Howl for help in movieland." *Los Angeles Times*, February 11, 1917, sec 3, p. 1.
11. "Films firm for the open shop." *Los Angeles Times*, August 31, 1918, sec 2, pp. 1, 7.
12. "Agitators busy." *Los Angeles Times*, September 16, 1918, sec 2, p. 6.
13. "Film actors' union." *Los Angeles Times*, November 13, 1918, p. 9.
14. "M. P. players' union gets separate Four A's charter." *Billboard*, February 7, 1920, p. 5.
15. "Equity absorbs M.P.P.A." *Variety*, April 2, 1920, p. 96.
16. "Doubts Equity strike." *New York Times*, November 1, 1920, p. 16.
17. "Equity may absorb coast film actors' association." *Variety*, January 21, 1921, p. 45.
18. "New York picture folks would break with Equity." *Variety*, February 11, 1921, p. 1.
19. "Los Angeles film players look for 100% Equity casts." *Variety*, March 25, 1921, p. 46.
20. "Remedy in friendly dealing." *Variety*, April 29, 1921, p. 47.
21. "General strike." *Variety*, July 22, 1921, p. 39.
22. *Ibid.*

183

Notes. Chapter 2

23. "Equity's M. P. branch finds rival in Film Players' Club." *Variety*, February 17, 1922, p. 46.
24. "Equity's picture branch closed in New York." *Variety*, November 17, 1922, p. 46.

Chapter 2

1. "Equity starting after picture field." *Variety*, June 4, 1924, p. 19.
2. "Film producers on coast agree not to raise salaries." *Variety*, June 25, 1924, p. 1.
3. "Speeding up film productions but overworking actors." *Variety*, July 23, 1924, p. 20.
4. "Equity's standard form of contract handed to Hays upon leaving L.A." *Variety*, August 6, 1924, p. 19.
5. *Ibid.*, pp. 19, 43.
6. *Ibid.*, p. 43.
7. "Railroading actors ends." *Variety*, September 17, 1924, pp. 1, 53.
8. "Extras steamed up against U manager." *Variety*, October 8, 1924, p. 20.
9. "10 per centers for extras noticed." *Variety*, January 28, 1925, p. 30.
10. "Rush by producers to sign players for 1925." *Variety*, March 4, 1925, p. 27.
11. "Extras' agents and commish all through." *Variety*, March 25, 1925, p. 1.
12. "Equity collected $90,000 due actors." *New York Times*, June 2, 1925, p. 7.
13. "Extra people in Hollywood." *Variety*, October 21, 1925, p. 26.
14. "Regulating extras." *Variety*, January 20, 1926, p. 29.
15. "Extras in movies to be considered." *Fresno Bee*, December 11, 1925, p. 25.
16. "Movie vagrants to be eliminated." *Fresno Bee*, January 25, 1926, p. 4.
17. "Hays begins clean-up of Hollywood today." *New York Times*, January 25, 1926, p. 22.
18. "Hays back." *Variety*, February 3, 1926, p. 29.
19. "22,500 idle at Hollywood." *Variety*, June 9, 1926, p. 1.
20. *Ibid.*, pp. 1, 18.
21. "2,300 out of 3,500 extras in Eastern films don't belong." *Variety*, July 7, 1926, p. 1.
22. "Average daily earning of Hollywood extras—$8.64." *Variety*, July 7, 1926, pp. 1, 12.
23. "Amusement people head list of white collar labor unions." *Variety*, August 18, 1926, p. 1.
24. "Franchising film agencies." *Variety*, August 18, 1926, p. 43.
25. "Picture actors asking for franchise booking office." *Variety*, January 19, 1927, p. 8.
26. "K.-A. contract clause can tie up all acts' screen services." *Variety*, April 27, 1927, pp. 1, 31.
27. "Easing out bad actors." *Variety*, October 6, 1926, p. 1.
28. "Studio strike situation." *Variety*, November 17, 1926, pp. 5, 18.
29. "Settlement of union demand may be reached in time." *Variety*, November 24, 1926, p. 13.
30. "More picture extras." *Variety*, January 19, 1927, pp. 1, 9.
31. "No more doubling by soldiers as extras." *Variety*, March 23, 1927, p. 1.

Chapter 3

1. "Closed shop and the stage." *Los Angeles Times*, March 27, 1927, p. B4.
2. "Academy of film art is started by industry." *Washington Post*, May 5, 1927, p. 4.
3. Felicia Pearson. "Chats on stage and screen folk." *Washington Post*, May 8, 1927, p. F3.
4. "Mary Pickford on A.M.P.A.S." *Variety*, May 18, 1927, p. 9.
5. *Ibid.*, pp. 9, 18.
6. "Tearle's issue up to Academy against M.P.P." *Variety*, June 8, 1927, p. 12.
7. "Regulating Hollywood." *Variety*, June 15, 1927, pp. 5, 8.
8. "Film actors and Equity again on the coast." *Variety*, June 22, 1927, p. 5.
9. "Actors' Equity urges delay in wage cut." *Washington Post*, June 27, 1927, p. 5.
10. "War now looming on movie pay cut." *New York Times*, June 28, 1927, p. 29.
11. "Cuts so far, $350,000 weekly." *Variety*, June 29, 1927, p. 5.
12. "Film workers win delay on cuts in salary." *Christian Science Monitor*, July 1, 1927, p. 5A.
13. "Salary cutting fluke." *Variety*, July 6, 1927, pp. 1, 17.
14. "Salary cutting may lead to Equity organizing picture actors on coast." *Variety*, July 6, 1927, p. 4.
15. "Is the Academy up-stage." *Variety*, July 6, 1927, p. 12.
16. "700 film players at meeting vote to join Equity." *Fresno Bee*, July 7, 1927, p. 4.
17. "Equity snares film players." *Los Angeles Times*, July 7, 1927, p. A1.
18. "Film industry rent by clash." *Los Angeles Times*, July 8, 1927, p. A1.
19. "Hollywood a closed shop." *Los Angeles Times*, July 11, 1927, p. A4.
20. *Ibid.*
21. "Equity gaining strength in motion picture ranks." *Billboard*, July 16, 1927, p. 6.
22. Wood Soanes. "Curtain calls." *Oakland Tribune*, July 13, 1927, p. 20.
23. "Salary cut flop may take Equity into coast studios." *Variety*, July 13, 1927, pp. 4, 15.
24. "The Los Angeles spirit." *Los Angeles Times*, July 15, 1927 p. A4.
25. *Ibid.*
26. "Producers unlikely to give Equity recognition in Hollywood studios." *Variety*, July 20, 1927, p. 9.
27. "Stars' salaries and ages." *Variety*, July 27, 1927, pp. 5, 11.
28. "Extra day averages $8.18." *Variety*, July 13, 1927, pp. 1, 24.
29. "Studios win over Equity." *Variety*, July 27, 1927, p. 9.
30. *Ibid.*, p. 10.
31. *Ibid.*
32. "Film actors pass up chance to get organized protection." *Billboard*, July 30, 1927, pp. 5, 105.
33. "Film stars' pay uncut; temperament given up." *Washington Post*, July 30, 1927, p. 3.
34. "A.F. of L. brands Academy as producers' company-union." *Billboard*, August 1, 1927, p. 9.
35. "Film stars facing pay cut or eclipse." *Washington Post*, August 17, 1927, p. 16.

Notes. Chapter 4

36. "Academy takes up matter of actors' standard contract." *Variety*, September 28, 1927, p. 5.
37. "Mayer's resolutions and don'ts; actors without representation." *Variety*, October 12, 1927, p. 5.
38. "Producer resolutions." *Variety*, October 19, 1927, p. 26
39. "Uniform system charging 3 weeks' salary for farming." *Variety*, October 19, 1927, p. 25.
40. "11,000 film extras on coast average $6,556 daily payroll." *Variety*, October 26, 1927, p. 5.
41. "Movie chiefs deny plan to cut salaries." *New York Times*, November 16, 1927, p. 2.
42. "Too many picture actors." *Variety*, November 30, 1927, p. 1.
43. "Coast not dealing with Actors' Equity on contract." *Variety*, December 7, 1927, p. 4.
44. "Equity scraps coast committee, seemingly gives up pictures." *Variety*, December 14, 1927, pp. 1, 39.
45. "Equity dissolves movie committee." *New York Times*, December 15, 1927, p. 33.
46. "Hollywood stars." *Washington Post*, December 19, 1927, p. 5.
47. "Actors form of contract." *Variety*, December 21, 1927, p. 9.
48. "Contract actors not subject to standard form contracts." *Variety*, December 28, 1927, p. 9.
49. "42,546 coast studio workers make 82% of world's supply." *Variety*, January 11, 1928, p. 1.

Chapter 4

1. "New actors' ass'n forms on coast." *Variety*, January 11, 1928, p. 3.
2. "New film contract exposed by Equity." *New York Times*, January 17, 1928, p. 23.
3. "Studios' average pay." *Variety*, February 1, 1928, p. 3.
4. "Extras' high daily average in '27." *Variety*, February 1, 1928, p. 5.
5. "Equity's coast branch voting for new advisory board." *Variety*, February 8, 1928, p. 9.
6. "Hersholt's contract may be bought by MGM." *Variety*, February 8, 1928, p. 9.
7. "Free lance contract back for revision." *Variety*, February 22, 1928, p. 4.
8. "Revised standard contract form accepted." *Variety*, March 21, 1928, p. 15.
9. "Equity plans new drive due to sound." *Variety*, June 13, 1928, p. 5.
10. "Equity expects 100% members of picture colony players within month, due to talkers." *Variety*, July 4, 1928, p. 5.
11. "Equity will warn members to watch talkie contracts." *Billboard*, July 14, 1928, p. 4.
12. "Wealthy tourists, acting as extras." *Variety*, October 3, 1928, p. 5.
13. "33% of film actors are out." *Variety*, October 10, 1928, pp. 1, 56.
14. "Coast extras burning up over studios' alleged labor violations." *Variety*, October 24, 1928, p. 15.
15. "Union invasion of film nears." *Los Angeles Times*, November 22, 1928, p. A1.

16. "Equity making preparations to organize talkie field." *Billboard*, November 24, 1928, pp. 3, 89.
17. "Coast extras cut down." *Variety*, January 16, 1929, p. 7.
18. "A picture players' union." *New York Times*, March 16, 1929, p. 12.
19. "Secrecy surrounds Equity plans in talkie campaign." *Billboard*, April 20, 1929, p. 3.
20. "Equity's film contract on the way." *Variety*, May 22, 1929, p. 4.
21. "4,000 actors for 600 jobs on coast." *Variety*, May 22, 1929, p. 4.

Chapter 5

1. "Equity shop starts now." *Variety*, June 5, 1929, pp. 5, 50, 55.
2. "Equity defied by movie producers." *Fresno Bee*, June 6, 1929, p. 5.
3. "Movie producers defy Actors' Equity." *New York Times*, June 7, 1929, p. 32.
4. "Equity shop in talkies." *Billboard*, June 8, 1929, pp. 3–4.
5. "The answer to Equity." *Los Angeles Times*, June 8, 1929, p. A4.
6. "Barrymore decries closed film shop." *New York Times*, June 10, 1929, p. 3.
7. "Mack scores closed shop." *New York Times*, June 11, 1929, p. 34.
8. "Equity's picture list." *Variety*, June 12, 1929, p. 4.
9. "Inside stuff—pictures." *Variety*, June 12, 1929, p. 53.
10. "Use around 700 screen credit players at peak." *Variety*, June 12, 1929, p. 5.
11. "Opposing forces on coast lining up silently for offense and defense ends." *Variety*, June 12, 1929, p. 5.
12. "Equity-studio matter." *Variety*, June 12, 1929, p. 5.
13. *Ibid.*, pp. 5, 34.
14. "Wait next step in talkie shop." *Billboard*, June 15, 1929, pp. 3, 15.
15. "Gillmore gets aid by Powers for Equity." *New York Times*, June 13, 1929, p. 35.
16. "Gilbert joins Equity foes." *Los Angeles Times*, June 13, 1929, p. A12.
17. "Protest Equity film move." *New York Times*, June 15, 1929, p. 22.
18. "Miss Bow can't emote by clock." *Los Angeles Times*, June 15, 1929, p. A6.
19. "Equity actors win skirmish as battle of movies begins." *Washington Post*, June 18, 1929, p. 11.
20. "100 Equity actors now under old studio form contract." *Variety*, June 19, 1926, pp 4–5.
21. "English actor is first Equity coast suspension." *Variety*, June 19, 1929, p. 5.
22. "Equity's meeting on coast Monday not so hot." *Variety*, June 19, 1929, p. 5.
23. "Coast's quiet battle." *Variety*, June 19, 1929, pp. 5, 52.
24. "Green offers aid to Equity in talkies." *New York Times*, June 20, 1929, p. 26.
25. "Labor ready to aid Equity in talkie fight." *Billboard*, June 22, 1929, pp. 3, 89.
26. "Unionizing the movies." *Washington Post*, June 22, 1929, p. 6.
27. "Actors defy Equity on movie contracts." *New York Times*, June 22, 1929, p. 3.
28. Lillian Albertson. "Equity's chief draws censure." *Los Angeles Times*, June 23, 1929, p. 8.
29. "Equity ballot not sent to them, say members." *Variety*, June 26, 1929, p. 6.

Notes. Chapter 5

30. "More Equityites sign old form studio contracts since June 18." *Variety*, June 26, 1929, p. 6.
31. "Stand against Gillmore." *Variety*, June 26, 1929, pp. 7, 29.
32. "3d Equity rally on coast draws crowd." *Variety*, June 26, 1929, p. 7.
33. "Equity considering calling its contract players out of studios." *Variety*, June 26, 1929, p. 7.
34. "Green backs Equity in film conflict." *New York Times*, June 27, 1929, p. 24.
35. "Film folk row at session of EQ program." *Modesto News-Herald*, June 27, 1929, p. 9.
36. "Equity's coast meetings." *Variety*, July 3, 1929, p. 6.
37. "Campaign plan urgent need of Equity." *Variety*, July 3, 1929, p. 6.
38. "Discounts for actors for food and gas." *Variety*, July 3, 1929, p. 7.
39. "Equity in strange position in deadlock with film producers." *Variety*, July 3, 1929, p. 7.
40. "26 pictures now in works." *Variety*, July 3, 1929, p. 7.
41. "Official out." *Variety*, July 3, 1929, p. 8.
42. "Studio noises when suspended actors on stage." *Variety*, July 3, 1929, p. 8.
43. "More Equityites sign old form studio contracts since June 25." *Variety*, July 3, 1929, p. 8.
44. "Urge loyalty and obedience at 4th Equity rally." *Variety*, July 3, 1929, p. 8.
45. "Organization of indie film producers looms as Equity possibility in East." *Billboard*, July 6, 1929, pp, 3, 86.
46. "DeMille says actors suffer." *Los Angeles Times*, July 5, 1929, p. A3.
47. "Green on organization." *Los Angeles Times*, July 6, 1929, p. A4.
48. "F. X. Bushman in tilt in Equity movie row." *New York Times*, July 7, 1929, p. 18.
49. "New contract — no Equity." *Variety*, July 10, 1929, pp. 1, 21.
50. "Equity rift out west explained by N.Y. actors now coast defenders." *Variety*, July 10, 1929, p. 7.
51. "Actors balk at 10% of salary for fund." *Variety*, July 10, 1929, p. 7.
52. "Equity not asking extras to join at this time." *Variety*, July 10, 1929, p. 7.
53. "Producers admit 200 refused work since Equity fight." *Variety*, July 10, 1929, p. 7.
54. "Bushman-Silvernail clash." *Variety*, July 10, 1929, pp. 7, 21.
55. "Equity campaign gains momentum." *Billboard*, July 13, 1929, pp. 3, 86–87.
56. "Equity orders film strike." *New York Times*, July 10, 1929, p. 14.
57. "Extras stay on job; no Hollywood strike." *New York Times*, July 12, 1929, p. 28.
58. "Equity in Hollywood." *New York Times*, July 12, 1929, p. 14.
59. "Government mediator enters Equity-film producers fight." *Billboard*, July 20, 1929, pp. 3, 86–87.
60. "Small part Equity players turn to fruit picking." *Variety*, July 17, 1929, p. 7.
61. "Compromise reports, chorus girls' walkout." *Variety*, July 17, 1929, p. 7.
62. "Equity broadcasts." *Variety*, July 17, 1929, p. 7.
63. "Equity mass meeting hears Academy, Casting Co., denounced." *Variety*, July 17, 1929, p. 7.
64. Somerset Logan. "Revolt in Hollywood." *The Nation* 129 (July 17, 1929): 61–62.
65. *Ibid.*, p. 62.

Notes. Chapter 5

66. "Equity asks actors to finance film fight." *New York Times*, July 23, 1929, p. 32.
67. "Turning tables by Equity in injunction." *Variety*, July 24, 1929, p. 6.
68. "Equity appeals for funds on radio." *Variety*, July 24, 1929, p. 7.
69. "1,500 volunteers on coast for Equity." *Variety*, July 24, 1929, p. 7.
70. "Equity's $4,500 weekly." *Variety*, July 24, 1929, p. 7
71. *Ibid.*, p. 42.
72. "Equity's first big threat." *Billboard*, July 27, 1929, p. 3.
73. "Weekly studio production." *Variety*, July 31, 1929, p. 6.
74. "Preparedness." *Variety*, July 31, 1929, p. 6.
75. "Equity plans own casting office." *Variety*, July 31, 1929, p. 7.
76. Somerset Logan. "The battle of Hollywood." *The New Republic* 59 (August 7, 1929): 308–309.
77. "Movie men agree to Equity parley." *New York Times*, August 2, 1929, p. 21.
78. "Calls film stars unfair." *New York Times*, August 5, 1929, p. 24.
79. "Compromise in Equity fight in films sought." *Oakland Tribune*, August 5, 1929, p. 12.
80. "Peace pact is likely." *Variety*, August 7, 1929, p. 191.
81. "Film producers yield to pressure by labor." *Billboard*, August 10, 1929, pp. 3, 7.
82. "Boycott and blacklist on." *Los Angeles Times*, August 6, 1929, pp. A1-A2.
83. "Ethel Barrymore says Gillmore misled meeting." *Fresno Bee*, August 12, 1929, p. 2.
84. "Ethel Barrymore opposes Gillmore." *New York Times*, August 13, 1929, p. 29.
85. "Two factions in Equity.' *Variety*, August 14, 1929, pp. 1, 27.
86. *Ibid.*, p. 27.
87. "Labor unions uncommitted to Equity." *Variety*, August 14, 1929, p. 6.
88. "Equity's 80–20 proposal is rejected by producers." *Variety*, August 17, 1929, pp. 3, 85.
89. "100% Equity always, says Ethel Barrymore." *Variety*, August 14, 1929, p. 6.
90. "Two big actors go non-Equity." *Variety*, August 14, 1929, p. 7.
91. "Equity badly whipped." *Variety*, August 21, 1929, pp. 1, 54.
92. "Equity suspends film fight." *Billboard*, August 24, 1929, pp. 3, 85.
93. "Equity's setback." *New York Times*, August 20, 1929, p. 21.
94. "DeMille elated by Equity decision." *New York Times*, August 21, 1929, p. 30.
95. "Unionism in filmland." *The Nation* 129 (August 28, 1929): 211.
96. "Gillmore ascribes defeat to threats." *New York Times*, August 27, 1929, p. 36.
97. "Equity defers action on Ethel Barrymore." *New York Times*, August 28, 1929, p. 28.
98. "Equity actors return to work in film studios." *Billboard*, August 31, 1929, p. 101.
99. "Studio labor survey." *Variety*, January 8, 1930, p. 91.
100. Simon Louvish. *Cecil B. DeMille and the Golden Calf*. London: Faber and Faber, 2007, p. 297.
101. "Retreat from Hollywood." *The Outlook and Independent* 153 (September 4, 1929): 13.

Chapter 6

1. "Academy handled 27 complaints in '29; 19 from actors." *Variety*, January 15, 1930, p. 11.
2. "Coast actors' own group." *Variety*, January 29, 1930, pp. 9–10.
3. "Hollywood moves to check Equity." *New York Times*, February 7, 1930, p. 28.
4. "12-hour rest period assures film players protection." *Variety*, February 12 1930, p. 10.
5. "Equity wipes out strike ban." *Billboard*, April 5, 1930, p. 5.
6. "Gillmore again nominated; Ethel Barrymore dropped." *Billboard*, April 19, 1930, p. 4.
7. "Equity may invade." *Billboard*, May 31, 1930, p. 3.
8. "Equity's next for film." *Variety*, June 25, 1930, pp. 101, 104.
9. "Economy in film colony." *Variety*, August 27, 1930, pp. 3, 76.
10. "Useless extras pile in." *Variety*, November 12, 1930, p. 3.
11. "Lower film player salaries." *Variety*, December 24, 1930, p. 5.
12. "Actors approve Academy contract as trial year ends." *Variety*, January 28, 1931, p. 4.
13. "Newer and cheaper stars." *Variety*, May 13, 1931, pp. 1, 34.
14. "Producers tying up actors to cover all work by 4-way contract." *Variety*, May 20, 1931, p. 2.
15. "Studio cuts and outs." *Variety*, May 27, 1931, pp. 3, 32.
16. "Salary cuts — good films." *Variety*, May 27, 1931, p. 5.
17. "New stars much cheaper." *Variety*, September 1, 1931, p. 3.
18. "Equity's 3rd film attack." *Variety*, October 20, 1931, p. 3.
19. "Equity says picture and B'way actors are both overpaid." *Variety*, November 3, 1931, p. 6.
20. "Coast secret meeting." *Variety*, December 1, 1931, pp. 3, 42.
21. "$5,000,000 salary cut." *Variety*, December 22, 1931, p. 3.
22. "Film mob's toughest year." *Variety*, February 9, 1932, pp. 1, 21.
23. "Actors vigorously protest producers' agreement in first Academy session." *Variety*, April 5, 1932, p. 3.
24. "Waiver system for stars." *Variety*, May 17, 1932, p. 5.
25. "Movie industry slashes all pay." *New York Times*, March 9, 1933, p. 19.
26. "Majority of players accept film pay cuts." *New York Times*, March 10, 1933, p. 18.
27. "No production shut-down." *Variety*, March 14, 1933, p. 25.
28. "Movie plants shut over union wage." *New York Times*, March 13, 1933, p. 14.
29. "Hollywood goes back to work." *New York Times*, March 19, 1933, sec 10, p. 3.
30. "Sees no closed studios." *New York Times*, March 23, 1933, p. 13.
31. "New players' union move." *Variety*, March 28, 1933, pp. 1, 48.
32. "Nagel no longer head of Academy." *New York Times*, April 21, 1933, p. 24.
33. "M.P. Academy-producer split in open over service bureau." *Billboard*, April 29, 1933, p. 4.
34. "Slim pickin' in Hollywood." *Variety*, May 9, 1933, p. 7.
35. "Actors largest Academy branch." *Billboard*, May 27, 1933, p. 5.

Notes. Chapter 7

Chapter 7

1. "Actors under new law." *Billboard*, July 1, 1933, pp. 3, 63.
2. "Anti-Academy ex-stage actor forming closed shop coast union similar to Equity setup." *Variety*, July 25, 1933, pp. 5, 29; George Frazier. "Nobody pushes Bob around." *Collier's* 123 (June, 4, 1949); 25.
3. "Actors organizing." *Billboard*, August 19, 1933, pp. 5, 55.
4. "Academy-producers-agents' pact." *Variety*, August 29, 1933, p. 7.
5. "Actors demand NRA guarantee on year round bidding for jobs." *Variety*, September 5, 1933, p. 2.
6. "Trickery hurled at agents' move." *Variety*, September 12, 1933, p. 7
7. "Sweat shop charge of penny-ante pay takes extras' plight to code." *Variety*, September 12, 1933, p. 7.
8. "AMPAS is socked." *Billboard*, September 23, 1933, p. 5.
9. "New film-actor group." *Variety*, October 3, 1933, p. 7.
10. "Film actors quit Academy over code." *New York Times*, October 3, 1933, p. 26.
11. "Actors Guild to fight cuts." *Oakland Tribune*, October 9, 1933, p. 5.
12. "Cantor gives reasons for Actors' Guild." *Oakland Tribune*, October 11, 1933, p. 11.
13. "Hollywood's open shop." *Variety*, October 3, 1933, p. 11.
14. "Picture actors wise up." *Billboard*, October 14, 1933, pp. 3, 10.
15. "100% Screen Actors' Guild." *Variety*, October 10, 1933, p. 7.
16. "Supporting players and pic extras get organization fever." *Variety*, October 31, 1933, p. 7.
17. "Studio players plenty het up over the code." *Variety*, October 17, 1933, p. 7.
18. "Screen Guild builds." *Billboard*, October 21, 1933, p. 5.
19. "Movie Guild opens doors to extras." *New York Times*, October 27, 1933, p. 22.
20. "A Chinese army." *Billboard*, November 4, 1933, p. 26.
21. "Actors Guild denies union." *Billboard*, November 18, 1933, p. 4.
22. "Screen Actors Guild asserts it doesn't want AFL or Equity ties." *Variety*, November 21, 1933, p. 5.
23. "Screen Actors' Guild sets back election." *Variety*, March 27, 1934, p. 2.
24. "Cantor slams pix Academy." *Billboard*, May 26, 1934, pp. 3–4.
25. "Screen Guild closed shop." *Billboard*, September 22, 1934, pp. 3, 16.
26. "Hollywood extra list being pruned from 17,000 to 2,500." *Billboard*, September 29, 1934, p. 3.
27. "Hollywood to control." *New York Times*, October 21, 1934, p. 33.
28. "Picture Guild nixes NRA." *Variety*, October 23, 1934, pp 3, 15.
29. "Screen Guild's prez, Eddie Cantor in N.Y." *Variety*, October 23, 1934, p. 3.
30. "A mistaken move." *Los Angeles Times*, October 23, 1934, p. A4.
31. "Equity's Guild control." *Variety*, October 30, 1934, pp. 3, 28.
32. "Guild-Equity tieup set." *Billboard*, November 3, 1934, pp. 3, 61.
33. "Anti-raiding pact given boot by all but three major studios." *Variety*, November 6, 1934, p. 4.
34. "Producers bow-out from Academy." *Variety*, November 13, 1934, pp. 4, 62.
35. "Equity OK's Screen Guild." *Variety*, November 20, 1934, p. 51.
36. "Actors lash film execs." *Variety*, January 8, 1935, p. 3.

Notes. Chapter 8

37. "Equity completes screen alliance." *New York Times*, January 17, 1935, p. 23.
38. "Hollywood actors nix Academy studio no strike pact in March." *Variety*, January 22, 1935, pp. 1, 59.
39. "Strike threat dwindles." *Variety*, February 5, 1935, pp. 3, 34.
40. "Screen actors stand pat." *Billboard*, February 9, 1935, pp. 3, 20.
41. "Screen Actors' Guild cold to producers." *Billboard*, February 16, 1935, p. 4.
42. Wood Soanes. "Curtain calls." *Oakland Tribune*, February 27, 1935, p. 14.
43. "Film players ignore Academy." *Billboard*, March 30, 1935, pp. 4, 20.
44. "Montgomery to succeed Cantor as Screen Actors' Guild prexy." *Billboard*, May 18, 1935, pp. 4, 6.
45. "Study of Academy contract shows majors offer little." *Billboard*, May 25, 1935, pp. 4, 20.
46. "Actors' film chances." *Variety*, July 3, 1935, pp. 1, 44.
47. "Montgomery heads Guild." *Billboard*, August 10, 1935, p. 5.
48. "Acad survey shows 974 players earned screen credit last year." *Variety*, January 29, 1936, p. 3.
49. "$9.25 average for extras." *Variety*, January 29, 1936, pp. 3, 31.
50. "Actor-labor U.S. peeve." *Variety*, February 17, 1936, pp. 5, 68.
51. *Ibid.*
52. "Academy adjusted 550 contracts of 4,000 free-lancers during year." *Variety*, April 1, 1936, p. 3.
53. Douglas W. Churchill. "Extra trouble in the Hollywood paradise." *New York Times*, August 30, 1936, sec 10, p. 3.
54. "SAG forces studio action against salary chiseling." *Billboard*, September 5, 1936, p. 3.

Chapter 8

1. "Pic actors union demand." *Variety*, September 23, 1936, pp. 3, 62.
2. Douglas W. Churchill. "Solidarity forever in Hollywood." *New York Times*, September 27, 1936, sec 10, p. 5.
3. "1st the indies, if a strike." *Variety*, September 30, 1936, p. 5.
4. "Thompson in D. C. wooing labor's cooperation for screen actors." *Variety*, March 24, 1937, p. 2.
5. "Film Guild seeks recognition again." *New York Times*, April 4, 1937, p. 22.
6. "Film Guild talks strike." *New York Times*, April 5, 1937, p. 16.
7. "10% pay rise given by film producers." *New York Times*, April 6, 1937, p. 21.
8. "Screen Actors' Guild gets no look-in." *Variety*, April 7, 1937, pp. 2, 27.
9. "Wagner disturbs H'Wood." *Variety*, April 14, 1937, pp. 1-2.
10. "Pic crafts' strike talk." *Variety*, April 28, 1937, pp. 5, 55.
11. "Studios picketed in movie walkout." *New York Times*, May 2, 1937, p. 28.
12. *Ibid.*
13. "Studio picketing halted for parley." *Washington Post*, May 3, 1937, p. 5.
14. "The Hollywood strike." *Washington Post*, May 4, 1937, p. 8.
15. "Screen Actors' Guild defers action on strike." *Washington Post*, May 4, 1937, pp. 1, 24.
16. Alan McElwain. "Strikers ask boycott of U.S. movies." *Oakland Tribune*, May 4, 1937, pp. 1, 5.

Notes. Chapter 8

17. "Movie stars vote strike for Monday." *Oakland Tribune*, May 9, 1937, p. 1.
18. Douglas W. Churchill. "Strife-torn Hollywood." *New York Times*, May 9, 1937, sec 10, p. 3.
19. "Movie men split by strike." *New York Times*, May 9, 1937, p. E10.
20. "Film actors' strike averted as Guild accord is reached." *Christian Science Monitor*, May 10, 1937, p. 4.
21. Morrie Ryskind. "It happened one night." *The Nation* 144 (May 15, 1937): 563.
22. "Actors sold us out, says strike head." *Oakland Tribune*, May 10, 1937, p. 1.
23. "National boycott of films is asked." *New York Times*, May 11, 1937, p. 4.
24. "Movie strikers seek help in picketing of theaters." *Christian Science Monitor*, May 11, 1937, p. 5.
25. "Actors rejoice but craftsmen continue strike." *Washington Post*, May 11, 1937, p. 24.
26. "Pix strike now nat'l." *Variety*, May 12, 1937, pp. 1–2.
27. "Picture crafts reject verbal peace proposal." *Washington Post*, May 15, 1937, p. 7.
28. "Film actors sign pact ban strikes." *Oakland Tribune*, May 17, 1937, p. 1.
29. "Boycott is called on 5 movie actors." *New York Times*, May 19, 1937, p. 12.
30. "Film strike heads repudiate boycott." *New York Times*, May 20, 1937, p. 11.
31. "SAG activity hits new high." *Billboard*, May 22, 1937, pp. 4, 91.
32. Hubbard Keavy. "Actors' strike left leaders out on limb." *Washington Post*, June 13, 1937, p. T3.
33. "Screen Guild roster now 15,000." *Variety*, July 21, 1937, p. 2.
34. Paul Ackerman. "New 4A setup okehed." *Billboard*, August 7, 1937, pp. 3, 10.
35. "Four A org's long road." *Billboard*, November 27, 1937, pp. 4, 10.
36. "Producers fight SAG move to force recognition beyond 300 mile limit." *Variety*, September 8, 1937, p. 4.
37. "100% SAG shop in the East, except M.T." *Variety*, September 22, 1937, p. 7.
38. Morton Thompson. "Hollywood is a union town." *The Nation* 146 (April 2, 1938): 381.

Bibliography

"Acad survey shows 974 players earned screen credits last year." *Variety*, January 29, 1936, p. 3.
"Academy adjusted 550 contracts of 4,000 free-lancers during year." *Variety*, April 1, 1936, p. 3.
"Academy handled 27 complaints in '29; 19 from actors." *Variety*, January 15, 1930, p. 11.
"Academy of film art is started by industry." *Washington Post*, May 5, 1927, p. 4.
"Academy-producers-agents' pact." *Variety*, August 29, 1933, p. 7.
"Academy takes up matter of actors' standard contract." *Variety*, September 28, 1927, p. 5.
Ackerman, Paul. "New 4A setup okened." *Billboard*, August 7, 1937, pp. 3, 10.
"Actor Guild denies union." *Billboard*, November 18, 1933, p. 4.
"Actor-labor U.S. peeve." *Variety*, February 17, 1936, pp. 5, 68.
"Actors approve Academy contract as trial year ends." *Variety*, January 28, 1931, p. 4.
"Actors balk at 10% of salary for fund." *Variety*, July 10, 1929, p. 7.
"Actors defy Equity on movie contracts." *New York Times*, June 22, 1929, p. 3.
"Actors demand NRA guarantee on year round bidding for jobs." *Variety*, September 5, 1933, p. 2.
"Actors' Equity urges delay in wage cut." *Washington Post*, June 27, 1927, p. 5.
"Actors' film chances." *Variety*, July 3, 1935, pp. 1, 44.
"Actors form of contract." *Variety*, December 21, 1927, p. 9.
"Actors Guild denies union." *Billboard*, November 18, 1933, p. 4.
"Actors Guild to fight cut." *Oakland Tribune*, October 9, 1933, p. 5.
"Actors largest Academy branch." *Billboard*, May 27, 1933, p. 5.
"Actors lash film execs." *Variety*, January 8, 1935, p. 3.
"Actors organizing." *Billboard*, August 19, 1933, pp. 5, 55.
"Actors rejoice but craftsmen continue strike." *Washington Post*, May 11, 1937, p. 24.
"Actors sold us out, says strike head." *Oakland Tribune*, May 10, 1937, p. 1.
"Actors under new law." *Billboard*, July 1, 1933, pp. 3, 63.
"Actors vigorously protest producers' agreement in first Academy session." *Variety*, April 5, 1932, p. 3.
"A.E.A. film membership." *Variety*, December 21, 1917, p. 50.

Bibliography

"A.F. of L. brands Academy as producers' company union." *Billboard*, August 1, 1927, p. 9.
"Agitators busy." *Los Angeles Times*, September 16, 1918, sec 2, p. 6.
Albertson, Lillian. "Equity's chief draws censure." *Los Angeles Times*, June 23, 1929, p. 8.
"AMPAS is socked." *Billboard*, September 23, 1933, p. 5.
"Amusement people head list of white collar labor unions." *Variety*, August 18, 1926, p. 1.
"The answer to Equity." *Los Angeles Times*, June 8, 1929, p. A4.
"Anti-Academy ex-stage actors forming closed shop coast union similar to Equity setup." *Variety*, July 25, 1933, pp. 5, 29.
"Anti-raiding pact given boost by all but three major studios." *Variety*, November 6, 1934, p. 4.
"Average daily earning of Hollywood extras—$8.64." *Variety*, July 7, 1926, pp. 1, 12.
"Barrymore decries closed film shop." *New York Times*, June 10, 1929, p. 3.
"Boycott and blacklist on." *Los Angeles Times*, August 6, 1929, pp. A1–A2.
"Boycott is called on 5 movie actors." *New York Times*, May 19, 1937, p. 12.
"Bushman-Silvernail clash." *Variety*, July 10, 1929, pp. 7, 21.
"Calls film stars unfair." *New York Times*, August 5, 1929, p. 24.
"Campaign plan urgent need of Equity." *Variety*, July 3, 1929, p. 6.
"Cantor gives reasons for Actors' Guild." *Oakland Tribune*, October 11, 1933, p. 11.
"Cantor slams pix Academy." *Billboard*, May 26, 1934, pp. 3–4.
"A Chinese army." *Billboard*, November 4, 1933, p. 26.
Churchill, Douglas W. "Extra trouble in the Hollywood paradise." *New York Times*, August 30, 1936, sec 10, p. 3.
_____. "Solidarity forever in Hollywood." *New York Times*, September 27, 1936, sec 10, p. 5.
_____. "Strife-torn Hollywood." *New York Times*, May 9, 1937, sec 10, p. 3.
"Closed shop and the stage." *Los Angeles Times*, March 27, 1927, p. B4.
"Coast actors' own group." *Variety*, January 29, 1930, pp. 9–10.
"Coast extras burning up over studios' alleged labor violations." *Variety*, October 24, 1928, p. 15.
"Coast extras cut down." *Variety*, January 16, 1929, p. 7.
"Coast not dealing with Actors' Equity on contract." *Variety*, December 7, 1927, p. 4.
"Coast secret meeting." *Variety*, December 1, 1931, pp. 3, 42.
"Coast's quiet battle." *Variety*, June 19, 1929, pp. 5, 52.
"Compromise in Equity fight in films sought." *Oakland Tribune*, August 5, 1929, p. 12.
"Compromise reports, chorus girls' walkout." *Variety*, July 17, 1929, p. 7.
"Contract actors not subject to standard form contracts." *Variety*, December 28, 1927, p. 9.
"Cuts so far, $350,000 wkly." *Variety*, June 29, 1927, pp. 5, 14.
"DeMille elated by Equity decision." *New York Times*, August 21, 1929, p. 30.
"DeMille says actors suffer." *Los Angeles Times*, July 5, 1929, p. A3.
"Discounts for actors for food and gas." *Variety*, July 3, 1929, p. 7.
"Doubts Equity strike." *New York Times*, November 1, 1920, p. 16.
"Easing out bad actors." *Variety*, October 6, 1926, p. 1.
"Economy in film colony." *Variety*, August 27, 1930, pp. 3, 76.
"11,000 film extras on coast average $6,556 daily payroll." *Variety*, October 26, 1927, p. 5.

Bibliography

"English actor is first Equity coast suspension." *Variety*, June 19, 1929, p. 5.
"Equity absorbs M.P.P.A." *Variety*, April 2, 1920, p. 96.
"Equity actions win skirmish as battle of movies begins." *Washington Post*, June 18, 1929, p. 11.
"Equity actors return to work in film studios." *Billboard*, August 31, 1929, pp. 3, 101.
"Equity appeals for funds on radio." *Variety*, July 24, 1929, p. 7.
"Equity asks actors to finance film fight." *New York Times*, July 23, 1929, p. 32.
"Equity badly whipped." *Variety*, August 21, 1929, pp. 1, 54.
"Equity ballot not sent them, say members." *Variety*, June 26, 1929, p. 6.
"Equity broadcasts." *Variety*, July 17, 1929, p. 7.
"Equity campaign gains momentum." *Billboard*, July 13, 1929, pp. 3, 86–87.
"Equity collected $90,000 due actors." *New York Times*, June 2, 1925, p. 7.
"Equity completes screen alliance." *New York Times*, January 17, 1935, p. 23.
"Equity considering calling its contract players out of studios." *Variety*, June 26, 1929, p. 7.
"Equity defers action on Ethel Barrymore." *New York Times*, August 28, 1929, p. 28.
"Equity defied by movie producers." *Fresno Bee*, June 6, 1929, p. 5.
"Equity dissolves movie committee." *New York Times*, December 15, 1927, p. 33.
"Equity expects 100% members of picture colony's players within month, due to talkers." *Variety*, July 4, 1928, p. 5.
"Equity gaining strength in motion picture ranks." *Billboard*, July 16, 1927, p. 6.
"Equity in Hollywood." *New York Times*, July 12, 1929, p. 14.
"Equity in strange position in deadlock with film producers." *Variety*, July 3, 1929, p. 7.
"Equity making preparations to organize talkie field." *Billboard*, November 24, 1928, pp. 3, 89.
"Equity mass meeting hears Academy, Casting Co., denounced." *Variety*, July 17, 1929, p. 7.
"Equity may absorb coast film actors' association." *Variety*, January 21, 1921, p. 45.
"Equity may invade." *Billboard*, May 31, 1930, p. 3.
"Equity not asking extras to join at this time." *Variety*, July 10, 1929, p. 7.
"Equity OK's Screen Guild." *Variety*, November 20, 1934, pp. 3, 51.
"Equity orders film strike." *New York Times*, July 10, 1929, p. 14.
"Equity plans new drive due to sound." *Variety*, June 13, 1928, p. 5.
"Equity plans own casting office." *Variety*, July 31, 1929, p. 7.
"Equity rift out west explained by N.Y. actors now coast defenders." *Variety*, July 10, 1929, p. 7.
"Equity says picture and B'way actors are both overpaid." *Variety*, November 3, 1931, pp. 3, 6.
"Equity scraps coast comm.; seemingly gives up pictures." *Variety*, December 14, 1927, pp. 1, 39.
"Equity shop in talkies." *Billboard*, June 8, 1929, pp. 3–4.
"Equity shop starts now." *Variety*, June 5, 1929, pp. 5, 50, 55.
"Equity snares film players." *Los Angeles Times*, July 7, 1927, p. A1.
"Equity starting after picture field." *Variety*, June 4, 1924, p. 19.
"Equity-studio matter." *Variety*, June 12, 1929, pp. 5, 34.
"Equity suspends film fight." *Billboard*, August 24, 1925, pp. 3, 85.
"Equity will warn members to watch talkie contracts." *Billboard*, July 14, 1928, p. 4.
"Equity wipes out strike ban." *Billboard*, April 5, 1930, p. 5.
"Equity's coast branch voting for new advisory board." *Variety*, February 8, 1928, p. 9.

Bibliography

"Equity's coast meetings." *Variety*, July 3, 1929, p. 6.
"Equity's 80–20 proposal is rejected by producers." *Variety*, August 17, 1929, pp. 3, 85.
"Equity's film contract on the way." *Variety*, May 22, 1929, p. 4.
"Equity's first big threat." *Billboard*, July 27, 1929, pp. 3, 6–7.
"Equity's $4,500 weekly." *Variety*, July 24, 1929, pp. 7, 42.
"Equity's Guild control." *Variety*, October 30, 1934, pp. 3, 28.
"Equity's meeting on coast Monday not so hot." *Variety*, June 19, 1929, p. 5.
"Equity's M. P. branch finds rival in film players' club." *Variety*, February 17, 1922, p. 46.
"Equity's next for film." *Variety*, June 25, 1930, pp. 101, 104.
"Equity's picture branch closed in New York." *Variety*, November 17, 1922, p. 46.
"Equity's picture list." *Variety*, June 12, 1929, p. 4.
"Equity's setback." *New York Times*, August 20, 1929, p. 21.
"Equity's standard form of contract handed to Hays upon leaving L.A." *Variety*, August 6, 1924, pp. 19, 43.
"Equity's 3rd film attack." *Variety*, October 20, 1931, p. 3.
"Ethel Barrymore opposes Gillmore." *New York Times*, August 13, 1929, p. 29.
"Ethel Barrymore says Gillmore misled meeting." *Fresno Bee*, August 12, 1929, p. 2.
"Extra day averages $8.18." *Variety*, July 13, 1927, pp. 1, 24.
"Extra people in Hollywood." *Variety*, October 21, 1925, p. 26.
"Extras agents and commish all through." *Variety*, March 25, 1925, p. 1.
"Extras forming union for mutual protection." *Variety*, August 25, 1916, p. 20.
"Extras high daily average in '27." *Variety*, February 1, 1928, p. 5.
"Extras in movies to be considered." *Fresno Bee*, December 11, 1925, p. 25.
"Extras stay on job; no Hollywood strike." *New York Times*, July 12, 1929, p. 28.
"Extras steamed up against U manager." *Variety*, October 8, 1924, p. 20.
"1,500 volunteers on coast for Equity." *Variety*, July 24, 1929, p. 7.
"Film actors and Equity again on the coast." *Variety*, June 22, 1927, p. 5.
"Film actors pass up chance to get organized protection." *Billboard*, July 30, 1927, pp. 5, 105.
"Film actors quit Academy over code." *New York Times*, October 3, 1933, p. 26.
"Film actors sign pact, ban strikes." *Oakland Tribune*, May 17, 1937, p. 1.
"Film actors' strike averted as Guild accord is reached." *Christian Science Monitor*, May 10, 1937, p. 4.
"Film actors' union." *Los Angeles Times*, November 13, 1918, p. 9.
"Film folk row at session of EQ program." *Modesto News-Herald*, June 27, 1929, p. 9.
"Film Guild seeks recognition again." *New York Times*, April 4, 1937, p. 22.
"Film Guild talks strike." *New York Times*, April 5, 1937, p. 16.
"Film industry rent by clash." *Los Angeles Times*, July 8, 1927, p. A1.
"Film mob's toughest year." *Variety*, February 9, 1932, pp. 1, 21.
"Film players ignore Academy." *Billboard*, March 30, 1935, pp. 4, 20.
"Film producers on coast agree not to raise salaries." *Variety*, June 25, 1924, p. 1.
"Film producers yield to pressure by labor." *Billboard*, August 10, 1929, pp. 3, 7.
"Film stars facing pay cut or eclipse." *Washington Post*, August 17, 1927, p. 16.
"Film stars' pay uncut, temperament given up." *Washington Post*, July 30, 1927, p. 3.
"Film strike heads repudiate boycott." *New York Times*, May 20, 1937, p. 11.
"Film workers win delay on cuts in salary." *Christian Science Monitor*, July 1, 1927, p. 5A.
"Films firm for the open shop." *Los Angeles Times*, August 31, 1918, sec 2, pp. 1, 7.

Bibliography

"1st the indies, if a strike." *Variety*, September 30, 1936, p. 5.
"$5,000,000 salary cut." *Variety*, December 22, 1931, p. 3.
"42,546 coast studio workers make 82% of world's supply." *Variety*, January 11, 1928, p. 1.
"Four A org's long road." *Billboard*, November 27, 1937, pp. 4, 10.
"4,000 actors for 600 jobs on coast." *Variety*, May 22, 1929, p. 4.
"Franchising film agencies." *Variety*, August 18, 1926, p. 43.
Frazier, George. "Nobody pushes Bob around." *Collier's* 123 (June 4, 1949): 24–25+.
"Free lance contract back for revision." *Variety*, February 22, 1928, p. 4.
"F. X. Bushman in tilt in Equity movie row." *New York Times*, July 7, 1929, p. 18.
"General strike." *Variety*, July 22, 1921, p. 39.
"Gilbert joins Equity foes." *Los Angeles Times*, June 13, 1929, p. A12.
"Gillmore again nominated; Ethel Barrymore dropped." *Billboard*, April 19, 1930, p. 4, 7.
"Gillmore ascribes defeat to threats." *New York Times*, August 27, 1929, p. 36.
"Gillmore gets aid by Powers for Equity." *New York Times*, June 13, 1929, p. 35.
"Government mediator enters Equity-film producer fight." *Billboard*, July 20, 1929, pp. 3, 86–87.
"Green backs Equity in film conflict." *New York Times*, June 27, 1929, p. 24.
"Green offers aid to Equity in talkies." *New York Times*, June 20, 1929, p. 26.
"Green on organization." *Los Angeles Times*, July 6, 1929, p. A4.
"Guild-Equity tieup set." *Billboard*, November 3, 1934, pp. 3, 61.
"Hays back." *Variety*, February 3, 1926, p. 29.
"Hays begins clean-up of Hollywood today." *New York Times*, January 25, 1926, p. 22.
"Hersholt's contract may be bought by MGM." *Variety*, February 8, 1928, p. 9.
"Hollywood actors nix Academy studio no strike pact in March." *Variety*, January 22, 1935, pp. 1, 59.
"Hollywood closed shop." *Los Angeles Times*, July 11, 1927, p. A4.
"Hollywood extra list being pruned from 17,000 to 2,500." *Billboard*, September 29, 1934, p. 3.
"Hollywood goes back to work." *New York Times*, March 19, 1933, sec 10, p. 3.
"Hollywood moves to check Equity." *New York Times*, February 7, 1930, p. 28.
"Hollywood stars." *Washington Post*, December 19, 1927, p. 5.
"The Hollywood strike." *Washington Post*, May 4, 1937, p. 8.
"Hollywood to control." *New York Times*, October 21, 1934, p. 33.
"Hollywood's open shop." *Variety*, October 3, 1933, p. 11.
"Howl for help in movieland." *Los Angeles Times*, February 11, 1917, sec 3, p. 1.
"Inside stuff—pictures." *Variety*, June 12, 1929, p. 53.
"Is the Academy up-stage." *Variety*, July 6, 1927, p. 12.
"K.-A. contract clause can tie up all acts' screen services." *Variety*, April 27, 1927, pp. 1, 31.
Keavy, Hubbard. "Actors' strike left leaders out on limb." *Washington Post*, June 13, 19367, p. T3.
"Labor ready to aid Equity in talkie fight." *Billboard*, June 22, 1929, pp. 3, 89.
"Labor unions uncommitted to Equity." *Variety*, August 14, 1929, p. 6.
Logan, Somerset. "The battle of Hollywood." *The New Republic* 59 (August 7, 1929): 308–310.
_____. "Revolt in Hollywood." *The Nation* 129 (July 17, 1929): 61–62.
"Los Angeles film players look for 100% Equity casts." *Variety*, March 25, 1921, p. 46.

Bibliography

"The Los Angeles spirit." *Los Angeles Times*, July 15, 1927, p. A4.
Louvish, Simon. *Cecil B. DeMille and the Golden Calf.* London: Faber and Faber, 2007.
"Lower film player salaries." *Variety*, December 24, 1930, p. 5.
"Mack scores closed shop." *New York Times*, June 11, 1929, p. 34.
"Majority of players accept film pay cut." *New York Times*, March 10, 1933, p. 18.
"Mary Pickford on A.M.P.A.S." *Variety*, May 18, 1927, pp. 9, 17–18.
"Mayer's resolution and don'ts; actors without representation." *Variety*, October 12, 1927, p. 5.
McElwain, Alan. "Strikers ask boycott of U.S. movies." *Oakland Tribune*, May 4, 1937, pp. 1, 5.
"Miss Bow can't emote by clock." *Los Angeles Times*, June 15, 1929, p. A6.
"A mistaken move." *Los Angeles Times*, October 23, 1934, p. A4.
"Montgomery heads Guild." *Billboard*, August 10, 1935, p. 5.
"Montgomery to succeed Cantor as Screen Actors' Guild prexy." *Billboard*, May 18, 1935, pp. 4, 6.
"More Equityites sign old form studio contracts since June 18." *Variety*, June 26, 1929, p. 6.
"More Equityites sign old form studio contracts since June 25." *Variety*, July 3, 1929, p. 8.
"More picture extras." *Variety*, January 19, 1927, pp. 1, 9.
"Movie chiefs deny plan to cut salaries." *New York Times*, November 16, 1927, p. 2.
"Movie Guild opens doors to extras." *New York Times*, October 27, 1933, p. 22.
"Movie industry slashes all pay." *New York Times*, March 9, 1933, p. 19.
"Movie men agree to Equity parley." *New York Times*, August 2, 1929, p. 21.
"Movie men split by strike." *New York Times*, May 9, 1937, p. E10.
"Movie plants shut over union wage." *New York Times*, March 13, 1933, p. 14.
"Movie producers defy Actors' Equity." *New York Times*, June 7, 1929, p. 32.
"Movie stars vote strike for Monday." *Oakland Tribune*, May 9, 1937, p. 1.
"Movie strikers seek help in picketing of theaters." *Christian Science Monitor*, May 11, 1937, p. 5.
"Movie vagrants to be eliminated." *Fresno Bee*, January 25, 1926, p. 4.
"M.P. Academy-producer split in open over service bureau." *Billboard*, April 29, 1933, p. 4.
"M.P. players' union gets separate Four A's charter." *Billboard*, February 7, 1920, p. 5.
"Nagel no longer head of Academy." *New York Times*, April 21, 1933, p. 24.
"National boycott of films is asked." *New York Times*, May 11, 1937, p. 4.
"New actors' ass'n forms on coast." *Variety*, January 11, 1928, p. 3.
"New contract — no Equity." *Variety*, July 10, 1929, pp. 1, 21.
"New film-actor group." *Variety*, October 3, 1933, p. 7.
"New film contract exposed by Equity." *New York Times*, January 17, 1928, p. 23.
"New players' union move." *Variety*, March 28, 1933, pp. 1, 48.
"New stars much cheaper." *Variety*, September 1, 1931, p. 3.
"New York picture folks would break with Equity." *Variety*, February 11, 1921, p. 1.
"Newer and cheaper stars." *Variety*, May 13, 1931, pp. 1, 34.
"$9.25 average for extras." *Variety*, January 29, 1936, pp. 3, 31.
"No more doubling by soldiers as extras." *Variety*, March 23, 1927, p. 1.
"No production shut-down." *Variety*, March 14, 1933, pp. 5, 25, 40.
"Official out." *Variety*, July 3, 1929, p. 8.
"100 Equity actors now under old studio form contracts, all signed since June 5th." *Variety*, June 19, 1929, p. 4.

Bibliography

"100% Equity always, says Ethel Barrymore." *Variety*, August 14, 1929, p. 6.
"100% SAG shop in the East, except M.T." *Variety*, September 22, 1937, p. 7.
"100% Screen Actors' Guild " *Variety*, October 10, 1933, p. 7.
"Opposing forces on coast lining up silently for offense and defense ends." *Variety*, June 12, 1929, p. 5.
"Organization of indie film producers looms as Equity possibility in East." *Billboard*, July 6, 1929, pp. 3, 86.
"Peace pact is likely." *Variety*, August 7, 1929, p. 191.
Pearson, Felicia. "Chats on stage and screen folk." *Washington Post*, May 8, 1927, p. F3.
"Photoplay actors fail to form new organization." *Variety*, July 25, 1913, p. 8.
"Pic actors union demand." *Variety*, September 23, 1936, pp. 3, 62.
"Pic crafts' strike talk." *Variety*, April 28, 1937, pp. 5, 55.
"Picture actors asking for franchise booking office." *Variety*, January 19, 1927, p. 8.
"Picture actors wise up." *Billboard*, October 14, 1933, pp. 3, 10
"Picture crafts reject verbal peace proposal." *Washington Post*, May 15, 1937, p. 7.
"Picture Guild nixes NRA." *Variety*, October 23, 1934, pp. 3, 15.
"A picture players' union." *New York Times*, March 16, 1929, p. 12.
"Pix strike now nat'l." *Variety*, May 12, 1937, pp. 1–2.
"Preparedness." *Variety*, July 31, 1929, p. 6.
"Producer resolutions." *Variety*, October 19, 1927, p. 26.
"Producers admit 200 refused work since Equity fight." *Variety*, July 10, 1929, p. 7.
"Producers bow-out from Academy." *Variety*, November 13, 1934, pp. 4, 62.
"Producers fight SAG move to force recognition beyond 300 mile limit." *Variety*, September 8, 1937, p. 4.
"Producers tying up actors to cover all work by 4-way contract." *Variety*, May 20, 1931, p. 2.
"Producers unlikely to give Equity recognition in Hollywood studios." *Variety*, July 20, 1927, p. 9.
"Protect Equity film move." *New York Times*, June 15, 1929, p. 22.
"Railroading actors ends." *Variety*, September 17, 1924, pp. 1, 53.
"Regulating extras." *Variety*, January 20, 1926, p. 29.
"Regulating Hollywood." *Variety*, June 15, 1927, pp. 5, 8.
"Remedy in friendly dealing." *Variety*, April 29, 1921, p. 47.
"Retreat from Hollywood." *The Outlook and Independent* 153 (September 4, 1929): 13–14.
"Revised standard contract form accepted." *Variety*, March 21, 1928, p. 15.
"Row in extras' association." *Variety*, November 3, 1916, p. 23.
"Rush by producers to sign players for 1925." *Variety*, March 4, 1925, p. 27.
Ryskind, Morrie. "It happened one night." *The Nation* 144 (May 15, 1937): 563.
"SAG activity hits new high." *Billboard*, May 22, 1937, pp. 4, 51.
"SAG forces studio action against salary chiseling." *Billboard*, September 5, 1936, pp. 3, 15.
"Salary cut flop may take Equity into coast studios." *Variety*, July 13, 1927, pp. 4, 15.
"Salary cuts — good films." *Variety*, May 27, 1931, pp. 5, 51.
"Salary cutting may lead to Equity organizing picture actors on coast." *Variety*, July 6, 1927, p. 4.
"Salary cutting fluke." *Variety*, July 6, 1927, pp. 1, 17.
"Screen Actors Guild asserts it doesn't want AFL or Equity ties." *Variety*, November 21, 1933, p. 5.

Bibliography

"Screen Actors' Guild cold to producers." *Billboard*, February 16, 1935, p. 4.
"Screen Actors' Guild defers action on strike." *Washington Post*, May 4, 1937, pp. 1, 24.
"Screen Actors' Guild gets no look-in." *Variety*, April 7, 1937, pp. 2, 27.
"Screen Actors' Guild sets back election." *Variety*, March 27, 1934, p. 2.
"Screen actors stand pat." *Billboard*, February 9, 1935, pp. 3, 20.
"Screen Guild builds." *Billboard*, October 21, 1933, p. 5.
"Screen Guild closed shop." *Billboard*, September 22, 1934, pp. 3, 16.
"Screen Guild roster now 10,000." *Variety*, July 21, 1937, p. 2.
"Screen Guild's prexy, Eddie Cantor in N.Y." *Variety*, October 23, 1934, p. 3.
"Secrecy surrounds Equity plan in talkie campaign." *Billboard*, April 20, 1929, p. 3.
"Sees no closed studios." *New York Times*, March 23, 1933, p. 13.
"Settlement of union demand may be reached in time." *Variety*, November 24, 1926, pp. 9, 13.
"700 film players at meeting vote to join Equity." *Fresno Bee*, July 7, 1927, p. 4.
"Slim pickin' in Hollywood." *Variety*, May 9, 1933, pp. 7, 46.
"Small part Equity players turn to fruit picking." *Variety*, July 7, 1929, p. 7.
Soanes, Wood. "Curtain calls." *Oakland Tribune*, July 13, 1927, p. 20.
Soanes, Wood. "Curtain calls." *Oakland Tribune*, February 27, 1935, p. 14.
"Speeding up film productions but overworking actors." *Variety*, July 23, 1924, p. 20.
"Stand against Gillmore." *Variety*, June 26, 1929, pp. 7, 29.
"Star's salaries and ages." *Variety*, July 27, 1927, pp. 5, 11.
"Strike threat dwindles." *Variety*, February 5, 1935, pp. 3, 34.
"Studio cuts and outs." *Variety*, May 27, 1931, pp. 3, 32.
"Studio labor survey." *Variety*, January 8, 1930, p. 91.
"Studio noises when suspended actors on stage." *Variety*, July 3, 1929, p. 8.
"Studio picketing halted for parley." *Washington Post*, May 3, 1937, p. 5.
"Studio players plenty het up over the code." *Variety*, October 17, 1933, p. 7.
"Studio strike situation." *Variety*, November 17, 1926, pp. 5, 18.
"Studios' average pay." *Variety*, February 1, 1928, p. 3.
"Studios picketed in movie walkout." *New York Times*, May 2, 1937, p. 28.
"Studios win over Equity." *Variety*, July 27, 1927, pp. 9, 10.
"Study of Academy contract shows majors offer little." *Billboard*, May 25, 1935, pp. 4, 20.
"Supers call mass meeting and arrange for a charter." *Variety*, September 1, 1916, p. 13.
"Supporting players and pic extras get organization fever." *Variety*, October 17, 1933, p. 7.
"Sweat shop charge of penny-ante pay takes extras' plight to code." *Variety*, September 12, 1938, p. 7.
"Tearle's issue up to Academy against M.P.P." *Variety*, June 8, 1927, p. 12.
"10% pay rise given by film producers." *New York Times*, April 6, 1937, p. 21.
"10 per centers for extras noticed." *Variety*, January 28, 1925, p. 30.
"3d Equity rally on coast draws crowd." *Variety*, June 26, 1929, p. 7.
"33% of film actors are out." *Variety*, October 10, 1928, pp. 1, 56.
"Thomson in D.C. wooing labor's cooperation for screen actors." *Variety*, March 24, 1937, p. 2.
Thompson, Morton. "Hollywood is a union town." *The Nation* 146 (April 2, 1938): 381–383.
"Too many picture actors." *Variety*, November 30, 1927, pp. 1–2.
"Trickery hurled at agents' move." *Variety*, September 12, 1933, p. 7.

Bibliography

"Turning tables by Equity in injunction." *Variety*, July 24, 1929, p. 6.
"12-hour rest period assures film players protection." *Variety*, February 12, 1930, p. 10.
"26 pictures now in works." *Variety*, July 3, 1929, p. 7.
"2,300 out of 3,500 extras in Eastern films don't belong." *Variety*, July 7, 1926, pp. 1, 12.
"22,500 idle at Hollywood.' *Variety*, June 9, 1926, pp. 1, 18.
"Two big actors go non-Equity." *Variety*, August 14, 1929, p. 7.
"Two factions in Equity." *Variety*, August 14, 1929, pp. 1, 27.
"Uniform system charging 3 weeks salary for farming." *Variety*, October 19, 1927, p. 25.
"Union invasion of film nears." *Los Angeles Times*, November 22, 1928, p. A1.
"Unionism in filmland." *The Nation* 129 (August 28, 1929): 211.
"Unionists plan to shackle film workers flat failure." *Los Angeles Times*, August 20, 1916, sec 2, p. 1.
"Unionizing the movies." *Washington Post*, June 22, 1929, p. 6.
"Urge loyalty and obedience at 4th Equity rally." *Variety*, July 3, 1929, p. 8.
"Use around 700 screen credit players at peak." *Variety*, June 12, 1929, p. 5.
"Useless extras pile in." *Variety*, November 12, 1930, p. 3.
"Wagner disturbs H'Wood." *Variety*, April 14, 1937, pp. 1-2.
"Wait next stop in talkie shop." *Billboard*, June 15, 1929, pp. 3. 15.
"Waiver system for stars." *Variety*, May 17, 1932, p. 5.
"War now looming on movie pay cut." *New York Times*, June 28, 1927, p. 29.
"Wealthy tourists, acting as extras." *Variety*, October 3, 1928, p. 5.
"Weekly studio production.' *Variety*, July 31, 1929, p. 6.

Index

Academy Awards (Oscars) 36
Academy of Motion Picture Arts and Sciences (AMPAS) 34–37, 41–42, 48, 49–50, 51–52, 66–67, 77, 87, 111–113, 117–118, 121–125, 127–133, 136, 139, 142–144, 147; complaints to 111; dues 41; and the media 46–47; membership 36, 41–42, 125; public relations aspect 36
actors, attitudes 68–69
Actors' Betterment Association 126–127
actors: employment 125, 145, 146; numbers of 22–23, 27–28, 55, 57, 66; salaries 47–48, 54, 141; statistics 109
Actors' Equity Association (AEA) see Equity
Actors Fidelity League 34
agencies 21–22, 23, 30; film 14
agents 5–6, 7–8, 86
Albertson, Lillian 80–81
All Quiet on the Western Front 147
Allen, Dave 28, 89
American Federation of Actors 165
American Federation of Labor (AFL) 5, 52, 65–66, 77, 80, 87, 93, 112, 157; affiliation with 7, 15, 135–146; support from 104
American Federation of Musicians 30, 165
American Federation of Radio Artists 165
anti-trust aspects 37–38, 53
anti-union atmosphere, California 5
anti-union sentiments 71–75
arbitration 37, 45, 58–59, 68
Arnold, Edward 163
Artist Managers' Association 123–124
Association of Actors and Artists of America (4As) 9, 13, 130, 136–137, 142, 164
attitudes, of actors 44–45
Atwill, Lionel 149
Balaban, Barney 152
Ball, J.A. 35
bank holiday (1933) 121
bankers, financing by 116
Banky, Vilma 56
Barrymore, Ethel 7, 79, 100–109, 113; versus Gillmore 102–109
Barrymore, John 79, 81, 149
Barrymore, Lionel 71–72, 79, 81, 97, 149
Barthelmess, Richard 56, 117
baseball 119–120
Beery, Noah 81, 97, 100
Beery, Wallace 42, 49, 56, 112
Beetson, Fred W. 22
Bell, George H. 7
Bellamy, Ralph 131
Ben Hur 28
Beranger, Andre 88, 95
Besserer, Eugenie 93
Bielenson, Laurence W. 145
Billboard 34, 79, 86, 133, 135
blacklisting: of actors 37; for moral reasons 31
Blackton, J.S. 7
Blair, Aubrey 158, 152
Blue, Monte 78, 90
Bogart, Humphrey 163
Boles, John 81
Bosworth, Hobart 81
Bow, Clara 75–76, 91, 97
boycotts 11–12, 91, 96–97, 158–159, 163
Brady, Alice 149
Brady, William A. 7

205

Index

Brent, Evelyn 81
Brooke, Clive 81
Browne, George E. 151
Buckley, Harry 152
Burlesque Artists' Association 128
Bushman, Francis X. 88, 90
Buzzell, J.W. 97

Cagney, James 131, 158
California, anti-union 70
California Industrial Welfare Commission 25–236
California State Department of Industrial Relations 63
California State Federation of Labor 150
California State Labor Commission 23
call-ins, to set 20–21
Cantor, Eddie 128, 131–132, 134, 136, 158
Captured 147
Casey, Pat 152, 156
Cavalcade 147
Central Casting Bureau (CCB) 26–29, 47–48, 59, 115, 119
Chatterton, Ruth 139
chorus workers 91, 97
Churchill, Berton 127
Churchill, Douglas 150, 159
closed shop 15
Cochrane, Robert 152
Colman, Ronald 103, 117
Columbia studio 120
commissaries 4, 6, 21
company union 41–42, 46–47
complaints, over conditions 29
Congress of Industrial Organizations (CIO) 151
Conklin, Chester 90, 104
contractors 7–8
contracts: AMPAS 59–60, 69, 147; form of 42; forms 14–15, 21; language 60; long-term 19, 23–24, 57, 120, 150; non-Equity 76, 77, 78–79, 80, 84–85, 90, 94; standard 47, 52–53, 56–57, 66, 111–124; studio, signed in defiance of Equity 73; union, for extras 73–74
Cooley, Hallam 52, 58
Cooper, Gary 131, 161
cooperation 51
cost cutting measures, by producers 37–40
Cowles, Jules 88
Crane, Phyllis 93, 95
Crane, William H. 44
Crawford, Joan 117, 158
Cullen, William 158

Dale, A.B. 12
Datig, Fred 93
Davies, Marion 56, 106
de Cordoba, Pedro 76
demands, actors 6
DeMille, Cecil B. 51, 69, 72, 86–87, 88, 89, 107–108, 109–110
DeMille, William 112
Denny, Reginald 44, 56
Depression (economic) 114–115
Dietrich, Marlene 161
directors: casting 23; film 7, 51, 122
discounts, retail 84
dispute settlement 37
Dix, Richard 56, 117, 158
Doran, Mary 81
Dowling, Eddie 127
Dresser, Louise 74, 79–80, 81, 91, 97
Dressler, Marie 74, 97
Dullzell, Paul 39, 42, 50–51, 61, 79, 84, 92, 107
Dynamite 98–99

Earnham, Joseph 34
economics, studio 115–120
efficiencies, production 51–52
Emerson, John 13–14
Equity 7, 9–10, 24–25, 34, 58, 61–64, 112, 113–114, 117–118, 127–130, 136–144; abandons campaign 1927 48–51; and AMPAS 39–41, 70, 87–88; attacked by actors 71–73; attempt to organize 1929 68–110; blacklisted by media 78–79; discipline of actors 90; dissension within 82–85, 100–109; dormancy 18; employment agency 92, 95–96; expenses 95–96; film disruptions by 88; industrial action 1929 68–102; and Los Angeles branch 55–56; membership, statistics 69, 72, 93; organizing effort 1920–1921 13–17; radio broadcasting 90, 92–93; resignation from 73; resistance to 15; seeking actor opinion 64; standard contract 66; and strike call 70, 90; support for other unions 16–17; suspensions 76–77, 85, 88, 91, 93, 113, 118; unionization effort 1927 38–56
extras, film 4–5, 22–23, 25–29, 47–48, 54, 59, 62, 78, 81, 89, 109, 115, 119, 129, 146, 148; statistics 29, 32, 64–65

Fairbanks, Douglas 34, 35
Farrell, Charles 115
Fazenda, Louise 81

206

Index

Federated Motion Picture Crafts (FMPC) 154–163
film code, industrial 126–132, 141–143
film industry, statistics 10–11
Film Players' Club 17
film producers, tactics 4
film production: disrupted 98; geography of 3
film production code 20
film receipts, actors share 134, 141–142
film workers: rate of unionization 30; technical 10
The Fleet's In 147
Forbes, Mary 88
Forbes, Ralph 82, 100
Fox studio 7
Francis, Kay 139
Franklin, Harold B. 98
Frayne, Hugh 6
fundraising 106

Gable, Clark 128, 156, 161
Garbo, Greta 117, 161
Gaynor, Janet 115
Gibbons, Cedric 35
Gilbert, John 74–75, 81
Gillingham, Claude 96
Gillmore, Frank 13, 15–17, 24–25, 38, 41, 45, 48, 49–50, 55, 66, 69–70, 72, 73–74, 77–78, 81, 82–83, 86, 91, 93, 100–109, 117–118, 129–130, 149
Gleason, Lucille 127
Goldwyn, Samuel 122, 160–161
Gran, Albert 85
Grant, Lawrence 112, 122
Green, Kempton 14
Green, William 77, 79, 87, 92, 104, 130, 151

Haines, William 56, 81
Hall, Fraser 14
Hall, James 81
Harding, Alfred 65–66
Hardy, Sam 112
Hatton, Raymond 56, 91, 95
Hays, Will 20, 26–27, 34, 118, 122
Hearst, William 74, 80, 92
Herbert, Holmes 95
Here Comes the Navy 147
Hersholt, Jean 56, 60, 106, 112
hiring, direct 6
Hollywood Picture Players' Association 134
Hopkins, Miriam 128
Hopper, Hedda 88, 95

hours of work 4, 42, 68, 93
Howard, William K. 128
Huston, Walter 106

International Alliance of Stage Employees (IATSE) 5, 12, 17, 30, 76, 151, 159
International Longshoremen's Association 162
Jessel, George 81, 84
Joy, Leatrice 56
jurisdictional disputes, unions 13

Kane, Robert 76
Karloff, Boris 131
Keavy, Hubbard 164
Keckley, Jane 90
Keith-Albee (vaudeville chain) 30
KELW (radio, Burbank) 95
Kent, Sidney R. 122, 130, 152
KGFG (radio, Los Angeles) 95
KMIC (radio, Los Angeles) 92–93
KMTR (radio, Los Angeles) 92
Kornblum, I.B. 95
KTM (radio, Los Angeles) 95
Kyle, Howard 10

labor laws, state, and producers 62
Laemmle, Carl 118
Landi, Elissa 158
Landis, Kenesaw Mountain 120
La Rocque, Rod 56, 82
Lasky, Jesse L. 39
The Leathernecks Have Landed 147
legislation, of extras 25–26
Lessing, Charles 161, 162
Levee, M.C. 34, 52, 100, 112
Lindelof, L.P. 152
Lloyd, Frank 35
loan-outs, of players 23–24, 52–53, 54, 60, 73, 76–77
location, films, travel to 21
Loeb, Edwin 120
Logan, Somerset 93–94, 99
Los Angeles 3
Los Angeles Actors' Association 14
Los Angeles Central Labor Council 78, 93, 96–97, 159
Los Angeles Examiner 74
Los Angeles Labor Council 16
Los Angeles Record 33
Los Angeles Times 10, 33, 42–43, 45–46, 63–64, 70–71, 74, 80–81, 87, 101–102, 138
Love, Montagu 103
Lowe, Edmund 81, 100

Index

Mack, Willard 71–72
Maclean, Douglas 58
March, Frederic 131, 158
Marsh, Ernest 91–92, 99
Marshall, Tully 91, 94
Marx, Groucho 128
Mayer, Louis B. 34, 35, 88, 118
McFadden, Hamilton 76
McPherson, Jeanie 34
media, anti-union 42–43, 74
media: blacklisting 92; coverage of Equity 86; Equity blacklist 83
mediator, federal government 91–92, 99
Meighan, Thomas 42
Mel, Marian 25
Menjou, Adolphe 56, 128
merchants, Los Angeles 84
MGM 115
military personnel: in film production 146–147; as free extras 32
Millard, Helen 88
Miller, Charles 73
Miller, George 127
Miller, Patsy Ruth 81
Mitchell, Grant 127
Montgomery, Robert 131, 134, 144, 158, 161, 163
morality, and Hollywood 20
Morgan, Frank 163
Morgan, Ralph 127
Morris, Chester 131, 159
Motion Picture Extra People's Association 6–7
Motion Picture Players' Association 13
Motion Picture Players' Union 12–13
Motion Picture Producers and Distributors Association (MPPDA) 16–17, 19, 22, 24, 26–27, 30, 36, 40, 47, 53, 69–70, 78, 86–87, 90, 94, 99, 114–120, 148, 150; and Equity 55–56; policing studios 89
Mountford, Harry 6, 8, 13
Mowbray, Alan 127
Muir, Jean 158
Mulhall, Jack 56
Muni, Paul 131
Murray, Mae 106

Nagel, Conrad 34, 35–36, 38, 44, 48–49, 51, 52, 56, 58, 66, 72, 82, 85, 97, 99–100, 112, 124
The Nation 108
National Industrial Recovery Act 126
National Labor Relations Act 145
National Recovery Administration (NRA) 126, 127–132, 137, 141–143

National Vaudeville Artists 34
New York City 7
New York Times 107
newspapers: anti-union 70–71, 74, 80–81, 87; biased reporting 94, 96, 99; blacklisting 94
newssheet, Equity 78
Niblo, Fred 34, 51
Nolan, Lloyd 149
Novarro, Ramon 103
Nowell, Wedgewood 19, 20
Nugent, Edward 81

Oakie, Jack 81, 149
Oakman, Wheeler 88
Ober, Robert 81
Oland, Warner 81
On the Stairs 76
O'Neil, Nance 106
open shop policy 10–11, 44, 70–71, 132
organizing, cross 9–10
Otto, Henry 91
overtime 6, 14–15, 68

Paramount 116–117
payment, of actors, statistics 25–26
payrolls, studio 119
Pearson, Felicia 35
performers, percentage unionized 165
phones, union, tapped 88–89
Pickford, Mary 34 35, 89
poaching, of actors by studios 19, 23–24, 37–40, 53, 60, 115, 139
Pomeroy, Roy 35
Powell, Eleanor 161
Powell, William 103, 139
Producers Arbitration Agreement 139
production code 53

Quartermaine, Charles 76, 85

racketeering 71
Raft, George 128, 131
Randolph, Anders 91
Rathbone, Basil 82, 103
reforms, cosmetic, by producers 24
rehearsals 93
relief, for actors 90
Rendezvous 147
riot, preparations for 98–99
Roach, Bert 81
Rogers, Charles (Buddy) 75
Rogers, Will 16
Rolfe, B.A. 8
Roosevelt, Franklin D. 126

208

Index

Rosenblatt, Sol 133
Rubin, J. Robert 54
Russell, Rosalind 149

sabotage, in studios 89–90
salaries 37; cuts 19, 32, 37, 40, 51, 54–55, 114–124; donations from 89, 94; film industry 59
scabs 157
Schenck, Joseph 22, 34, 36, 100, 118
Schenck, Nicholas 118, 122, 152
Schulberg, B.P. 52
Schulberg, Ben 100
Schwartz, Charles 152
Screen Actors' Guild (SAG) 7, 34, 134–135; class divisions 136; and Equity 136–144, 149–150; first contract 162–165; formation 127, 131–132; membership 151, 152; negotiations 149–160
Screen Club 5
Screen Writers' Guild (SWG) 127
screenwriters 51, 122
Seattle Central Labor Council 91
Selznick, Lewis J. 6
Shearer, Norma 117
Sheehan, Winifred R. 88, 100, 113
Sheer, George 5
Sheer, William A. 5–6
Sherman, Lowell 81
Sherrill, William A. 7
silent films 61–62, 92
Sills, Milton 34, 48
Silverman, Clark 88
Soanes, Wood 44–45
soldiers, as free extras 32
sped-ups, production 14, 19–20
Spits, Leo 152
stage actors 62
stage, legitimate 33–34
Stahl, John 35, 128
stars, film status 14, 18, 43, 44, 48, 50
Stern, Isador 7–8
Stone, Lewis S. 78, 98
Strange, Philip 103
strike, FMPC, 1937 155–162
strikebreakers 159
strikes, film, technical workers 12, 16–17, 31
studio basic agreement 150–151, 158–159
Swanson, Gloria 117

talking movies 60–62, 64–65, 92

Talmadge, Norma 75, 81
The Taming of the Shrew 89
Tashman, Lilyan 81
Taurog, Norman 128
Tearle, Conway 37
temperament, artistic 51
Thalberg, Irving 100, 112
Thompson, Morton 166
Thomson, Alden Gay 127
Thomson, Kenneth 127, 149, 150
Tobin, Daniel J. 151
Tone, Franchot 158, 163
tourists, as unpaid extras 62
Tracy, Dan W. 151
trade conference, film 52–53
Turner, Paul 100
Tyron, Glen 81

Ulric, Lenore 81
unions: company 34–37; coverage, geography 3, 165; craft 18, 76, 151–152; membership 7, 14, 31, 76, 82, 93, 144; organizing efforts 11–12; shops 33–34, 43, 48, 61, 80, 102, 161, 163
United States Navy 147
United States Supreme Court 126
United States War Department 32
Universal 116

Variety 34, 72, 76, 82, 85, 132
Vaverka, Anton 91

Wagner Act 145–146, 153
waiver system (baseball) 119–120
wardrobes, film 27
Ware, Helen 96
Warner, Albert 152
Warner, Harry 118
Warner, Jack 100, 118
Warner Brothers 94–95, 147
Washington Post 80, 156–157
Weiss, Ben 8
Wellman, William 128
White Rats Actors Union of America 6–7, 8–9, 34
Wilson, Carey 34
Wilson, Lois 82, 100
Woods, Frank 34
working conditions 70, 93–94; actors 4–5, 19–23; hazardous 21

Zucker, Adolph 118

www.ingramcontent.com/pod-product-compliance
Lightning Source LLC
Chambersburg PA
CBHW032057300426
44116CB00007B/775